**DISCOURSE AND REFERENCE
IN THE NUCLEAR AGE**

OKLAHOMA PROJECT FOR DISCOURSE AND THEORY

OKLAHOMA PROJECT FOR DISCOURSE AND THEORY

SERIES EDITORS

Robert Con Davis, University of Oklahoma
Ronald Schleifer, University of Oklahoma

ADVISORY BOARD

Maya Angelou, Wake Forest University
Jonathan Culler, Cornell University
Jacques Derrida, University of California, Irvine
Shoshana Felman, Yale University
Henry Louis Gates, Jr., Cornell University
Sandra M. Gilbert, Princeton University
Edmund Leach, Oxford University
Richard Macksey, Johns Hopkins University
J. Hillis Miller, University of California, Irvine
Marjorie Perloff, Stanford University
Edward W. Said, Columbia University
Thomas A. Sebeok, Indiana University at Bloomington
Gayatri Chakravorty Spivak, University of Pittsburgh

Discourse and Reference
in the Nuclear Age

By J. FISHER SOLOMON

UNIVERSITY OF OKLAHOMA PRESS : NORMAN AND LONDON

Library of Congress Cataloging-in-Publication Data

Solomon, J. Fisher (James Fisher), 1954–
Discourse and reference in the nuclear age.

(Oklahoma project for discourse and theory ; v. 2)
Bibliography: p.
Includes index.
1. Criticism. 2. Languages—Philosophy.
3. Literature and society. 4. Civilization, Modern—20th century. 5. Nuclear warfare—Moral and ethical aspects.
6. Metaphysics. 7. Hermeneutics. 8. Semiotics.
I. Title. II. Series: Oklahoma project for discourse and theory ; no. 2.
PN98.M67S65   1988   801'.95   87-40558
ISBN 0-8061-2135-1 (alk. paper)

Publication of this work has been made possible in part by a grant from the Andrew W. Mellon Foundation.

The paper in this book meets the guidelines for permanence and durability of the Committee on Production Guidelines for Book Longevity of the Council on Library Resources, Inc.

Copyright © 1988 by the University of Oklahoma Press, Norman, Publishing Division of the University. All rights reserved. Manufactured in the U.S.A. First edition.

Discourse and Reference in the Nuclear Age is Volume 2 of the Oklahoma Project for Discourse and Theory.

For Sonia

Contents

Series Editors' Foreword		ix
Acknowledgments		xiii

PART 1   INTRODUCTION

CHAPTER		
1	A "Nuclear" Agenda	5
2	"No Apocalypse, Not Now": Deconstructing the Nuclear Referent	18
3	Critical Realism in a Nuclear Era: Toward a Potentialist Metaphysics	34

PART 2   FIRST PRINCIPLES: THE CASE FOR REALISM

CHAPTER		
4	History, Metahistory, and War: The Example of Thucydides	41
5	Natural Genesis: Aristotle's *Physics* and the Problem of Change	51
6	Aristotle's *Metaphysics* and the Potentiality of the Real	62
7	Realism in the Quantum Age: Karl Popper and the Debate Between Determinism and Indeterminism	74

PART 3   A POTENTIALIST HERMENEUTICS

CHAPTER		
8	A Rhetoric of the Real	109
9	Reader-Response Theory and the Hermeneutics of Potentiality	115
10	Naming and Referring in a Potential World	129
11	"Necessary Equivocation": An Allegory of Reading	155

PART 4   THE POTENTIAL SIGN

CHAPTER 12	Substance and/or Form: Saussure, Semiology, and Ontology	169
13	Producing the Referent: C. S. Peirce's Semiotic Realism	183
14	From Difference to Differance: A Derridean Solicitation	207

PART 5   LIVED EXPERIENCE

CHAPTER 15	Martin Heidegger and Ontological Difference in the Atomic Age	223
16	Marxism and the Categories of Historical Presentation	244
17	Power and Difference in the Nuclear Era	263

Notes	277
Bibliography	281
Index	289

Series Editors' Foreword

FRENCH CLASSICIST LOUIS GERNET once remarked that there are some human activities and investments it is entirely possible for a culture to forget. Citing examples from classical Athenian culture, he mentioned the impact of a political or monetary system and the foundation of cultural values as things that could be forgotten. Gernet was referring both to the temporary loss of values or memories of events that later reemerge and prove to be crucial as well as to cultural forgetting, or loss, of a reference. This latter kind of forgetting has a structural and social intention and constitutes a necessary cloak of obscurity thrown over functions or practices that, if contextualized and scrutinized, would be altered—as if too much had been revealed. The retrieval, or "remembering," of lost cultural connections, therefore, can entail the rediscovery of a cultural impact already made but somehow obscured, the delayed recognition of a reference that has been camouflaged, as if to protect against articulations that are too harsh or too far-reaching in their implications.

The force of J. Fisher Solomon's *Discourse and Reference in the Nuclear Age* is that it creates precisely this sense of a once "forgotten" and now regained connection in modern culture. Solomon's dramatic reframing of culture within the possibility of nuclear war is the "remembering" of a recognition that has been made only peripherally in the past three decades. By focusing on language and the study of language in contemporary culture and on the possibility of nuclear annihilation, Solomon "remembers" nuclear death, a subject that, since World War II, has been discussed only at the margins and in the gaps of academic and institutional discourse. Solomon marks and helps to effect this remembering by "thinking crudely," as Bertolt Brecht urged, and making the seemingly all too evident but previously deferred connection (as if, like Edgar Allen Poe's purloined letter, it had been too obvious to be seen) between the semiotic ultimacy of a nuclear referent and the local practices of textuality—the possibility of significance against the absolute cancellation of reference.

We believe that *Discourse and Reference in the Nuclear Age* is an important contribution to the contemporary debate about discourse theory and that it will help define the place of discourse, in an urgent way, in our social and individual lives. This book also fulfills our own best vision for the Oklahoma Project for Discourse and Theory in that it combines literary theory, philosophy, politics, and discourse theory in the exploration of a subject that is timely and of the utmost importance. We can think of no more important issue that contemporary intellectual life should address, and we can think of no issue that contemporary intellectual life has avoided more assiduously in the confines of the various disciplines of the academy.

This combination of urgency and avoidance in facing the issues of war and peace—in facing, that is, the "life" of the human sciences in a absolute way—is the subject of Solomon's study. Solomon first examines the status of discourse concerning nuclear war. What is the nature of language and discourse that "speaks" about nuclear war? Is discourse that "refers" to nuclear war of the same status as fictional discourse that refers to Captain Ahab or Moby Dick, for instance? Or does the social and political nature of nuclear war require that, although it is "contrary to fact," discourse treating nuclear war nevertheless must rethink the referential function of language, something contemporary philosophy of language has failed to do? In pursuing his topic, Solomon ranges through the major tenets of current language philosophy, but he turns to Aristotle for the intellectual framework of his discussion of Saussure, Peirce, Popper, Derrida, and others, always returning to the pressing question, the defining question, of discourse theory—namely, the referential status of "potential" political events which discourse articulates.

Solomon's discussion is not simply of the effect of the possibility of nuclear war on intellectual endeavor, although this is a crucial sub-theme of the book. More generally, Solomon deals with what he calls the "concrete historical and political experience" in all the discursive formations that constitute our social life. In this way Solomon addresses the question of the "enunciation" of discourse, the difficult relationship between the general structures and forms of language—what Paul de Man calls the "grammatical" aspect of language and what Kierkegaard calls its "universalizing" tendency—and the particular enunciations of concrete situations. This, as Solomon suggests, is a pressing area of discourse theory, and *Discourse and Reference in the Nuclear Age* offers an important contribution to this debate.

But the more particular focus of this book—its own concrete historical and political situation—attempts to situate discourse theory within the experience of our times. That is, Solomon attempts to describe a discourse theory that "would be by nature both pluralistic and interdisciplinary, attempting to constitute ... a 'thick description' of the structure of that complex system of interrelated national and international effects that we include under the umbrella of the 'nuclear referent.'"

We do not need to point out the details of this discussion—Solomon's text is both impassioned and clear in its "rememberings" of these issues—but we do want to situate this study in the context of the Oklahoma Project's aims and ambitions. To begin with, Solomon's book places discourse theory within the social and political experience of our time by its very topic, especially in that such a discussion requires the kind of interdisciplinary focus that Solomon brings to the task. The book, like the Oklahoma Project as a whole, is based upon the assumption that the study of discourse and discursive formations—in this case the language that refers to and defines the strategic nature of nuclear conflicts—demands an interdisciplinary approach. Solomon, thus, forges connections between the philosophy of language, the post-structuralist critique of structuralism and of continental and Anglo-American language philosophy, and political discourse. More important, Solomon suggests ways in which these divergent "disciplines" serve particular historical and political ends.

Solomon uses this analysis to conceive of nuclear war as a referent of discourse by "remembering" another model—an Aristotelian model—that attempts to account for the referential problem that nuclear war suggests, a model somewhat different from the contemporary structural models of discourse. The importance of this book, finally, is that it defines the problem of discourse in our time in ways that cannot and should not again be forgotten or deferred. This is an immensely important book that will help describe the engagement that "discourse theory" should provide to our intellectual and social lives. It opens a consideration that brings together, in the most pressing of contemporary concerns, divergent areas of intellectual pursuit. There are no more important concerns than those "remembered" in *Discourse and Reference in the Nuclear Age,* and we are pleased that this significant study has found a home in the Oklahoma Project.

ROBERT CON DAVIS
RONALD SCHLEIFER

Norman, Oklahoma

Acknowledgments

IT IS WITH SOME SADNESS that I complete these notes of acknowledgment and thanks, for only in the midst of their revision did I learn of the passing of the man who perhaps more than anyone else has made this book possible. I will not be alone in mourning the departure of Professor Morton Bloomfield, but among all those who have owed so much to him I feel that mine is a special debt, the debt not of a medievalist but of a student of critical theory to whom he offered support and guidance above and beyond an already full load of academic responsibilities. Long before this book had even been dreamed of, Professor Bloomfield allowed me the precious freedom to explore my own theoretical speculations and conjectures, the critical explorations that led to the writing of this book. Whatever mistakes I may have made along the way are my own, but I shall always owe to Morton Bloomfield's memory the opportunities I was granted to take the risks I believed necessary to take.

On a happier note, I wish to thank Professors Jurij Striedter and Claudio Guillén, who with Professor Bloomfield guided my earliest critical efforts with an open-minded generosity that I can only appreciate more as the years go by. I would also like to thank Joel Weinsheimer, Thomas Winner, Kelsie Harder, Dean MacCannell, and Juliet Flower MacCannell for their judicious criticism of earlier versions of some of the ideas found in these pages. Especial thanks are due in this regard to Professor Thomas Sebeok, to the editorial staff of *Semiotica*, and to the Semiotic Society of

America for encouraging and enlightening my semiotic explorations over the years.

To Joseph Riddel, I extend the thanks of a colleague who has learned much from him about how to (and how not to) read Jacques Derrida. Maximillian Novak, Frederick Burwick, Richard Lehan, Bob Maniquis, and Anne Mellor have all offered collegial guidance and encouragement when both were much needed and appreciated. The Research Committee of the Academic Senate at UCLA has consistently provided material support in the form of annual grants that have considerably facilitated the research and writing of this book.

I am pleased also to be able to thank Geoffrey Hartman and the faculty and students of the School of Criticism and Theory for enlarging my critical horizons and lending an immediacy to the controversies that I have tackled in this study. My summer with them at Northwestern University successfully transformed the abstractions of critical discussion into the flesh and blood of intellectual give-and-take, and I would be poorer without that experience.

I cannot begin to thank Marjorie Perloff for her friendship and guidance, both of which have been crucial to the successful completion of this book. So many of us owe so much to her generosity that we could form a society. To Jerome McGann, my heartfelt gratitude for moral support when it was most needed. To Richard Martin, Arden Reed, and Jim Holstun, the same.

Carolyn Porter, Robert Con Davis, and Ronald Schleifer have all been instrumental in shaping the final form of this book through both their clear-sighted criticism and their liberal reception of ideas that may challenge many of their own critical beliefs. I would also like to thank Tom Radko, who carefully guided this project through the publication process from start to finish, and Patty Dornbusch, for her attentive editing of my manuscript. I also wish to acknowledge the journal *Names* for permission to reprint portions of my article "Speaking of No One: The Logical Status of Fictional

Proper Names," vol. 33, no. 3(1985): 145–57, and the journal *SubStance* for permission to reprint portions of my article "Between Determinism and Indeterminism" (forthcoming, 1988).

I owe heavy intellectual debts to Christopher Norris, who charted a path between post-structural and analytic philosophy, and to Floyd Merrell, who explored the critical connections between physics and metaphysics. In following their example, I may not always draw the same conclusions, but without their pioneering work my own would have been weaker.

If there are debts of friendship, then I shall never be able to repay mine to Martin Irvine and Radha Radhakrushnan. I have valued their intelligence, sympathy, and comradeship more than they may know. Their infectious enthusiasm for ideas has kept me going time and again in the darker moments of scholarship. Without such friends I doubt that any books would ever get written at all.

No economic metaphors will be of any use in my final note of acknowledgment, because I can find no adequate words to express my gratitude for Sonia Maasik's intelligence and comradeship beyond dedicating to her a book whose every word she has read more often than any editor, or wife, should ever be asked to read.

J. Fisher Solomon

Los Angeles, California

DISCOURSE AND REFERENCE
IN THE NUCLEAR AGE

PART 1

INTRODUCTION

CHAPTER 1

A "Nuclear" Agenda

IN THE SPRING OF 1984 the Department of Romance Studies at Cornell University was host to a colloquium designed to inaugurate a dialogue among advanced literary theorists concerning a possible agenda for critical theory in a nuclear age. Soon after the conference a representative sampling of the papers presented at the meeting appeared in a special issue of *Diacritics* (1984) along with a preface outlining the general profile of an emerging "nuclear criticism."[1] "By Nuclear Criticism," the preface explains,

> is meant something positive and something unavowed, a new topic and an explicitation of what is already everywhere being done. This proposal arises, on the one hand, out of reading a certain amount of recent criticism and critical theory and feeling that without exception it recounts an allegory of nuclear survival; and on the other, out of the sense that critical theory ought to be making a more important contribution to the public discussion of nuclear issues. The field would invite both kinds of criticism, the sort that reads other critical or canonical texts for the purpose of uncovering the unknown shapes of our unconscious nuclear fears, and that which aims to show how the terms of the current nuclear discussion are being shaped by literary or critical assumptions whose implications are often, perhaps systematically ignored. [*Diacritics* 1984:2]

Immediately following this programmatic description there appears an eclectic agenda for a prospective nuclear criticism, including suggestions for applying the rhetorical, semiological, and interpretational skills that literary theorists have developed in their textual studies to the complex political questions of the nuclear era.[2] But the assumption "that critical theory ought to be making a more important contribution to the public discussion of nuclear issues" may raise a number of questions both inside and outside the critical community. Since the nuclear era is now well over a quarter century old, one might ask why such a critical agenda is emerging *now*. Why, that is, has no such agenda been so fully and programmatically articulated before? What was it about the spring of 1984 that caused so many literary theorists to converge upon Ithaca, New York, to draft and exemplify a coherently defined nuclear criticism? Certainly the Cornell conferees met during a moment of particular global tension, but why did former global crises not result in similar meetings of American literary theorists?

Implicit in such questions, however, is a further, more general one: Why are literary scholars now turning their attention to political questions at all? What has made possible the mixture of aesthetic, linguistic, and political discourse that characterizes, for example, Zoë Sofia's contribution to the Cornell meeting, "Exterminating Fetuses: Abortion, Disarmament, and the Sexo-Semiotics of Extraterrestrialism," or Mary Ann Caws's feminist interpretation, "Singing in Another Key: Surrealism Through a Feminist Eye?" What has enabled American criticism's recent turn from strictly aesthetic and textual research toward a more engaged relation between critical theory and political action?

The answers to such questions lie in a complex of professional, political, and technological upheavals that, taken together, sharply identify the specific historical context of the Cornell colloquium. Perhaps the most dramatic of these upheavals appears in the history of nuclear technology itself. As late as 1962 the politics of nuclear brinkmanship still enjoyed the support of a public for whom a nuclear conflict still had the cast of conventional warfare. In the Cold War aftermath of the Cuban Missile Crisis, for example, many Americans ordered the construction of personal bomb shelters, not a cessation to the politics of confrontation. Nuclear war seemed awful but not unthinkable. No one wanted it, but it did exert a certain appeal, a morbid fascination that we may find reflected in the aesthetic representations of the period. In *On the Beach* (1959), for instance, a film designed to warn Americans against the disastrous futility of a nuclear exchange, audiences could imaginatively witness a noble, if moribund, postnuclear world in which surviving individuals played out their final romantic fantasies before painlessly disappearing in the reassuring company of their fellow survivors. The inspired black humor of *Doctor Strangelove* (1964) was less compromising, but in it we find some seductive intimations of a postnuclear liberation from the constraints of civil society that might be enjoyed by the few survivors of a nuclear holocaust. Paradoxically, and probably unintentionally, both of these films subtly appealed to the selfish side of the American character, to the ingrained individualism for which the imagined survivability of an absolute war has a certain anarchic appeal.

When we compare such films as *On the Beach* and *Doctor Strangelove* to *Testament* or *The Day After*, we can see that something has changed. It is not likely, however, that this same change can be found in the American character. A *survivable* nuclear war probably still retains its appeal to the peculiarly anarchic temper of Jeffersonian America. Few Americans, however, are still able to believe in the *possibility* of such an event. Quantitative and qualitative changes in our nuclear arsenals have effaced the popular image of a survivable nuclear exchange and have prompted a substantial number of Americans to demand a cessation to the development and stockpiling of nuclear weapons. New imagery, accordingly, has replaced the old imagery. There is no romance for the pathetic survivors of *The Day After*; there is no comic relief in *Testament*. These films have not been made to appeal to our aesthetic sensibilities: their purpose is ultimately more political than aesthetically formal. One can, of course, still respond to such representations aesthetically and critically, but that response, by itself, would be somehow to miss the point.

To understand more fully the motivation behind the Cornell conference, however, we must look to political as well as to technological change. To name just one such change, we might recall how in the forties, fifties, and early sixties, America was engaged in a cold war with the Soviet Union that rendered impracticable any full-scale attempt by literary intellectuals to affect strategic policy. Such an attempt, of course, might have been made, but it would have been regarded with suspicion. Oddly enough, however, the apparent calling off of the Cold War in the détente years also may have reduced the likelihood of a critical intervention into the nuclear controversy. With Washington and Moscow actively negotiating with each other, the world appeared to be a less dangerous place than it had been. America in the mid-seventies was more or less at peace, and the SALT negotiations *appeared* to be progressing toward a solution to the arms race. Under such circumstances, literary critics could continue their more traditional pursuits without feeling any strong pressures to get involved in the nuclear debate.

What changed all this was the apparent resumption of the Cold War following the election of the Reagan administration. Having become accustomed to the unthinkability of nuclear warfare and to the necessity, therefore, for arms negotiations, many Americans (literary critics included) were startled by the new talk emanating from Washington. For the first time in almost twenty years an American administration had begun to prefer confrontation to negotiation; and for the first time ever the authors of American strategic policy had begun to speak of a nuclear conflict that would be not only survivable but winnable. No American administration had ever hinted at the possibility of *prevailing* in a nuclear war: suddenly, one was. The new rhetoric was thus doubly startling, at once disrupting the assumptions of the era of détente while apparently going the Cold War years one better. Washington seemed to be contemplating a "hot" war with the Soviet Union, and it is in the context of the spontaneous worldwide response to this disturbing new rhetoric that we can situate at least the emotions behind the Cornell meeting.

Still, with a long tradition of apolitical aestheticism behind it, American literary criticism might yet have held itself aloof. That a meeting such as Cornell's could have been organized at all, then, suggests that there has been a certain upheaval within the critical community itself, an ideological shift relatively independent of the external technological and political pressures briefly outlined above. And, in fact, there has been an upheaval in the profession, an upheaval that, taken in conjunction with the sufficient causation provided by an extraprofessional history, defines what we might call the necessary cause behind the Cornell meeting. To determine the precise nature of the professional revolution before us, then, we might look briefly at the recent history of American literary criticism itself.

This history, of course, is now well known. As a discrete profession academically distinct from the traditional curricular study of the classics or of grammar, literary criticism emerged in the early-twentieth-century American university as something of a subset of philology and biography. By midcentury, however, a "New Critical" revolution had effectively overturned this "Old Critical" regime by declaring a formal distinction between the study of "history" and the criticism of "poetry." Being humanists themselves, the "New Critics" did not attack the study of history in itself, but argued that the social, or moral, value of literature could be best conveyed by treating poems as formally autonomous aesthetic objects whose "ironic" function was to call attention to the properties of poetic language itself, not to the extraliterary, referential realities of scientific or historical discourse. With Immanuel Kant and Samuel Taylor Coleridge as their major authorities, the New Critics successfully launched an American poetics parallel in certain respects to the formalistic analyses simultaneously being developed by the Russian and Czechoslovakian critics on the Continent. The self-referring subject of poetry, each school argued, was poetry. The referential subjects of historical and scientific discourse belonged to a separate study.

The success of the New Critics helps explain the reluctance of American critics in the post–World War II era to get involved, in a professional capacity, with strictly political issues. Given the implicit and explicit authority among the New Critics of Matthew Arnold's passionate call for a politically disassociated and ideologically disinterested critical community, it is not surprising that American criticism saw little place for itself within the nuclear debates of the early sixties. Our question, rather, is why American criticism today is forging a place for itself not only within the nuclear debate but within a larger range of political issues including Marxist and feminist politics. A partial answer to this question might be found within the even more recent history of American avant-garde criticism from the midsixties to the present.

Perhaps the greatest single theoretical change in recent American criticism has been the violent disruption, or deconstruction, of its traditional, essentially identitarian, ontology. The New Critics, though champions of aesthetic irony and ambiguity, assumed nonetheless the unitary identity of the poetic tradition and of the forms of poetic discourse as well. Northrop Frye, in spite of his challenge to New Critical universalism, similarly treated the literary tradition as a self-contained formal unity whose history is independent of social and political necessity. In much the same way, the existentialists, following the lead of Jean-Paul Sartre, Wallace Stevens, and Frank Kermode, opposed the unconstrained realm of fiction to an existential Being whose determinate identity could only fetter the free rein of the imagination. And the phenomenologists, whether following the lead of Edmund Husserl or of Georges Poulet, grounded their inquiries in the self-present identity of the transcendental ego, or the critic's own aesthetic consciousness.

But ironically, as Frank Lentricchia has reminded us (1980), even as archetypal, existentialist, and phenomenological critics jockeyed for position during the waning of the New Criticism in America, structuralist theorists on the Continent had, by the middle of the 1960s, demolished the identitarian foundations of phenomenology and existentialism through their attention to the anti-identitarian principle of *difference*, which Ferdinand de Saussure had introduced into theoretical discourse three-quarters of a century before. Thus, even as Anglo-American semanticists were exploring the logical relationships between words and things, Continental and American linguists were deconstructing the referent on behalf of the systematically codified play of structural differences. At the same time, such structuralist anthropologists as Claude Lévi-Strauss were undoing the "universal" identity of cultural consciousness, while the ever-roving figure of Roland Barthes could be found demythologizing the naturalizing myths of bourgeois culture by exposing the ideologically motivated codes upon which they rested. In an era, then, when structuralism had essentially announced the dissolution of the human sciences as a unified totality, American critics were still looking for a foundational method to center their criticism.

In spite of their apparent triumphs, however, the structuralists were to face their own paradoxes by the middle 1960s, for it was not until then that anyone fully noticed the contradiction at the heart of the structuralist enterprise: the contradiction, that is, implicit in the structuralists' attempt to ground their analyses upon a principle of structural differences. The structuralists, that is to say, had not fully realized that by centering their inquiries upon the systematic play of difference, they had essentially come to treat the "other" of identity as if it were itself an identity. But how can one identify a difference? Is difference not simply another center that cannot hold, another nostalgic attempt to ground the human sciences in a presence or identity that might justify and universalize our knowledge?

Such were the observations, of course, of a young, then relatively unknown philosopher named Jacques Derrida, whose work, paradoxically, first appeared in America precisely at the moment when American criticism was preparing to make its inaugural contact with structuralist thinking. The principle of structural difference, we might say, entered the discourse of American criticism *already in the form of differance*. Frank Lentricchia has narrated the historical outline of this "event" of difference/differance nicely. "When in late October of 1966," he writes,

> over one hundred humanists and social scientists from the United States and eight other countries gathered at the Johns Hopkins Humanities Center to participate in a symposium called "The Languages of Criticism and the Sciences of Man," the reigning avant-garde theoretical presences for literary critics in this country were Georges Poulet, to a lesser extent members of the "Geneva School" associated with him, and, in the distant background, in uncertain relationship to the critics of consciousness, the forbidding philosophical analyses of Heidegger (*Being and Time*), Sartre (*Being and Nothingness*), and Merleau-Ponty (*The Phenomenology of Perception*). [1980:157]

The Hopkins symposium was called to introduce American criticism to the as yet little-known structuralist critique already in full cry on the Continent. With the last-minute inclusion in the program of Jacques Derrida's essay "Structure, Sign, and Play in the Discourse of the Human Sciences," however, the case for an American structuralist poetics was undermined from the very beginning. For while Derrida challenged neither structuralism's dissolution of phenomenological consciousness nor its deconstruction of referential realism, he effectively undermined the implicit claims of both Lévi-Strauss and Saussure to have found a self-consistent method for the human sciences, an indifferent master code with which to unlock the manifold codes of culture. Once the structuralists had essentially deconstructed the figure of ontological identity, in other words, they implicitly forbade any attempt to reconstruct the discourse of the human sciences upon an indifferent method outside the play of differences. If all knowledge is codified knowledge, grounded neither in a transcendental consciousness nor in an objectively subsisting referential reality, then "structural" knowledge is itself just another code among a potentially unlimited number of codes. A "structuralist science," as Derrida pointed out to his audience at Johns Hopkins, is a contradiction. And so, it was not Lévi-Strauss, and not Roland Barthes, who emerged from the Hopkins series of colloquiums as the new guide for American avant-garde criticism: it was Derrida. Paradoxically, structuralism could only be born in America in the posthumous figure of post-structuralism.

As American criticism assimilated itself to Derrida in the early to middle seventies, the initial response (not too surprisingly, given both the linguistic emphasis of Derrida's early work in "grammatology" and the textual training and disposition of his American disciples) remained formalist and textual, not political. In the writings of such influential "Yale School" post-structuralist critics as the late Paul de Man, for example, one could find rigorous deconstructions of semiology and rhetoric through the painstaking recuperation of textual aporias, but little trace of "history." "Among all the deconstructive close readers," as Vincent Leitch has put it, "de Man pays least attention to intertextuality. Rarely does he focus on the pressing influences of forerunners or on the determining cultural forces operating upon or in texts.... So tangled up does de Man get in the epistemological abysses of figurative play that he never quite arrives at history" (1983:188). "History," that is to say, was not so much denied as deferred in the beginnings of the post-structural enterprise in America, subjected to a differential play of metaphors that effectively concealed the referents of historical realism behind the free-playing figures of tropological discourse. And no master language, or meta-language, the post-structuralists argued, could retrieve them.

Such a deferral of history occurred not only in the literary analyses of the Yale School: we also find it in the earliest metahistorical criticism of such American post-structural historians as Hayden White. Adapting the critical vocabulary of Northrop Frye to the genealogical historicity of Friedrich Nietzsche, White effectively textualized the criticism of historical narrative itself, arguing that even the writer of history is trapped inside his or her own governing tropes, unable to achieve unmediated contact with historical "reality," that is, with an objective historical referent. With no transcending master code for the writing of history, the historian becomes a metahistorian, a writer about writing, about the irreducibly deflecting tropes of historical narrative, inherently unable to represent an immediate historical presence.

The initial phase of American post-structural criticism, then, was essentially as apolitical as the formalisms that it overturned. While critical formalism tended to marginalize the diachrony of history, the early post-structuralists effectively obscured it by raising the principle of tropological play over the referential realism of traditional historical discourse. With "history" contained within an "intertextual" (or "archival") play of metaphors, the early post-structuralists apparently substituted their own antiformalist aestheticism for what had been a reigning formalist aestheticism. And some observers, in fact, complained that they could not tell the difference.

The first signs of a major change in the political consciousness of American criticism appeared in the late seventies and early eighties with the publication of influential works by such critics as Fredric Jameson, Edward Said, Gayatri Spivak, and Frank Lentricchia. Without abandoning the post-structural critique of representational realism, each of these writers began to search for a way of shifting criticism's focus from a strictly textual analysis to a more broadly political analysis, often blending a Nietzschean distrust of historical dialectics and referential realism with a Marxian attentiveness to the social forces behind the writing of both literary and critical texts.

In Jameson's *The Political Unconscious* (1981), for example, we find an amalgamation of both structuralist and post-structuralist discourses articulated around a specifically Marxist theory of historical *presentation* (*Darstellung*) rather than representation. In Michael Ryan's *Marxism and Deconstruction: A Critical Articulation* (1982), we are challenged to conceive of a revolutionary agenda based upon what Ryan perceives to be a logical continuity between Derridean deconstruction and Marxian social analysis. Focusing upon the destabilizing play of class differences that he finds in Marx's historical theory, Ryan proposes a model for a politically committed criticism dedicated to the constant undermining of political and textual authority in the name of differance itself. Similarly, in a special issue of *Boundary 2* (1982-83), American critics were invited to explore the possible engagements that might be negotiated between Marxist and postmodern discourse. By the early 1980s, then, it was becoming increasingly clear that a new brand of political criticism was emerging in America, a "new historicism," distinguishable from the "old historicism" precisely in its rigorous opposition to dialectics, referential realism, and identitarian metaphysics.

It is against the backdrop of this epochal shift within the critical community itself that we can finally place the Cornell conference. With geopolitical tensions rising and with American theorists increasingly exploring a new political agenda of their own for post-structural criticism, the Cornell gathering assumes a certain air of inevitability. Still, while we can explain the reasons for the meeting, we may yet be asked to justify it. Richard Macksey and Eugenio Donato, the organizers of the Johns Hopkins symposium on "The Languages of Criticism and the Sciences of Man," had no need to justify their introduction of European critical trends to American criticism; but can American criticism justify its desire to make an "important contribution to the public discussion of nuclear issues?" This question can be enlarged: Can American criticism justify its desire to make an important contribution to political discussion at all? A "nuclear criticism," in other words, might be said to be a species of the larger genus of political criticism in general. But political discourse seeks results beyond those of literary discourse: it seeks to be extratextually as well as textually effective, directed toward the reality of the act as well as the tropology of the word. Given the recent politicizing of American criticism, one might expect that it would now be seeking a revived realism, a turn, perhaps, to Georg Lukács and his passionate defense of the realistic tradition, of Aristotle, and of the continuous dialectic between subjective individuality and objective nature.

But while critical *practice* in the eighties may indeed be pursuing the reality of the act, its *theory* remains post-structurally opposed to dialectics, to realism, and to the objectivity of the referent, maintaining still the differing/deferring tropes of the word. But this complex comingling of post-structural theory and political desire is not without its theoretical and practical effects. To return for a moment to Michael Ryan's *Marxism and Deconstruction*, for example, we can see that to articulate revolutionary Marxism with Derridean deconstruction, Ryan has to argue, essentially, that Marx himself authored no dialectically teleological revolutionary *program*, but simply deconstructed the Hegelian dialectic on behalf of a vision of an ever-unfolding, *de*totalizing, revolutionary *process* (see Ryan 1982, chaps. 2–3 especially). Whether this is indeed the case is less important than Ryan's so taking the dialectic out of Marx's hands. Ryan's gesture frees him to propose a permanent antidialectical revolution in the name of a Marxian-Derridean resistance to bourgeois authority, but once one begins to deconstruct, it is difficult to see where the process might stop. For if we follow the logic of differance rigorously, we find that the articulation between gnosis and praxis, between the *word* of the critic and the *act* of the politician, is a peculiarly troubled one, fissured by an irreducible *difference* between the two that would leave us undecidably suspended between word and act at the very point of our politico-critical inauguration.

This potential aporia of politico-critical discourse is not a wholly fanciful one, for it is precisely what is suggested in Jacques Derrida's invited contribution to the Cornell colloquium, "No Apocalypse, Not Now (full speed ahead, seven missiles, seven missives)," an essay that paradoxically repeats the essential effect of Derrida's inaugural performance in America. For just as Derrida's contribution to the Hopkins symposium undercut from the start the very project that the conference had been intended to inaugurate, so too does his contribution to the Cornell meeting complicate the very idea of a nuclear criticism, questioning not the competence of literary scholars before such extraliterary issues as nuclear war but the "scientific" competence of anyone before the nuclear referent, the competence of anyone, that is to say, to distinguish between the realities of the world and the tropological "fictions" by which they are apprehended. And by looking closely at the series of logical aporias that Derrida's essay uncovers in the face of the nuclear referent, we may find not only a challenge that a nuclear criticism might well have to take up before establishing its theory and agenda but a challenge to anyone seeking to cross unambiguously from the critical text into an extracritical reality, a challenge, in other words, to reassess historical and referential realism in a nuclear age.

CHAPTER 2

"No Apocalypse, Not Now": Deconstructing the Nuclear Referent

IN THE STYLE OF ITS DELIVERY and textual presentation, "No Apocalypse, Not Now" (Derrida 1984) resembles a sermon more than it does a conventional academic discourse. Its text is divided into seven parts: seven "missiles," or gnomic statements, each followed by an explanatory, or exegetical, "missive," itself divided into a varying number of "reasons." Indeed, there is something parodically "sacred" about the entire proceeding as we follow it from its apocalyptic inauguration to its apocalyptic concluding reference to the Revelation of John. But this "sacred" missive is hardly conventionally sermonic, since unlike a conventional sermon its purpose is not to propose doctrinal guidance but to suspend in a series of unresolved aporias any possible conclusion that a nuclear criticism might accomplish.

"Let me first say a word about speed," Derrida accordingly begins, thereby preparing his first paradox: "*At the beginning there will have been speed*" (1984:20). Why do we find "speed," motion, change, at the origin, that is to say, at the non-origin of a nuclear criticism? Because, Derrida observes, while we may "find it easy to say that in nuclear war 'humanity' runs the risk of its self-destruction, with nothing left over, no remainder," we still have to recognize that what is at stake in the nuclear era appears to us all the same "in the experience of a race, or more precisely of a *competition*, a rivalry between two rates of speed" (1984:20). East versus West. The Warsaw Pact versus the Free World. Us versus Them. But "Is this new?" Derrida asks. Have not the "most classical wars" been "speed races, in their preparation and in the actual pursuit of hostilities" (1984:20)? What historical era, that is to say, has not experienced its own geopolitical agon, its own competitive balance of power? So can we really say, Derrida continues, that we are "having, today, *another*, a different experience of speed," or "must we speak prudently of an extraordinary—although qualitatively homogeneous—acceleration of the same experience" (1984:20)?

Thus Derrida begins to elaborate his first aporia, beginning with the very form of his own question, namely, "Is the war of (over, for) speed (with all that it entails) an irreducibly new phenomenon, an invention linked to a set of inventions of the so-called nuclear age, or is it rather the brutal acceleration of a movement that has always already been at work" (1984:20–21)? There are two apparently irreconcilable answers to this question. On the one hand, says Derrida, we might say that, no, there "is perhaps no invention, no radically new predicate in the situation known as the 'nuclear age,'" for of "all the dimensions of such an 'age' we may always say one thing: it is neither the first time nor the last. The historian's critical vigilance can always help us verify that repetitiveness; and the historian's patience, the lucidity of memory must always shed their light on 'nuclear criticism,' must oblige it to decelerate, dissuade it from rushing to a conclusion on the subject of speed itself" (1984:21). Be calm, such words advise. The crises of the present are not the world's first. This is not the millenium; it is not the first time that humanity has imagined its apocalypse. Consider history. The present is not unprecedented. There have been other wars, other cataclysms, other premonitions of the "end."

But then, on the other hand, we cannot ignore the possibility that perhaps there *is* some "radically new predicate" in this the "nuclear age." For, as Derrida continues, "this dissuasion and deceleration I am urging carry their own risks: the critical zeal that leads us to recognize precedents, continuities, repetitions at every turn can make us look like suicidal sleepwalkers, blind and deaf *alongside the unheard-of*.... One may still die after spending one's life recognizing, as a lucid historian, to what extent all that was not new, telling oneself that the inventors of the nuclear age or of nuclear criticism did not invent the wheel, or, as we French say, 'invent gunpowder.' That's the way one always dies, moreover, and the death of what is still now and then called humanity might well not escape the rule" (1984:21).

So what, then, would be the *right* answer, the right rate of speed: historical prudence or apocalyptic zeal? Critical deceleration or political acceleration? The word of the historian or the act of the activist? Somehow we "need to move both slowly and quickly" in the nuclear era (1984:21): but what speed is that? Derrida does not say, chooses neither the historian's soothing text nor the activist's zeal. Instead he commits himself only to his own rhetoric, his decision to address himself to the nuclear referent in the "rhetorical form of tiny atomic nuclei (in the process of fission or division in an uninterruptable chain)"—a rhetorical movement that should not be unfamiliar to us, since it essentially exemplifies the movement of the "trace," of differance, itself (1984:21).

And so, with the aporia of speed Derrida's first "missile" concludes, with a suspension, that is, of the relationship between word and act. Because, Derrida observes, prior to the mimetic text of the historian, to the word that might enable us "to translate the unknown into a known, to metaphorize, allegorize, domesticate the terror" (1984:21), and prior to the program of the nuclear activist certain of the irreducible uniqueness of the nuclear era, there will have been speed, the primordial competition between the Word and the Act, the inaugural brisure between creation and representation. "At the beginning was the word," Derrida muses, "at the beginning was the act. No! At the beginning—faster than word or act—there will have been *speed*, and a speed race between them" (1984:22).

Derrida's second missile shifts direction to consider the question of the competence of literary critics to address the nuclear referent, the competence, that is to say, of humanists, of "specialists in texts, all sorts of texts" relative to the "professionals of strategy, diplomacy, or nuclear technoscience" (1984:22). Again, the question admits two irreconcilable answers. From the perspective of the nuclear "experts" the humanist can have no such competence at all. What does criticism know of diplomacy, strategy, or technology? But the humanist, Derrida suggests, can always retort that "inasmuch as we are representative of humanity and of the incompetent humanities," and because "the stakes of the nuclear question are those of humanity, of the humanities," then it is simply our *responsibility* "to concern ourselves with the nuclear issue," especially in the light of our suspicion that "in this area in particular, there is a multiplicity of dissociated, heterogeneous competencies" (1984: 22). Is it not *more* dangerous, Derrida asks, to entrust this "dice game to so few hands," to the military officials and scientists who are "in the position of inventing, inaugurating, improvising procedures and giving orders where no model . . . can help them at all" (1984:22)?

Every voice in such an era, Derrida suggests, is needed in the face of something that has never been experienced before. For who can claim expertise before an event that has never occurred? Upon what historical precedents can a total nuclear war be conceived? We have to make our decisions, in Derrida's words, "at the moment of a decision that has no common ground with any other," which means that to think *pragmatically* through the dilemmas of the nuclear era we would "have to reinvent invention or conceive of another 'pragmatics'" (1984:23).

But can criticism conceive such a pragmatics? Can it supplement the technical competence of the nuclear experts? An attempt to elaborate a pragmatics for nuclear decision making would face a substantial epistemological difficulty from the beginning, and the difficulty would be metaphysical as well as epistemological. How could we begin to conceive, how could we possibly represent, something that, as Derrida writes, "has no precedent," that "has never occurred" (1984:23), that, properly speaking, does not exist? To what *do* the words "total nuclear war" refer? Wherein can we find the nuclear referent outside of speaking and writing about it? Indeed, Derrida suggests, the "terrifying reality of the nuclear conflict can only be the signified referent, never the real referent (present or past) of a discourse or a text" (1984:23). "Nuclear war," in other words, is, *today*, a sign, not a "reality" outside the play of signs. In a certain sense, Derrida provisionally implies, there *is* no nuclear referent.

Such might be our second aporia. But, paradoxically, it is precisely the apparently textual nature of "nuclear war," Derrida continues, that "entitles us . . . to concern ourselves seriously with the nuclear issue." We are so entitled, Derrida suggests, because in "our techno-scientifico-militaro-diplomatic incompetence, we may consider ourselves . . . as competent as others to deal with a phenomenon whose essential feature is that of being *fabulously textual* through and through," fabulously textual because "for the moment, a nuclear war has not taken place: one can only talk and write about it" (1984:23). And so, Derrida remarks, one "might call it a fable . . . a pure invention: in the sense in which it is said that a myth, an image, a fiction, a utopia, a rhetorical figure, a fantasy, a phantasm, are inventions" (1984:23).

"You will perhaps find it shocking to find the nuclear issue reduced to a fable," Derrida observes,

> but then I haven't simply said that. I have recalled that a nuclear war is for the time being a fable, that is, something one can only talk about. But who can fail to recognize the massive "reality" of nuclear weaponry and of the terrible forces of destruction that are being stockpiled and capitalized everywhere, that are coming to constitute the very movement of capitalization. [1984:23]

Thus we encounter a third aporia, as Derrida presents us with two peculiarly interrelated phenomena. On the one hand, we have the historical "reality" of a nuclear arms race; on the other, we have a "fabulous" representation of a war that has never happened. But the two are difficult to separate from each other, for the "reality" of the arms race has itself been predicated upon the "fiction" of the war. Our nuclear stockpile has been stockpiled in the *name* of the war, and in the name of deterring that war.

Derrida's nuclear critic must accordingly be able "to distinguish between this 'reality' of the nuclear age and the fiction of war," even as he or she "must also be careful to interpret critically this critical or diacritical distinction":

> For the "reality" of the nuclear age and the fable of nuclear war are perhaps distinct, but they are not two separate things. It is the war (in other words the fable) that triggers this fabulous war effort, this senseless capitalization of sophisticated weaponry, this speed race in search of speed. [1984:23]

In the face of this paradoxical interrelation of fact and fiction, scientific knowledge itself begins to break down. "There is nothing but *doxa*, opinion, 'belief' " in the face of the nuclear referent, Derrida suggests, because one "can no longer oppose belief and science, *doxa* and *épistémè*, once one has reached the decisive place of the nuclear age, in other words, once one has arrived at the critical place of the nuclear age." For in "this critical place, there is no more room for a distinction between belief and science, thus no more space for a 'nuclear criticism' strictly speaking. Nor even for a truth in that sense. No truth, no apocalypse. (As you know, Apocalypse means Revelation, of Truth, *Un-Veiling*)" (1984:24).

Perhaps, in the practical, pragmatic sense, this is the most disturbing of Derrida's nuclear aporias, because it essentially undermines the objective, scientific claims of every voice in the nuclear debate. Whose "belief" could claim "truth," and upon what basis? How could we test the relative merits of our various speculations? To demonstrate his implied argument, Derrida briefly deconstructs Leslie Gelb's critique of the apparent "belief" present in the early months of the first Reagan administration that the United States could achieve nuclear superiority over the Soviets. But in Gelb's criticism, Derrida can find what is only another "belief." Gelb, Derrida writes, "believes" that the "'Reagan' belief is not based on proofs. But by definition it could not be," Derrida adds, "for there are no proofs in this area. There is only one proof, that is war, and moreover it proves nothing. The only thing the adverse discourse can oppose to the 'Reagan' belief is another belief, its own hermeneutics and its own rhetoric" (1984:26).

And so, Derrida implies, no matter which side one is on in the nuclear debate, one cannot escape one's own rhetoric, indeed, one's own text, writing, literature. It is not the war itself that is so confined but our knowledge of it, a knowledge that cannot transcend its own rhetorical tropes, its own "literature." Thus, in his fourth "missile" Derrida considers the relationship between literature itself and the nuclear referent, a relationship, Derrida suggests, that is perhaps more decisive than that between the war and human life as a whole. For while some fragment of humanity, some fragment of life, certainly of being, might survive a nuclear holocaust, literature, which cannot exist without its "archive," without "the development of a positive law implying authors' rights, the identification of the signatory, of the corpus, of names, titles, the distinction between the original and the copy, the original and the plagiarized version, and so forth," could not.

"Literature is not reduced to this form of archivizing and this form of law," Derrida adds, "but it could not outlive them and still be called literature" (1984:26). It is literature, the archive, that is most certainly threatened with extinction by a total nuclear exchange, Derrida writes; it is literature that is best able to imagine our historical fragility. Indeed, Europe survived the collapse of classical civilization, but its literature very nearly did not. The same might be true for contemporary civilization. And so, Derrida suggests, "what allows us perhaps to think the uniqueness of nuclear war, its being-for-the-first-time-and-perhaps-for-the-last-time, its absolute inventiveness, what it prompts us to think even if it remains a decoy, a belief, a phantasmic projection, is obviously the possibility of an irreversible destruction, leaving no trace of the juridico-literary archive—that is, total destruction of the basis of literature and criticism" (1984:26).

Thus, in a sense, literature and criticism both belong to the nuclear age, Derrida writes, for both have always dealt "hypothetically with a total and remainderless destruction of the archive, a destruction that would take place for the first time and . . . would lack any common proportion with, for example, the burning of a library":

> That is why deconstruction . . . belongs to the nuclear age. And to the age of literature. If "literature" is the name we give to the body of texts whose existence, possibility, and significance are the most radically threatened, for the first and last time, by the nuclear catastrophe, that definition allows our thought to grasp the essence of literature, its radical precariousness and the radical form of its historicity. . . . We may henceforth assert that the historicity of literature is contemporaneous through and through, or rather structurally indissociable, from something like a nuclear *epoch* (by nuclear "epoch," I also mean the *épochè* suspending judgment before the absolute decision). The nuclear age is not an epoch, it is the absolute *épochè*; it is not absolute knowledge and the end of history, it is the *épochè* of absolute knowledge. [1984:27]

Suspended between our present knowledge and the symbolically empty "absolute knowledge" that only an actual experience of a total nuclear war would bring, we thus find ourselves telling stories about that future terror, stories that refer, Derrida suggests, not to the "reality" of the "war" (because that "war," as such, does not yet exist to be referred to) but to the rhetorical forms that are available to us in our intertextual archive. Our tendency to imagine "total nuclear war" as an "apocalypse," for example, comes to us from the archive, from a history of texts, of millenarian speculations, of dialectical dreams of some Absolute Knowledge to be achieved at the "end" of history. Nuclear war can bring no such "revelation." It can "reveal" nothing. It can be fought, what is more, "*in the name of*" nothing at all, because no name on whose behalf it might be fought today ("freedom," "democracy," "socialism") would survive it to be "transmitted, inherited by anything living" (1984:30). Thus the nuclear "apocalypse" itself belongs to the archive, appearing to us as "an invention in the sense of a fable or an invention to be invented in order to make a place for it or to prevent it from taking place" (1984:28). The "apocalypse," in other words, is a figure that can be exploited by all sides in the nuclear debate, by all players: by those who wish to eliminate nuclear weapons altogether and by those who mean to retain them in the name of "deterrence." Either way the nuclear referent is somehow part of a continuing story, framed by what our literary imagination gives us or by the terms that our metaphysics has developed. Nuclear war is not itself "archival," Derrida implies, but like all of the "referents" of our discourse it cannot be thought apart from the figures of the archive, cannot be thought outside of metaphor and rhetoric.

"Some might conclude that therefore it is not real, as it remains entirely suspended in its fabulous and literary *épochè*," Derrida proposes (1984:28). But, of course, this is yet another play in what is for Derrida an entirely incalculable game. There is another side to the question, another aporia. "But we do not believe, such is the other version or the other side of the same paradox, in any thing except the nuclear referent," Derrida continues, as he launches his fifth "missile." Again we face an aporia of decision. On the one hand the nuclear referent is the only absolute referent "of all possible literature," an "ultimate referent" that would be "on a par with the absolute effacement of any possible trace" (1984:28), outside the play of difference, language, and rhetoric, the only possible referent absolutely "outside" the archive, silent, asymbolic, a nameless name. But on the other hand the nuclear referent is no referent, as such, at all; it is only a figure, an invention of our discourse, a pure signifier without any existing signified. Thus our very ability to decide, to make a judgment, to determine the right rate of speed, the right ratio of word and act, has been suspended at a moment when we have achieved a certain kind of "absolute knowledge" (i.e., in our knowledge of nuclear fission and fusion) and "run the risk, precisely because of that, of not stopping," of destroying ourselves (1984:31). "Unless," Derrida adds, "it is the other way around" (1984:31). Perhaps we may learn that it is not worth it ("and this," Derrida adds, "would be absolute knowledge" too), that it would be better "to spend a little more time together, the time of a long colloquy with warriors in love with life, busy writing in all languages in order to make the conversation last" (1984:31).

Thus it appears that in the face of the nuclear referent we must resign ourselves to our own inability to descry our "destiny" through the crystal ball of dialectical or apocalyptic metaphysics. History has no destiny, Derrida suggests, but moves instead along the incalculable play of differences that he calls destinerrance: a historical "wandering that is its own end" (1984:29). *Either* we shall not stop before it is too late, *or* we shall. There is nothing to help us decide, no present determinants before an uncertain future. For in this moment of indecision, this fissuring difference between alternatives that we cannot resolve, Derrida finds no ground from which we might begin to calculate the latent potentialities of the future, of our political, not our metaphysical, destiny. "I am not speaking here of factors of undecidability or incalculability that function as reservations in a calculable decision," Derrida remarks. "It is a question here of an aleatory element that appears in a heterogeneous relation to every possible calculation and every possible decision" (1984:29). "An absolute missile," in other words, *does not abolish chance*" (1984:29).

It is difficult to argue with this, and certainly it is impossible to attribute Derrida's critique of certainty in the nuclear era to the "fashions" of contemporary criticism, no matter how urgently our practical reason might militate against fully accepting Derrida's paradoxical suspension of knowledge in the face of the nuclear referent. For even Aristotle, whose dialectical theory of contradictory change anticipates Hegel's rigorous attempt to reduce the negative play of history to determinate certainty, had to concede that "everything must either be or not be, whether in the present or the future, but it is not always possible to distinguish and state determinately which of the alternatives must necessarily come about" (*De Interpretatione* 19a27–29). "A sea-fight [or, we might add, a nuclear war] must either take place to-morrow or not," Aristotle explains, but "it is not necessary that it should take place to-morrow, neither is it necessary that it should not take place" (*De Interpretatione* 19a30–31). And, also like Derrida, Aristotle too is concerned with the problematic relationship between what our propositions (our words) say about the world and how the world will actually conform to them—a relationship that lands Aristotle in a "difficulty" (*aporia*) just as it does Derrida, because our words cannot determine in themselves what will or will not take place. The future, Aristotle believes, must establish the propositional truth of our predictions, but those predictions themselves, our words, cannot determine their truth from within, cannot cross over from the word to the act, cannot reduce to indifference the difference between the conformations of our knowledge and the reality that we seek to know.

And yet, there is still something missing from Derrida's analysis of the nuclear referent, from his suspension of calculation and belief in the face of the "unheard-of." For the reality to which the nuclear referent refers, a reality that Derrida does not deny but rather suspends, is, in Aristotelian terms, a *potential* reality as well as an actual one. The nuclear referent, in other words, refers to an actual situational configuration of political and technological conditions that bear within themselves their own concrete potentialities for future development. The futurity of the nuclear referent is bound to the present not only by a tie of logical possibility but by one of empirical potentiality as well, a potentiality that *can* be calculated through the calculus of probability.

There is a material difference, that is to say, between modal possibility and empirical potentiality. Logically speaking, there can indeed be no ranking, no hierarchization, of contradictory beliefs about an indeterminate future. But the opposing beliefs, for example, of the Union of Concerned Scientists and the Civil Defense Administration over the possibilities for a postnuclear survival of a recognizable American civilization are not *simply* equal, for the veracity of each belief must be judged on the basis of a rigorous calculation of known technological, meteorological, biological, and sociological potentialities and propensities. Few would deny such an apparently obvious observation, and there is little in Derrida's own essay to suggest that he would contest it. But I am suggesting here something more. I am suggesting that the ground for such a testing of propositional belief does not lie simply within the paradigms and norms of scientific discourse: it is to be found within the real existence of empirical potentialities and propensities that scientific research can reveal. I am suggesting that our apprehension, for example, of the nuclear referent is determined not only by our archival imagination but also by our knowledge of an extraarchival world that is as real in its dispositional potentialities as in its actuated formalities. And this, Derrida's essay leads me to believe, *would* be contested.

For the thrust not only of Derrida's work but of poststructural criticism in general has been precisely against such a ground, against any appeal to a referentially determinate "reality" outside the figural paradigms of our discourse. Whether structuralist, post-structuralist, or even Marxist, criticism has maintained the irreducibly discursive nature of our understanding and knowledge, attacking the identity of the referent on behalf of a play of historical and tropological differences. There is no "Archimedean point" outside the play of difference that might ground our knowledge, criticism has argued. There is no apprehension of reality that has not "always already" been historicized, subjectivized, relativized. And so indeed, according to such a perspective, not only the nuclear referent but all referents are figures for our discourse that nothing short of the destruction of the historical archive itself might reduce to indifference. Until that moment of destruction, as Derrida's essay rigorously points out, the logic of the trace, of the play of difference, must suspend the referential relation between word and act, between our knowledge of the world and the world that we seek to know. Derrida does not say that we cannot continue to interpret that world, cannot attempt to anticipate possible futures, but he does deconstruct the ground by which we might evaluate our interpretations, suspending our beliefs in a universal *épochè*.

A nuclear criticism that simultaneously assents to this deconstruction of the referent while maintaining its desire to cross from the word to the act, from the text of the critic to the goal-oriented world of political activity, is not really credible. It can only state its own "beliefs," even as it undermines the ground for those beliefs. In itself, perhaps, there is nothing very serious in this. The agenda for a nuclear criticism suggested by the editors of *Diacritics* leaves plenty of room for textual approaches to the problem (for example, the study of the literary allegorization of nuclear war), approaches that can be useful in exploring the rhetoric of nuclear brinkmanship. And at the same time, while the humanities can indeed be said to have a "humane" responsibility, we need not argue the necessity for a nuclear criticism conducted on a broad front. Individual critics can choose or choose not to enter the debate, and their political success or lack of it in that debate will not affect the conduct of criticism as a whole. The challenge presented to critical thought by the nuclear referent, in other words, need not be urgently political. All the same, the nuclear referent does present a challenge to criticism, an epistemological challenge to think through the consequences of our general textualization of critical knowledge, our unrelenting deconstruction of the referent, of the belief in a physical world whose behavioral properties and dispositions can be objectively calculated and known.

The consequences of this deconstruction, as we can see in "No Apocalypse, Not Now," involve a suspension of knowledge and belief, an inability to choose between beliefs, between logical possibilities. But, somehow, not only do we make such choices all the time (which no one would deny), but we do so on the basis of determinants that come from our knowledge of the world as well as of the word. Somehow, for example, we know that there is a very low probability that one might save oneself from a nuclear strike by digging a hole in the ground. But how do we know this? Is our calculation merely an expression of subjective belief? To argue that it is not, that such knowledge is "scientific" rather than "archival," is to argue that the basis of our beliefs lies in a reality that transcends our archival figurations. And this, I think, is the real challenge that the nuclear referent offers to criticism, a challenge to analyze the ways in which the word relates to the world, how our knowledge actuates the potentiality of a world that, I shall argue, is real, that subsists outside our discourse and referentially grounds it.

The challenge presented by the nuclear referent, in other words, is to conceive what might be called a "potentialist realism" or "potentialist metaphysics." Such a metaphysics would not be the same as classical realism, for a potentiality is not a transcendentally universal, static identity. It is dynamic. It is indeed in play. But this play is not an unlimited "free play." It is situationally delimited, and its dynamics can be defined only within specified circumstances. In a sense, the ontological reality of a potentiality lies somewhere between identity and difference, between a universal determinism and the unrestricted play of differance, appearing to us in the form of empirical propensities, behavioral regularities that can be calculated, and thus grounding our distinctions between beliefs rather than suspending our decision.

The defense of a potentialist metaphysics cannot be uncontroversial, for in our "nuclear epoch" we have suspended our knowledge not only of the nuclear referent but of the referent itself. Scientific realism is regarded as mere metaphysics, blind to its own governing tropes. Criticism today attacks rather than defends the reality of natural order, continuity, or law. So why should the attempt be made at all? Why search for a ground, for a basis for decision? After all, criticism is not at all likely to be asked for a defense of realism. The so-called "decision makers" will continue to operate without us. Still, I suggest that the need for such a defense comes from the pressure exerted by the nuclear referent itself, from the intellectual challenge that it presents to us: to think through the aporias of this potential phenomenon, which, somehow, we know is real and cannot be ignored, but whose "reality," like the reality of more ordinary referents, appears to be inexplicable.

Perhaps, it may be suggested, the resolution of this referential problem is a task for semantic, not critical, analysis—a task for referential logicians, not for critics. But in the face of the nuclear referent, the either/or, true or false paradigms of logical discourse are simply not adequate. For the ontological status of the nuclear referent falls somewhere between the logical alternatives "exists" and "does not exist," and so any proposition concerning it can be judged neither to be true nor to be false. The situation is simply too uncertain to admit truth conditions. But this does not mean that we must simply deconstruct the nuclear predicament, assimilating its uncertainties to the aporias of literary discourse. Neither should we turn the problem wholly over to the technical experts; for the challenge presented by the nuclear referent goes beyond any single discipline, scientific or otherwise, crossing from physics to politics to rhetoric and beyond. The function of criticism at the present time, we might say, is to exercise its essentially Arnoldian willingness to transcend disciplinary boundaries and bring together a spectrum of relevant perspectives. A criticism that rejects this role, insisting upon reducing the complex elements of the nuclear referent to its own aestheticized terms, will be as inadequate to the challenge as the most rigid logical dialectic.

At a time, what is more, when literary critics are making a political turn from the word to the world, it is also time for criticism to rethink its rejection of the referent on behalf of a renewed approach to a referential reality that subsists outside the forms of textuality. I shall attempt in this book to rethink that referent, using the figure of the nuclear referent as a concrete example to guide the search for a potentialist realism beyond the either/or choice between identitarian metaphysics and the deconstruction of metaphysics that seems so inevitable to so many critics today. In this way, I shall pursue not a solution to the political dilemmas of the nuclear era but another way of thinking through the more critical ones.

CHAPTER 3

Critical Realism in a Nuclear Era: Toward a Potentialist Metaphysics

"REALITY IS NOT A QUESTION of the absolute eyewitness, but a question of the future," Jean-François Lyotard has written (1984:13), but to what do the words "nuclear war" refer, now, in the present, when no such war has ever occurred, when its "reality" would be a pure future? Before answering this question, however, we might ask a few others like it. For example, to what do the words "Moby Dick" refer? Or "*la langue*?" Or "Being" itself? We use them all the time, but can we point to them? We know what they mean, but wherein do we find their "reality?" Or, to take another example, when a gambler calculates the odds on a horse race, to what kind of "reality" do his or her calculations refer? The race, after all, has not been run yet, but this horse is rated at five-to-one, and that horse is a twenty-to-one shot. But how can the gambler make such a prediction? And in the ultimate gamble of them all, how can we calculate the relative odds on this or that nuclear strategy when *no* strategy, except the absolutely wrong one, can ever be accomplished once and for all?

To ask such questions, however, is not to question the possibility of ever realistically addressing the nuclear referent; in fact, it is to indicate just the reverse. That is, it is not only the nuclear critic who is concerned with phenomena that are not wholly actual but whose potentiality is somehow real all the same. The most traditional of literary critics, as we shall see in these pages, is concerned with a text whose interpretation is only a virtual "reality" that the critic must actuate. The speaker of any language can never realize more than a fraction of the potential that his or her language holds. And the gambler too has before him or her nothing more than a potential race, although he or she must bet upon its outcome. All of these cases involve phenomena whose "reality" is at once *actual* (texts, languages, and horses are "really" there) and *potential* (as interpretations, speech acts, and payoffs). But how are we to speak of such "realities?" Have we any metaphysical authority to do so?

If we take the words "metaphysical authority" to mean "determinate authority," then our answer to this last question would have to be no. We cannot know for certain just how a given reader is going to respond to the words "Moby Dick." We cannot predict what any given speaker is going to say. And if we knew for certain how a horse race was going to turn out (i.e., if we "fixed" it), then we would not be gamblers. All of these phenomena are crossed with uncertainty, and similarly, we are all gamblers in the face of the nuclear referent. But although we cannot be certain of the course of phenomenal and historical development and cannot be sure which of our potential worlds will be realized, our uncertainty is not necessarily absolute. We cannot be certain of our destiny, but we are not therefore abandoned to a chartless destinerrance. We cannot be certain what *will* happen in any given historical or experimental situation, but somehow we can have a pretty good idea of what *will not*, or what *cannot*, or what is most *likely* to happen. Somehow there is a factor within specific empirical situations that delimits the possible and defines the probable, the regular, the typical. It is the purpose of this book to explore that factor.

That is, it is the purpose of this book to explore the metaphysics of potentiality, of empirical propensities and regularities. The goal of this exploration is the delineation of what we might call a "potentialist metaphysics" or "potentialist realism"—a realism in Karl Popper's sense of the term rather than in Plato's. That is, we shall be searching for a ground for the rational discussion of the calculable probabilities for the behavior of physical entities and situations that exist outside our own discussions of them, outside our own archive. We shall be searching for a ground for distinguishing between objective knowledge, *épistémè*, and subjective belief, *doxa*. And this ground, I shall argue, exists in a reality that, as Popper has written, "is implied in almost all the common sense statements we ever make" (1983:128). But realism entails more than a belief in existing entities; it equally entails "the existence of laws of nature," laws that, as Popper continues, also "imply realism" (1983:128). Such an entailment is indeed "metaphysical" (in Popper's sense of nonverifiability or nonfalsifiability), but it is not "metaphysical" in the sense of either a theological or a providential or a dialectical determinism. For the metaphysics we shall be pursuing here is a meta-physics, a discursive commentary on, and interpretation of, the observations of physicists, not theologians.

Thus, while the meta-physical hypothesis of a "potentialist realism" cannot be proved, as such, it can be presented as a kind of heuristic, enabling us to review a tradition that, extending from Aristotle to C. S. Peirce to Karl Popper, can help us think through in a different way some of the major questions of literary criticism: questions relating to metaphysics (see chaps. 5–7), hermeneutics (chaps. 8–11), semiotics (chaps. 12–13), historicity (chaps. 15–16), and, indeed, to the nuclear referent itself.

Our exploration, then, will begin with what might be called a reconstructive reading of Aristotle, that is, a reading that seeks in Aristotle's thought insights and intuitions that can speak to us today and stimulate our own thinking. If nothing else, such a reading can at least reintroduce to an audience of literary theorists a currently neglected voice whose complex redirecting of Platonic realism can guide us to a new kind of realism undeveloped, but anticipated, in the text of Aristotle. To complete this reading, we shall then look at Karl Popper's reinterpretation of Aristotelian metaphysics in the light of contemporary physical knowledge, seeking in Popper's interpretation the "first principles" for a potentialist realism. I shall not argue that we can absolutely transcend our historical subjectivity, but only that rational discussion, in Popper's words, "cannot exist without real problems, without the search for objective truth, without a task of discovery which we set ourselves: without a reality to be discovered—a reality to be explained by *structural universal laws*" (1983:157). Reality, I shall argue, exceeds our history precisely in the objectivity of its potentiality, its structural regularities and laws. And it will be through the exploration and defense of this potentiality that we shall conduct our own "rational discussion" of the nuclear referent and of the referent in general.

After establishing my potentialist "first principles," I shall explore their pertinence to the kinds of problems with which literary, as well as nuclear, critics are now concerned. Thus I shall review both hermeneutic and semiotic theory in the light of a potentialist realism, especially as it may be said to be at least tacitly assumed by both reader-response criticism and Peircean semiotics. I shall conclude with a "potentialist" inquiry into Fredric Jameson's and Michel Foucault's versions of historical narration and political practice. The purpose of such explorations will be to demonstrate the heuristic value of a concept often ignored in the debate between critical formalism and antiformalism, the value, that is to say, of a principle that mediates between, rather than suspends, the relationship between identity and difference.

In the course of these investigations I shall keep the nuclear referent in view as an example of precisely the kind of problem that baffles both classical realism and post-structural antirealism as well as traditional dialectics and the suspension of the dialectic. The difficulty of defining the nuclear referent, in other words, is a particularly striking example, a cogent test case, of the more general difficulties that criticism confronts in its analyses of the mimetic tradition. But rather than suspending or deconstructing this tradition, I shall attempt here to locate within it the possible terms for its own opening out toward a reality that exceeds it and that, while never completely contained by discourse, can be "realistically" apprehended beyond the archive.

PART 2

FIRST PRINCIPLES: THE CASE FOR REALISM

CHAPTER 4

History, Metahistory, and War: The Example of Thucydides

IN THE NINTH CHAPTER of the *Poetics*, Aristotle defines what appears to be the logical difference between the writing of history and the writing of poetry. This difference, Aristotle explains, is simply that "one relates what has happened [*ta genomena*] the other what may happen [*an genoito*]" (1971:53).[1] That is to say, "It is not the function of the poet to relate what has happened, but what may happen—what is possible [*ta dunata*] according to the law of probability or necessity" (1971:53). Poetry, accordingly, "is a more philosophical and a higher thing than history," Aristotle continues, "for poetry tends to express the universal, history the particular"; poetry, in other words, attempts to represent "how a person of a certain type will on occasion speak or act, according to the law of probability or necessity," while history describes what, "for example, ... Alcibiades did or suffered" (1971:53).

According to Aristotle, then, the historian's text is restricted to recording the imperfect generation of particular events, events whose historical actuation somehow falls short of the formal purposiveness of natural becoming. The poet, on the other hand, can represent that purposiveness as the historian cannot, can imitate, that is to say, the formal and final causality within nature that historical generation aspires toward but fails to achieve. Historical knowledge concerns what is corruptible, what changes, *ta phtharta*; poetic knowledge concerns what is organically whole, what remains, what fulfills its own formal necessity.

But what sort of text, then, would the following passage from *The Peloponnesian War* be according to Aristotle's distinction?

> With reference to the speeches in this history, some were delivered before the war began, others while it was going on; some I heard myself, others I got from various quarters; it was in all cases difficult to carry them word for word in one's memory, so my habit has been to make the speakers say what was in my opinion demanded of them by the various occasions, of course adhering as closely as possible to the general sense of what they really said. [Thucydides 1982:13]

Thucydides, of course, was not a poet but a historian. And yet he too, as if he were a latter-day Homer, felt compelled to draw upon "the law of probability or necessity" in the face of a task for which the "particulars" alone were neither adequate nor entirely available. Speaking as the occasion would have "demanded," Thucydides' generals often resemble epic heroes, nobly exhorting their comrades or threatening their enemies. For example, we can "hear" the Lacedaemonian king, Archidamus, threatening the Plataeans as if he were standing before the gates of Troy, crying out to the "gods and heroes" of the country before launching his invasion:

> Ye gods and heroes of the Plataean territory, be my witnesses that not as aggressors originally, nor until these had departed from the common oath, did we invade this land, in which our fathers offered you their prayers before defeating the Medes, and which you made auspicious to the Hellenic arms; nor shall we be aggressors in the measures to which we may now resort, since we have made many fair proposals but have not been successful. Graciously accord that those who were the first to offend may be punished for it, and that vengeance may be attained by those who would righteously inflict it. [1982:132]

Thucydides' oratorical transcriptions, of course, do not constitute his sole departure from historical particularity. For from the very beginning of his text, as he attempts to provide a causal explanation for the outbreak of the war,

Thucydides openly departs from the visible particulars of the case, discounting the actual reasons given by the combatants themselves and offering an interpretation of his own. "The real cause," Thucydides writes, "I consider to be the one which was formally kept out of sight. The growth and power of Athens, and the alarm which this inspired in Lacedaemon, made war inevitable" (1982:14). But while this is an entirely probable explanation, it is only that—a probability, a belief. There is no ostensively visible "fact" for it to refer to, no particular "what happened," no formally objective referent. We have only Thucydides' word: the war was "inevitable," he writes, and the buildup of Athenian power made it so.

In the strict terms of the *Poetics*, then, Thucydides' history thus appears to resemble poetry. Moving from ostensive particularity to probabalistic universality, the text of *The Peloponnesian War* seems to operate in two different realms, mixing historical fact and poetic interpretation in such a way that it is difficult to distinguish between the two. This aporia of poetic and historical representation has, of course, been generalized in contemporary historical scholarship by such post-structurally–influenced "metahistorians" as Hayden White, who has argued that no historical narrative, howsoever realistic its claims, can transcend the "dominant poetic mode in which its discourse is cast" (1980:33). The historian's text, metahistory argues, is determined by the constitutive tropes of historical consciousness, not by the uninterpreted identity of its referent. Historical narrative, accordingly, is essentially rhetorical rather than referential; it is *écriture* rather than representation; it is, in a sense, fiction rather than fact.

In Hayden White's terms, then, "poetic" interpretation "enters into historiography in at least three ways:"

aesthetically (in the choice of narrative strategy), epistemologically (in the choice of explanatory paradigm) and ethically (in the choice of a strategy by which the ideological implications of a given representation can be drawn for the comprehension of current social problems). [1985:69–70][2]

A metahistorical approach to *The Peloponnesian War* thus might involve an analysis of Thucydides' dominant narrative strategy, or what White calls the "Mode of Emplotment" (1980:29). Is it "romantic," we might inquire, or "tragic," or "comic," or "satiric?" The answer that we might give to this question will raise (still using White's terms) related questions concerning the "Mode of Argument" of Thucydides' text as well as its "Mode of Ideological Implication." Is Thucydides' argument "formist," "mechanistic," "organicist," or "contextualist?" Is his ideology "anarchistic," "radical," "conservative," or "liberal?" What, in short, are the dominant tropes that shape Thucydides' own apprehension and constitution of the events that he narrates? Such questions thus shift our attention away from the extratextual referent toward the differential play of tropology itself.

Still, while each of these questions can certainly help us unpack the *text* of Thucydides, would any of them, the historical realist might ask, help us understand the text as Thucydides himself invites us to understand it, that is, as "inquirers who desire an exact knowledge of the past as an aid to the interpretation of the future" (Thucydides 1982:13)? Can the questions of metahistory reveal anything about the content of *The Peloponnesian War*, about the real historical situation to which it refers—a situation that we might call the "Peloponnesian referent?" Can metahistory, that is to say, enable us to transcend, if only partially, the figural formations of historical narrative on behalf of the events that the historian interprets?

The answer to this question, of course, depends upon one's epistemological perspective. Answering either as structuralists or as post-structuralists, our answer not only would be in the negative but also should call into question the presuppositions that enabled its asking. To ask, that is to say, whether one may cross from the constitutive tropes of discourse to the referential realities that such tropes interpretatively mediate is apparently to assume not only that one can but that one, in a certain sense, already has—that one, in other words, has already found a key that can unlock the door of consciousness and make immediate contact with some historical "identity." But this is not what my question means to presuppose. I am not suggesting that we can entirely transcend our interpretational consciousness. I am not presupposing that there is any pure historical "identity," as such. What I am suggesting by the form of my question is that our interpretive activities are not *wholly* rhetorical. Rather, they are conditioned by something that exceeds discourse, that exceeds tropology and difference, and that, while not reducible to an absolutely determinate identity (dialectical or otherwise), is not to be found in the figure of differance. For while differance also denies us access to any historically certain identity or presence, its strategic effect is precisely to disrupt the very form of the question that I am asking. Differance is a figure that has been derived from the archive itself, and its effect is to complicate attempts to transcend archival textuality. The "something" to which I am referring is precisely that which, I shall argue, *does* transcend the archive. But if this something can be described neither as a wholly determinate identity nor as a wholly indeterminate play of differences, then what could it possibly be?

It is the purpose of these chapters (4–7) to explore the physical and metaphysical dimensions of such a question and to see what answers, or at least partial answers, certain traditional and contemporary metaphysical interpretations can offer to the enduring riddle of the referent, of the extratext, of the "something" that, somehow, conditions our discourse without absolutely determining it. Before turning directly to this analysis, however, we might discuss what we have called the "Peloponnesian referent" to indicate the direction our own exploration will take.

To begin with, to what does the Peloponnesian referent

refer? Certainly not to any monadic identity, not to any full historical presence, not to the simple totality of the Peloponnesian War, because the text in which the referent appears not only is incomplete but also was written, at least in part, as the war itself was being fought. The Peloponnesian referent, we might say instead, refers not to a completed totality but to a dynamically unfolding situation, a situation, what is more, with certain calculable propensities that Thucydides apprehended in his interpretation of the causes of the conflict. His interpretation, in Hayden White's terms, could be said to be "mechanistic," given Thucydides' apprehension of a certain historical "inevitability" at work within the situation. But while this "Mode of Argument" cannot claim any a priori superiority over any other possible epistemological paradigm with which we might approach the Peloponnesian referent, may we not discern, within the actual empirical circumstances of the rivalry between Athens and Lacedaemon, a certain factor that would "weight," so to speak, Thucydides' "mechanistic" interpretation more heavily than another and render it more probable? In other words, do not such political circumstances as those that led to the outbreak of the Peloponnesian War bear a certain empirical potentiality, a certain propensity for conflict, that we can take into account as we seek to interpret the course of similar events?

Let us hypothesize, for the purposes of further analysis, that the Peloponnesian referent refers to a dynamic synthesis of real, not subjective, historical actualities *and* potentialities. These potentialities do not absolutely determine our interpretations of the specific actualities that bear them, but they can help guide them. They can, that is to say, help us both evaluate and hierarchize our possible interpretations. It will be asked: Why *should* we hierarchize our interpretational beliefs? Certainly there is no *scholarly* reason to do so. The scholar can certainly be content with a pluralistic analysis of the ways in which other scholars have sought to interpret the movement of history. But if the scholar wishes to move from the word to the world, from gnosis and analysis to praxis and decision, he or she will have to take some kind of stand, and to take that stand, he or she will require some ground to stand on. And as criticism begins to turn toward the nuclear referent, in particular, and to the political referent, in general, it might well consider the potentialist "ground" that is implicitly offered in Thucydides' own interpretation of the Peloponnesian referent. For in Thucydides' representation of the way in which two rather uneasy allies finally fell out over ideological and geopolitical differences, we may discern a not so very distant analogy to the superpower conflict of our own time, an analogy that is strengthened by the relative nontotality of both the nuclear and the Peloponnesian referents.[3]

For while the Peloponnesian referent and the nuclear referent each refer to different historical actualities, the concrete historical potentialities of the two situations are not dissimilar. When equal powers come into competitive conflict, there is always a propensity for mutual destruction. Perhaps this is what Thucydides wanted his readers, present and future, to learn from his coolly nonpartisan exposure of the disastrous consequences the Peloponnesian War had for both sides in the conflict.

It is true that this lesson may be pertinent only from the perspective of the major players in such "speed races," that the Peloponnesian referent may have meant something rather different to a Macedonian reader. But as citizens of a nation directly involved in precisely the kind of competition that has ruined many powers before us, we can learn something from the mistakes of the Greeks, not because the nuclear referent refers to a historical actuality that has simply repeated that of the Peloponnesian referent, but because our own, different, actuality bears a set of potentialities, or propensities, similar to those entailed by similar historical circumstances. History has not "returned" to anything in the nuclear era, has not repeated itself. I am not appealing to some model of simple historical iteration. Rather, what we can learn from the text of Thucydides, "as an aid to the interpretation of the future," is that similar historical circumstances bear similar historical propensities, that while ontological actualities differ from moment to moment, their potentialities need not. Thus, just as Thucydides could guess that, with "the preparations of both the combatants" in the Peloponnesian conflict being "in every department in the last state of perfection" (1982:1), a disastrous conflict was almost inevitable, so too can we make similar guesses. And my argument is that the basis for these guesses lies in the regular behavior, the real propensities and potentialities, of material history itself and not simply within the paradigms of our historical hermeneutics.

But what is the nature of this "potentiality," and how does it relate to differential actuality? How can we approach it? Dialectically? Deterministically? Do potentialities simply determine the course of historical becoming? My hypothesis is that they do not, that potentialities are not determinate in a dialectical sense; but at the same time they are not wholly indeterminate either, nor are they simply suspended between the poles of determination and indetermination. Rather, potentialities exceed the metaphysical figures of determination and indetermination and, in so doing, exceed the very figures of our archive. And while this may sound mysterious, the fact is that we refer to and base our decisions upon potentialities all the time: to do so is simply common sense. The question is: Can this common sense be defended from the perspective of realism, or is it, too, finally only a subjective illusion?

Robert Lifton has written how Hiroshima constitutes "a form of what the Greeks call *kairos*, an early event which is decisive for the outcome of actual and potential future events" (quoted in Zins 1985:393). I expect that few would challenge this interpretation, but what has made it possible? Simply the figures of our discourse, or something in the event of Hiroshima itself? Certainly this "something" cannot be identified with the completed totality, the full actuality, of the dropping of the bomb itself, because what happened at Hiroshima was not, as Derrida points out, a total nuclear war. Nor has it made a total nuclear war necessary. But at the same time, the decisiveness, the *kairos*, of Hiroshima is more than textual, is not *merely* an interpretation—at least from the perspective of commonsense realism. But for commonsense realism to defend itself, it would have to establish the extratextual reality of that "something," that dynamic potentiality, that has been projected out of the historical actuality of Hiroshima, and to do this it would have to be able to demonstrate the difference between a metahistorical, archival, or "poetic" representation of historical potentiality and a historically realistic one.

History and poetry, Aristotle tells us, are two different things, and if we are to recover the referential, as opposed to the rhetorical, reality of the nuclear referent, we will have to reinscribe, rather than deconstruct, this difference. But given the metahistorians' argument that both the writing of history and the writing of poetry share rhetorical characteristics, we cannot discover the terms for this distinction in rhetorical analysis: such a study can uncover only what is the same in the two kinds of text. The difference, rather, is to be found in the nature of the historical and the poetic referent. The referent of the poet, in Aristotle's terms, is an action that has achieved its final purposiveness, its formal essence and identity, and is thus ultimately ideal. The referent of the historian, on the other hand, the Aristotelian *phtharta*, is empirical, bearing a contingency that poetry—in Aristotle's sense—does not.

But this does not necessarily mean that historical, or natural, becoming, is absolutely contingent. For things, in Aristotle's philosophy, can become only what they have a capacity to become, and this capacity—which Aristotle equates with the material "potentiality" (*dunamis*) of an object—is an integral part of their "substance." Signifying "power" and "potentiality," as well as "possibility," *dunamis* supplements the formal "actuality" (*energeia*) of things and can be seen to limit the possibilities of their becoming. Aristotle's analysis of this power, of course, is not found in the *Poetics*, whose subject is the formal actuality of poetry. But we can find it in the texts that lie in the background of the *Poetics*, wherein Aristotle explores the role that potentiality, *dunamis*, plays in the course of natural becoming. Those texts, we shall see, are echoed by contemporary analyses of empirical potentiality. And through a critically reconstructive reading of those texts, we can begin to formulate the terms for a potentialist realism by which the extratextual reality of empirical potentiality (that "something" that exceeds the archive and delimits interpretation) might be defended in our search for the complex reality of the nuclear referent.

CHAPTER 5

Natural Genesis: Aristotle's *Physics* and the Problem of Change

AMONG THE MANY GROUPS competing for influence in the current debate over our national strategic policy, there is one with a rather metaphysically interesting name. It calls itself "The Committee on the Present Danger." What is interesting about this name is not simply its ambiguity (i.e., it can refer as easily to the "present danger" of an all-out nuclear war as to our strategic "unpreparedness") but its referent, "the present danger," which is at once definite and indefinite. It is definite insofar as it refers to a concrete historico-political situation, but it is indefinite insofar as a "danger" is a highly intangible phenomenon. For while a danger does appear to be sufficiently real to be named and announced, as in "Danger: Thin Ice," its reality is a peculiar thing, for a danger can remain what it is only as long as its present status continues to defer an absent future. The ice through which we have already fallen is no longer a danger: it has become something else. A nuclear war that has already been fought has relinquished its "dangerousness." So how are we to speak of such a thing when its reality relies so necessarily upon its own un-reality?

Defining the nature of a phenomenon and its potential for future actuation in terms of an opposition between a presence and an absence is one of the ways in which Aristotle formulates a solution to the problem of change in the *Physics* and the *Metaphysics*. But, as we shall see, this formulation can lead to the same paradox of the nuclear referent that Derrida has deconstructed in "No Apocalypse, Not Now" (1984:20–31); that is, the paradox of a nuclear present that has been constituted against the absence of any actual nuclear war. But Aristotle offers an alternative formulation of the problem of change that can enable us, after demythologizing his text, to define the danger of an ice pond, not to mention the danger of a nuclear war, in terms of a dynamic relationship not between "being" and "not-being" but between an existing formal actuality and an existing material potentiality. The danger of an ice pond, according to this formula, would involve the formal actuality of a sheet of thin ice and its material potentiality to buckle under pressure—a potentiality that is as much a constituent of the situation as is the actuality of the weakened ice itself. And as we confront the "present danger" of an actual nuclear exchange, that is to say, the nuclear referent as such, we might also conjecture that its nature too inheres in a configuration of actual political and technological circumstances along with the specific potentialities that such circumstances bear. But how are we to describe such a configuration of potentiality and actuality? And how can it be opposed to the metaphysics of presence and absence?

Let us broaden our question for a moment. What, we might ask, "is the difference between the potentiality of anything 'becoming' one of several things and the actuality of its being the one thing it is? And why are potentialities at once so varied and so strictly limited" (Cornford and Wicksteed 1957:xvii)? To put this another way, Why is there order in the world rather than chaos? These questions are not our own but rather are among "the fundamental questions and concepts with which Aristotle deals in the *Physics*" (Cornford and Wicksteed 1957:xvii), and they are worth further exploration as we seek to describe the complex nature of the nuclear referent. For in its detailed investigation of the process of natural becoming and change, the *Physics*, in spite of its overall distance from contemporary thinking, still harbors an insight that can guide us toward a metaphysical understanding of a phenomenal danger that is as real in its indefinite potentiality as in its definite actuality.

In the *Physics*, then, Aristotle explores two major solutions to the problem of natural genesis. The first results in a metaphysical opposition between presence and absence and thus entails a certain self-deconstruction, while the second suggests a different approach "based on the distinction between existing as a potentiality and existing as an actuality" (191b29). This second alternative is the one we will follow more closely in our search for the terms of a potentialist realism. In other words, my purpose is not to decide just which solution Aristotle himself ultimately preferred. My purpose is rather to show that, while the former solution falls into the mode of Western metaphysics that poststructuralist critics have deconstructed, the latter solution, the one less explored by critics, actually anticipates our contemporary understanding of the nature of material reality.

Our inquiry, then, can begin with an analysis of Aristotle's proposal that natural becoming proceeds through a course of formal contradiction or privation. As Aristotle states:

Anything that is articulated must rise out of something from which that particular articulation is absent; and if, in its turn, it falls out of articulation it must go back again to the absence of the particular articulation it had. [*Physics* 188b13–15]

That is, if someone (the "efficient" cause in the process) builds, say, a house or a statue, "what the house replaces by being made is the unordered relation of the materials to each other; and what passes away in the making of the statue, or any other shapely work, is the unshapeliness of the material" (188b18–20). In other words, when we build a house, we impose a certain form on a collection of materials that hitherto lacked that form, and it is that lack of form that is "replaced" by the efficiency of our formalizing activity. In the overall terms of the *Physics*, then, four causes are involved in the process of change: in the case of the house they are the builder's efficient activity in inaugurating a change, the finality of his or her purpose in building at all, the form of the thing built, and the materials of which it is made. But there is also an implied fifth principle here—that is, the *lack* of a given form—which causes certain problems for Aristotle's analysis.

To see what the problems are, we can begin by noting how Aristotle's analysis of physical change applies to the natural world the basic principles of his logical and metaphysical studies of "contrariety" and "privation." The difference between an articulated and a disarticulated house, in the terms of the *Metaphysics*, involves the "primary contrariety" of "possession and privation" (1055a34), according to which a house might be said either to possess or not to possess a given form. Such a logic of formal contradiction, of course, parallels Aristotle's analysis of propositional truth conditions in *De Interpretatione* (see 17b16ff.), which also assumes a binary logic of affirmation and denial, an up or down choice between the contrarieties of truth and falsity. In the *Physics*, we find this logical dialectic translated into a natural one, as Aristotle provisionally proposes that it "would seem that whenever anything comes into existence or passes out of it, the movement is along the determined line between the terms of some contrast," and so "it follows that all things that come into existence in the course of nature are either opposites themselves or are compounded of opposites" (188b21–25). Without negation, in other words, without the antithetical contrariety of possession and privation, there is no change.

But while Aristotle tentatively suggests that his analysis of antithetical change has "established antithesis as an ultimate constituent in Nature" (189a12), his dialectical inquiry into the ultimate constituents of natural reality does not conclude with the principle of antithetical contradiction. For in seeking to determine and number the ultimate principles of becoming and change, Aristotle considers a certain "difficulty [*aporia*] in supposing there to be nothing in Nature underlying the antithetical couple":

For we never see the antithetical principles, by themselves, constituting the substantive existence [*ousian*] of anything we know in

Nature, and a true principle cannot be the mere attribute of something else, for the subject [hupokeimenon] to which it was attributed would be a principle anterior to it, inasmuch as it would be presupposed in the very fact of having this attribute predicated of it. [189a27-33]

In other words, the formal nature of the antithetical principle must be supplemented by a third natural principle, because the form of an antithesis is ontologically empty unless it can have some subject to work on—unless it has, in other words, some nonantithetical substrate to accept the accidents of contradictory qualification. Thus, natural substances apparently must involve three principles: the two contradictory terms of an antithesis and the subject (hupokeimenon) upon which the antitheses act. As Aristotle states:

If our former insistence on the two terms of some antithesis being principles is sound, and if we are now convinced that these antithetical principles need something to work on, and if we are to preserve these conclusions, must we not necessarily posit a third principle as the subject on which the antithetical principles act? [189a35-b2]

This third principle constitutes the "material cause" of the Aristotelian philosophy, that is, the ungenerated substrate, prior even to the four elements of earth, air, fire, and water, which grounds the course of formal addition and privation without itself being subject to contradiction or change. The antitheses, then, act upon this substrate in the course of ontic generation, but rather than constituting *two* more causal principles, they can be considered under the single heading of the "formal cause," because each contradictory form that the material substrate may assume as it enters into generation can be, in Aristotle's words, "taken singly as competent, by its presence or absence, to accomplish the whole change" (191a6-8). But like the material cause of things, the formal cause is not generated either: only the things that are themselves constituted by the composition of matter and form are subject to generational change. In the *Physics*, Aristotle adds to these two causes the principles of efficiency and finality (which, as we shall see, can themselves be identified with the formal cause), but the point is that at this point in his analysis Aristotle has identified what he believes to be the two essential principles behind the course of natural generation: the material and the formal. Thus,

> there will only be the "ultimately underlying" factor in Nature in addition to this formal principle to reckon with. And of this "underlying" factor we can form a conception by analogy; for it will bear the same relation to concrete things in general, or to any specific concrete thing, which the bronze bears to the statue before it is founded, or the wood to the couch, or the crude material of any object that has determined form and quality to that object itself. This ultimate material will count as one principle ... and the collectivity of determining qualities implied by the thing's definition [*logos*, or "form"] is also one principle; *and further there is the opposite of this, namely the "being without" or "shortage" [steresis] of it.* [191a8–14; my italics]

The trouble, or difficulty, here is that Aristotle, while trying to identify the two positive principles of matter and form, has included a third principle, *steresis*, which raises an ontological question that cannot be resolved by Aristotle's hylomorphic philosophy as it has been so far described. This is the problem of negation, of the "being without," of not-being itself. How, that is, can we define the ontological nature of negation and contradiction? What *is* a "privation?" Aristotle says that it simply expresses the "incidental" absence of a given form with respect to a specific substantial presence, and yet privation seems essential if a thing is to change at all. But if it is essential to the course of change, in what might its essence lie?

The problem that the *Physics* faces here is the paradox of natural genesis itself, which consists in the apparent fact that for one thing or situation to change into another, it must first pass from a state of being through a state of not-being. But this, as Aristotle himself notes, Parmenides and his followers "proved" to be impossible, because not-being is nothing at all. "Keep your mind away from this way of inquiry," Parmenides had urged, "for never will you show that not-being is" (*Sophist* 237a9–10). And, as Aristotle also observes, the Parmenideans argued equally that nothing can come *into* existence either, because "if a thing comes into existence, it must proceed either out of the existent or out of the non-existent, both of which are impossible; for how could anything 'come out of' the existent, since it is already there? and obviously it could not come out of the non-existent, for what it comes out of must be there for it to come out of, and the non-existent is not there at all" (*Physics* 191a28–32). Thus, Parmenides concluded, ontic or natural genesis is not real at all: it is a mere appearance. "Reality" is both "one" and immutable. The very nothingness of not-being thus leads to a paradoxical denial of the reality of change itself. Such a paradox seems to frustrate in advance Aristotle's intentions of establishing the principles of *natural* genesis in the *Physics*, so how does he get around it?

In the *Sophist*, Plato's "Eleatic Stranger" proposes his own realistic (in the Platonic sense) solution to the problem of not-being by granting to it a Form of its own among the major Forms of his "eidetic alphabet:" i.e., the Form of "otherness" or "difference" (*Sophist* 255aff.). To so formalize not-being is, of course, to transcendentalize it, to contain it within the terms of Platonic realism. But such a solution cannot be satisfactory to a philosophy whose thrust (if not always its total effect) is against transcendental realism. So rather than rejecting outright the reality of not-being, as the Parmenideans did, or transcendentally formalizing it, as Platonic philosophy does, Aristotle brought not-being (absence, or negation) into ontic reality itself in the figure of privation. "The doctrine of privation," Stanley Rosen writes, "is thus Aristotle's revision of the Platonic doctrine of 'otherness' "—a revision that denies to privation any universal genus of its own, defining it only "with respect to a specific, actual form" (1974:85).

Aristotle's solution to the paradox of genetic negation, then, is to explain the nature of change as a process by which an ungenerated material substrate comes to possess a certain form (also ungenerated) that it had previously lacked. In Aristotle's terms, this relative presence or absence of a given form is only incidental with respect to the substrate, and in this way Aristotle seeks to resolve Parmenides' paradox. For while he accepts the argument "that nothing can 'come to be,' in the absolute sense, out of the non-existent," Aristotle declares "nevertheless that all things which come to be owe their existence to the incidental non-existence of something; for they owe it to the 'shortage' from which they started 'being no longer there'" (191b14–17). In other words, Aristotle draws a line between *absolute* not-being, which has no formal essence in his philosophy, and *incidental* not-being, which subsists only with respect to specific entities. What passes into not-being in the process of natural genesis, accordingly, is only the incidental nature of a thing, the presence or absence of a given form. The underlying subject of the change, on the other hand, endures in its material substrate:

> For what I mean by matter is precisely the ultimate underlying subject, common to all the Things of Nature, presupposed as their substantive, not incidental, constituent. And again, the destruction of a thing means the disappearance of everything that constitutes it except just that very underlying subject which its existence presupposes. [192a32–34]

Still, has Aristotle's "matter/form-plus-shortage" solution to the problem of not-being and change really resolved the difficulty? Is the "shortage" really so "incidental" to the process of natural becoming, or is it, rather, logically the most essential principle of change according to the formula? For if "all things which come to be owe their existence to the incidental non-existence of something," it appears that it is precisely this nonexistence, this privational shortage, that drives forward the play of change. In other words, since both the material and the formal cause do not, in themselves, suffer any privation, and because, according to the formula, change itself is a function of privation, then it seems that there must be some negative principle—privation—prior to the substantial ontological principles of matter and form that causes them to enter into generative movement. And this principle, the principle of absence or not-being that Aristotle subordinates to the substantial presence of matter and form, apparently would be better accounted for by Derrida's analysis of the movement of differance than by Aristotle's positive analysis of the fundamental categories of ontological presence.

It will be objected that in the *Physics* it is not privation but the final causes of things that determine their motions, causes that, in the case of heavenly motions, are grounded not in privation but in the full *actuality* of the Prime Mover. But still the paradox remains. Because between the full, immaterial actuality of the Prime Mover and the merely partial actualities of the sublunary entities that strive to imitate the Prime Mover's perfect motion, there lies an uncrossable difference, a difference constituted precisely by the imperfections, the shortages, the privations, in ontic things themselves. In other words, if motion is caused by the gap between sublunary imitation and the perfection that it imitates, then indeed it appears that the course of generation and change would have to turn upon the hinge of not-being after all, upon difference rather than upon presence.

To put all this another way, by privileging the categorically substantial "presence" of matter and form while seeking to reduce formal privation to an "incidental" feature in the "matter/form-plus-shortage" formula, Aristotle's text lands in a contradiction or, more precisely, inverts itself in a manner that will be familiar to post-structural criticism. But I have not conducted this analysis with the intention of simply deconstructing Aristotle's text. Rather, I mean to deconstruct only that part of it that relies on an ontological opposition between presence and absence, and which thus, against its own purposes, seems to lead us from the positive causational account that the *Physics* attempts to provide to the movement of the trace, of that which "produces" the positive categories of philosophy without belonging to any possible category of metaphysics.

My point here is not to intimate that the *Physics* thematizes Derridean concepts but only to assert that it falls into the same metaphysical difficulties that so much of the Western tradition has encountered. Still, there is a side, indeed a margin, to the *Physics* that I believe has been ignored. For while Aristotle's "matter/form-plus-shortage" solution to the paradox of natural genesis *is* grounded in an opposition between presence and absence, it is not the only account that Aristotle offers. After presenting his analysis of *steresis* in the first book of the *Physics*, Aristotle remarks that it is but "one way of formulating the solution of the problem" of change, and that "there is also an alternative formula based on the distinction between existing as a potentiality and existing as an actuality" (191b28–29). In this alternative view, what exists in potentia and in actuality still consists of the material and formal principles, but privative not-being does not generate their relation. Rather, the distinction enables us to reinterpret the material and formal causes of being and becoming in a way that avoids the paradoxes of not-being, for the hinge upon which change pivots in this view is not privation: it is the complex relation between the potential nature of a thing and its actual nature. But since, as Aristotle remarks, "this is developed more fully elsewhere" (191b29)— that is, in the *Metaphysics* (which perhaps explains why some commentators regard Aristotle's remark in 191b27–29 as a later interpolation in the text)—we will now turn our attention to the *Metaphysics*. Which of the two accounts Aristotle himself preferred is not easily judged, and I will not attempt to do so here. My concern, rather, is that the "matter/form-plus-shortage" formula can be shown to lead to its own deconstruction, that is, to a raising of the incidental principle of not-being over that of the substantial principles of matter and form. But to what does Aristotle's alternative formula lead? What is the ontology of potentiality and actuality?

CHAPTER 6

Aristotle's *Metaphysics* and the Potentiality of the Real

"THERE IS A SCIENCE which studies Being [*to on*] qua Being, and the properties inherent in it in virtue of its own nature," Aristotle writes in the *Metaphysics* (1947:1003a21).[1] And this science, he continues, "is not the same as any of the so-called particular sciences, for none of the others contemplates Being generally *qua* Being; they divide off some portion of it and study the attribute of this portion, as do for example the mathematical sciences" (1947:1003a21–26). There is a difference, then, between Aristotle's *Physics* and his *Metaphysics*. While their definitions and terminologies often overlap, the former is still a particular science insofar as it is concerned with the processes of *natural* becoming, while the latter is more universally concerned with the "being" of all things, corporeal and incorporeal, natural and divine. But while the *Metaphysics* is sometimes explicitly a "theology,"[2] seeking its "first principles" and "final causes" in the "highest Good" and in the Deity (see 1947:982b1–983a13), it is not everywhere a transcendental study. For the *Metaphysics* also describes a reality whose finality, or motivating purpose, ultimately may be found not on the other side of a privational gap between the corruptible and the divine but within the very things that suffer their own generation.

What, then, is the subject matter of a science of "Being qua Being?" What is it that we are investigating? Given the Scholastic history of Aristotelian interpretation, we might expect the "Being" of the *Metaphysics* to be the divine substance itself, the universal presence from which all particular "beings" spring. But the *Metaphysics* does not constitute such an onto-theologism, does not, that is to say, inscribe (in contemporary terms) an ontico-ontological difference between the beings of the world and a World of Being.[3] Indeed, there is a sense in the *Metaphysics* that there are as many kinds of "being" as there are discontinuous beings. But there is a continuous principle in Aristotle's metaphysics as well, an ontological continuity that we may find in the universal potentiality or power (*dunamis*) of the "matter" that is formally actuated in particular beings. My purpose in this chapter is to explore the nature of this ontic synthesis of formal particularity and material universality as well as the role that potentiality plays in it.

We can start this exploration by looking at the beginning of the Zeta treatise of the *Metaphysics*, which opens with a definition of the word "being" in what is indeed a more ontic than ontological sense, defining the term with respect to concrete things themselves:

> The term "being" [*to on*] has several senses, which we have classified in our discussion of the number of senses in which terms are used. It denotes first the "*what*" [*ti esti*] of a thing, i.e. the individuality [*tode ti*] and then the quality or quantity or any such category. Now of all these senses which "being" has, the primary sense is clearly the "what," which denotes the substance [*ousia*] (because when we describe the quality of a particular thing we say that it is "good" or "bad," and not "five feet high" or "a man;" but when we describe *what* it is, we say not that it is "white" or "hot" or "five feet high," but that it is "a man" or "a god"), and all other things are said to "be" because they are either quantities or qualities or affections of some other thing. [1947:1028a10–20]

Thus, in its primary sense, "being" signifies "substance," the "whatness" or essential individuality of a "this" (*tode ti*) that Aristotle predicates as the first category of ontic existence. Primary substance in itself, as the substrate of the "this," has no contrary: rather, it is that which accepts contrary predication (as a "man" can be either "white" or "black," "cultured" or "uncultured," without having any contrariety in himself). But this does not mean that the substance of a thing is a simple monad, for while Aristotle determines that it is the unpredicable "substrate" (*hupokeimenon*) that "is considered to be in the truest sense substance," the substrate involves not one but three interrelated metaphysical principles. Aristotle states that

> in one sense we call the matter [*hyle*] the substrate; in another the *shape*; and in a third, the combination [*sunolon*] of the two. By matter I mean, for instance, bronze; by shape, the arrangement of the form; and by the combination of the two, the concrete thing: the statue. [1947:1029a2-6]

By "substance," then, Aristotle can refer to at least three principles: matter, form, and the combination of matter and form in particular entities. Furthermore, the term "matter" alone can signify a number of meanings, including the "ultimate underlying subject" or "ultimate matter" referred to in the *Physics* as well as the relatively less universal material "genus," whose potential for formal actuation is realized in specific individuals. For the purposes of this study I will take the term in both of these senses, because in each sense "matter" signifies an unextended ontological potentiality that subsists in a complex relation to extensional actuality.

For example, to define the being of a particular "man," Aristotle begins with the "first genus" of the individual (viz., "animal"), which stands to that individual as abstract matter does to concrete form. Then he proceeds to divide that genus into its special differentiae: e.g., "two-footed animal" and then "two-footed wingless animal." At the end of this process of differential specification we find that "the last differentia will be the form and the *substance*" of a particular man, his definition or soul (1979:1037b29-38a21). Thus the final difference that defines, say, Socrates, constitutes his actuality (*energeia*) as such, his formal essence (*to ti ein einai*); for "by 'form,' " Aristotle explains, "I mean the essence of each thing, and the first *substance*" (1979:1032b2).

But while the form of an individual constitutes the individual's essential nature and identifying difference, it does not do so independently of that individual's material nature, that is, apart from what might be called the generic potentiality that the concrete individual has formally actuated. For just as, in Aristotle's words, "matter exists potentially in view of the fact that it might come to possesss a form; and when it exists *actually*, then it exists in a form" (1979:1050a15–16), so too does a genus exist in potentia with respect to its instantiating individuals. Matter, in this sense, is not some spatio-temporally extended "stuff." It constitutes the theoretically abstract but ontically real potentiality that has been actuated in each empirical individual belonging to a given genus.

In a sense, then, we might say that the actuating "form" of the "this" constitutes a specific *state* of a material substrate that must always subsist in one actual form or another. The "being of a triangular bronze," for example, "will be a composition of bronze and a triangle" (1979:1045b15), Aristotle writes. But, as H. G. Apostle explains, a "triangular bronze is not a composite of a triangle and a bronze in the sense that these two can be separated and exist apart and also be combined. Every instance of bronze has some shape, and every shape is with some matter, and bronze is to triangle as matter to *actuality*" (see *Metaphysics* 1979:353 n.13).

Thus, as Aristotle observes, "all things which are generated, whether by nature or by art, have matter; for there is a potentiality for each of them to be, and also not to be, and this potentiality is the matter in each" (1979:1032a20–22). We might say, then, that according to the "matter-form-composite" formula there is no ontological gap between the formal particularity of a thing and its material substrate: the relation is that of actuality to potentiality, that is, the formal actualization of an *existing*, though unextended, material capacity to be so informed. The formal principle is *theoretically* separable from the material and can be analyzed accordingly. But in the world of ontic being, the formal principle is not opposed, as such, to the material, but stands in essential relation to it.

This implies that specific things are generated not out

of a privative shortage but out of an unextended material potentiality to be actuated in spatio-temporally extended forms. In the Zeta treatise of the *Metaphysics*, Aristotle accordingly revises his "matter/form-plus-shortage" formula to observe how "that which is generated is generated by something (by 'something' here I mean the source which begins generation), and out of something (*let this be not the privation but the matter*) . . . and it becomes something (this is a sphere or a circle or whatever else it may happen to be)." [1979: 1033a24–28; my italics]

Now, Aristotle's equation of the "matter" of a thing, at least in one of its senses, with its "genus" ("for that which has a differentia or a quality is the underlying subject, which we call 'matter' " [1979: 1024b8–9]) might be further read as follows. A "genus," such as "animal," stands as a relatively universal natural class with respect to the individuals that differentially actuate its potential to be actuated in species and individuals. A species, in turn, stands as a less universal class relative to the particular individuals that actuate its specific potentiality. But while there can be no "Socrates" without the species of "two-footed animals" (or, in more modern terms, the species *Homo sapiens*), and there can be no "two-footed animals" without the genus "animal," neither the genus nor the species has an independent form of its own but subsists only in relation to the concrete individuals that actuate it. A genus, in other words, which Aristotle also defines as "a continuous generation of things which have the same form" (1979: 1024a29–31), must be instantiated by particular individuals, but it stands to those individuals as matter to form or as unextended potentiality to extended actuality.

If, then, a thing is generated out of a preexisting material potentiality, which we can specify through its generic identity, we should be able, in principle, to apprehend what it can potentially become on the basis of our knowledge of the general potentialities of the genus that it instantiates. In other words, we should be able, as Aristotle puts it, to "specify when something is potentially another thing and when it is not; for it is not potentially another at any time":

For example, is earth potentially a man? No, but rather when it has already become a seed, and perhaps not even then. This is similar to being healed, since not everything can be healed by the medical art or by luck, but only something which has this capability, and it is this thing which is potentially healthy. [1979:1049a1–5]

We might say here that what a thing is capable of becoming, its potentiality as such, is generic. Our knowledge of the capabilities of the genus to which a thing belongs can be at least partly transferred to the particular thing itself. This implies that our knowledge of the capacity of something for future development, while not being logically determinate, can be grounded in our objective experience of the typical behavior of the kinds of thing to which that individual thing belongs. The kind, then, stands as potential being, while the individual is actual, and so we might say that an individual thing is at once materially universal in its relationship to other things of its kind and formally particular in its own specific being. To put this another way, "each thing is a kind of unity," as Aristotle remarks in the Eta treatise, "and potentiality and actuality taken together exist somehow as one" (1979:1045b21).

Each generated "this," then, can be said to be constituted neither by a universal material potentiality alone nor by a particular formal actuality alone: rather each "this" instantiates a dynamic composition (*sunolon*) of what we might call *dunamis-kai-energeia*, or "potentiality-*and/also*-actuality." This composition includes at once the actual formal state of the thing as well as the material potentiality that it has actuated and that remains for further actuation. Relative to the "this," then, any future formal state might be said to exist as a positive potentiality rather than as a privative negation: as what a thing of its kind is capable of becoming. Indeed, we may even see privation itself as a function of potentiality. Aristotle states that "privation means (1) not having something which can be had by nature" as well as "(2) not having something which a thing, either itself or its genus, should by nature have." For example, a mole can be said to be deprived of sight "with respect to its genus," because as an "animal" a mole has the capacity for sight (see 1979:1022b22–27). The implication here, though it is not necessarily Aristotle's, is that our anticipations of potential developments can be grounded in our knowledge of the typical capacities of things as they are related to other things of the same type. Our anticipations do not determine what a thing will become, but they need not be regarded as merely subjective speculations either, for they can be grounded objectively in our knowledge of the typical powers (*dunamis*), or "dispositions," of the things of our experience.[4]

But to develop this interpretation of ontic potentiality, we must first make some concessions. I am not arguing that Aristotle's metaphysics as a whole is "realistic" in the sense that I am suggesting. After all, his analysis of *dunamis* (which, as we shall see in chapter 7, has been taken up and further developed by modern physicists and philosophers of science) does occur side by side with the development of an organicist and transcendental theology that is virtually impossible either to accept or to defend. It cannot be denied that Aristotle's belief in an "organic" finality or purposiveness in nature, his belief, that is to say, that the final cause of every motion is "the Good in each particular case, and in general the highest Good in the whole of nature" (1947: 982b6–8), constitutes a transcendentalism that retains a trace of the Platonic realism with which Aristotle contended throughout his philosophy. Still, I will suggest that, in Aristotle's attempt to qualify or refute Plato's transcendental realism, we may find a perhaps inchoate intuition of the terms by which that transcendentalism might be bracketed in a way that can be useful for contemporary thinking.

For even Aristotle's appeal to a transcendental set of purely *actual* movers, whose incorruptible motion, as Joseph Owens puts it, all "corruptible things imitate" as they seek that "goal sought by all things ... the 'eternal and the divine'" (1978:460-61), may be bracketed on principles offered by the *Metaphysics* itself. Because while Aristotle argues that formal actuality "is prior in substance to potency," and that "one *actuality* always precedes another in time until we come to the *actuality* of the eternal prime mover" (1979: 1050b4-6), the transcendental finality that this implies is qualified by the "tendency," as Hugh Tredennick has put it, "for the formal, final, and efficient causes to be merged in a single principle [the formal] opposed to the material" in the course of Aristotle's analysis (*Metaphysics* 1947:xxviii). The final cause of a thing, that is to say, once identified with its formal actuality, can be understood in empirical rather than transcendental terms. For the form of a thing can be shown to be purposive in itself, and this purposiveness does not require a final Good outside the realm of corruptible individuals to be actuated. For as Joseph Owens has suggested, the very "divinity" that corruptible things strive to imitate can itself be a function of empirical generation, as each corruptible individual is formed to perpetuate the species of which it is a part. Because in this respect, as Owens explains:

> It is the species that is divine and eternal. The singular thing does not matter in itself. It is only on account of the species; its every act naturally strives to perpetuate its species. That is the goal of itself and of all its activity. It is divine, as best it may be, by being perpetual in its kind. [1978:461]

A modern biologist, of course, would not put it quite this way, but Aristotle's intuition that the form of a thing expresses its generative purpose is not so very distant from our contemporary apprehension of the relationship between form and function in biological evolution. Today we would say that randomly generated organic structures tend to be genetically preserved if they offer some functional advantage in the struggle for survival. The form of an individual, in other words, has been shaped by a selective process that (for all practical purposes) also results in the perpetuation of a species.

Thus, as W. Wieland has written, while "teleology certainly plays an important role in Aristotle's science," it "is simply not that universal cosmic principle that it becomes in the course of time" (1975:142). Rather, according to Aristotle, as we reflect on the formal nature of specific kinds of things, we find that they are ordered with respect to specific purposes, but these purposes do not have universal forms of their own. Different purposes belong to the different kinds of things in the world without there being some final *telos* to which all things tend. Thus, again in Wieland's words, we may "see in Aristotle's conception of *telos* . . . a concept of reflection whose significance lies in its application to particular states of affairs" (1975:159) rather than to some transcendentally universal goal.

Of course, Aristotle's explicit privileging of the determinate principle of formal actuality cannot withstand a modern scrutiny, and I do not propose any sort of rehabilitation of this side of his metaphysics. In the light of our present cosmological understanding, it simply makes no sense to say that formal actuality *comes first* in the order of being. Indeed, if any ontological principle can be said to come "first," it seems that it would consist of an ungenerated, unactualized, principle of potentiality. How else could we characterize the pre-temporal, pre-spatial "moment" that "preceded" the Bang from which the present universe has apparently emerged? The actuality of our world, it now appears, has emerged neither ex nihilo nor from some fully actualized spatio-temporal presence. "Potentiality," although a weak term, comes closer to expressing that unimaginable origin than does any concept of formal "actuality"—or, for that matter, than does the Lucretian *clinamen*, or "swerve," which has proven so attractive to the post-structural imagination. For the Lucretian swerve is a departure from the paths of already falling atoms, and the point here is that before our universe existed, there was nothing to swerve *from* in the ordinary physical sense. To contemplate universal origins at all, we must necessarily pass from physical to metaphysical ways of thinking.

Still, to be of any practical value, our thought must remain within the universe as we find it in its empirical actuality, and thus we cannot contemplate pure, unactuated potentiality for very long. And so it is significant that to the eternality of material potentiality or power Aristotle adds the eternality of formal actuation. Aristotle's speculative remarks allow us to conceive the spatio-temporal nature of the empirical universe as a *composition* of material potentiality and formal actuality, an unceasing process of formal differentiation powered by a dynamic substrate of physical force: the fields and particles that constitute us all.

Aristotle, for his part, does attempt to separate these two principles in his positing of the eternally actual Prime Movers, but in doing so, he implies a privational difference between the being of things and the Being of their final purposiveness, thus contradicting his text where it attempts to locate the essential purposiveness of things in things themselves. But we can reconstruct, rather than deconstruct, Aristotle's antitranscendentalist impulse by accepting quite simply the universal coexistence of material potentiality and formal actuality in the present universe, a coexistence that might be conceived in the terms of the neither monistic nor precisely dualistic ontology that we have found in the dynamic expression of potentiality-*and/also*-actuality, or, we might say, "power-*and*-difference."

It is interesting to note that Aristotle's own characterization of an infinite process—say, an infinite course of arithmetical division or addition—consists in a formula including both actuality and potentiality. That is, "the infinite," Aristotle writes in the Theta treatise, "is potential not in such a way that it will be separate in *actuality*, but it is potential in knowledge. For to a never-ending process of division we attribute an *actuality* which exists potentially, but not a separate existence to the infinite" (1979: 1048b14–17).

H. G. Apostle's gloss of this passage is significant. "*Actuality* in the infinite," he writes, "is the never-ending process of division or addition; but such a process, in view of the fact that it never comes to an end, exists potentially. Thus, *actuality* and potentiality exist together, so to say, in the infinite" (see *Metaphysics* 1979:357 n. 6).

The universe as we know it, we might say, is never wholly actual, never closed, never totalized. Its material potentiality can never be realized in some final form. But this lack of an *arche* or a *telos* does not necessarily imply that the course of change is causally incoherent, because, as Aristotle suggests, material being can only become what it has a capacity or power to become. The material universe, that is to say, can be seen to determine its own formal constraints, its own potentiality to exist in one state or another.

This does not mean that the principle of difference, of formal actuation, can be left out of the formula, however. For to privilege material power, *dunamis*, alone would be to posit a universal substrate with no inherent power of self-formation and actuation. Such a substrate would, accordingly, require a transcendental principle to actuate it. On the other hand, however, to privilege immaterial difference alone would be to locate the ultimate nature of the world in an immaterial abyss. This view would, in its turn, leave unanswered the question how an infinite play of immaterial differences can "produce" a material world. Our only choice, then, appears to be acceptance of a formula simultaneously including the principles of "power-*and*-difference," or "potentiality-*and/also*-actuality." Such a formula would represent an apprehension of a reality that produces from within itself individual beings that are at once universal and particular. And while having neither a fully actual origin nor end, this reality is neither a chaos nor an absolutely determinate formal monad. Rather, the universe so conceived can be seen to generate its own formal order out of the reality of its own material potentiality, a potentiality that does not determine what must happen in the course of change, but which does objectively control what is possible or probable. Such a metaphysical formulation is not itself Aristotelian, but I believe that Aristotle's analyses offer the terms for this expression of a "potentialist metaphysics" or "potentialist realism." Still, before we can complete the description of the potentialist realism that I am suggesting here, more modifications are necessary. To complete a reconstructive reading of Aristotle, we need to see just how his insights into the nature of material potentiality and formal actuality fare in the context of our contemporary understanding of matter and natural law. At first sight, of course, he does not fare well at all. Post-Renaissance science has exploded both his physics and his metaphysics. And what is more, in an age of quantum "uncertainty," even the inorganic principles of Newtonian mechanics that replaced Aristotle's organicism have been called into question. For many physicists and philosophers of science today the "natural laws" that classical physics substituted for Aristotelian physics are no more "real" than the metaphysical principles that they overthrew. But, paradoxically, it is precisely in such a post-Newtonian climate that Aristotle's metaphysical insights have begun to be reexplored. For in Karl Popper's "propensity interpretation" of the probabilism of contemporary physics we may find a metaphysical paradigm that, in its defense of scientific realism and the reality of relational laws, explicitly refers itself to Aristotle's metaphysics. And through an analysis of Popper's reading of Aristotelian potentiality, we will complete our own reconstructive reading of Aristotle toward the articulation of a potentialist realism.

CHAPTER 7

Realism in the Quantum Age: Karl Popper and the Debate Between Determinism and Indeterminism

"IN THE LAST HUNDRED YEARS of onslaught by mathematics, philosophy and the hard sciences," writes Frank Coppay, "the clockwork universe has come unsprung":

> Axiomatics is reeling from an uppercut by Gödel's theorem. The biologist's pre-biotic soup bears a striking resemblance to Mallarmé's throw of the dice. Literary deconstruction, in its refusal to ascribe origins, centers, or identities to authors or texts, has introduced a wave of anti-causality into the analysis of works of art. [1983:7]

But at the same time, Coppay adds, "we can recursively describe a Drunkard's walk. We can tip over a probability board and watch in security the little beads spill pathwise into a bell curve: nearly every time. We can computer-generate random-number sequences. This means, irony of ironies, that we can program improbability" (1983:7).

What is perhaps most striking about Coppay's remarks is that they appear not in a scientific or mathematical journal but in a critical one, *SubStance*. That such a journal should devote a special issue to scientific determinism is indicative of a recent interest among literary theorists in exploring the possible continuities that may exist, in the words of the editors of *SubStance*, "between the 'natural' world and the 'symbolic' universe, as well as the question of the mutual relevance of the discourses elaborated in order to understand each of these two fields" (1983:3). The barriers between scientific discourse and symbolic, or textual, discourse thus appear to be disintegrating in an intellectual environment that is every day being "defined more clearly as the problematical place where writing practices, scientific theories and philosophical meditations encounter and question each other as much as do esthetic investigations" (1983:3).

For example, the drift of contemporary science away from Laplacean and Newtonian deterministic certainty has been of considerable interest to a critical community intent upon demonstrating the absolute uncertainty and indeterminacy of textual interpretation. Often, in fact, such scientific developments are used to defend deconstructive critical practices. This has been the case especially with Werner Heisenberg's famous statement of scientific "uncertainty" in the face of the quantum atom. This statement has been taken as a general metaphor for a global epistemological uncertainty that prevents any objectively determinate knowledge of the world. But while I would agree with the editors of *SubStance* that criticism, especially in the nuclear age, must be allowed to compare scientific theories with its own critical and philosophical practices to advance our general understanding of the world, I would caution against the tendency of post-structural criticism to assimilate the uncertainties of scientific investigation with the aporias of aesthetic inquiry. For critical uncertainty and quantum uncertainty are not equivalent: the former refers to aesthetic indeterminacy, while the latter refers to a specific interpretation of atomic measurement and experimentation.

What is more, my contention in this chapter will be that if we carefully review the implications of Heisenberg's uncertainty principle, we may discover a contemporary expression of the metaphysics of potentiality that we have explored in Aristotle—an expression whose Aristotelian connection is made explicit both in the work of Karl Popper and, rather surprisingly, in a lecture by Heisenberg himself. For, as I shall argue, quantum uncertainty expresses not the indeterminacy and subjectivism of our knowledge of reality but, rather, the means by which its potential development and potential behavior may be calculated and known.

So let us return to the apparent paradox that, as Coppay said, "we can program improbability" and ask just how we might interpret such an interplay between randomness and certainty from a potentialist perspective. When we program a computer to calculate the irrational sequence of the number pi, for example, which is the more "real:" the determinate ordering of our program or the random unpredictability of the number itself? Since an irrational number has no closure, must we conclude that, because we cannot represent it, we can have no definite knowledge of it? Or should we focus our attention on the definite knowledge that we do have of its formal algorithm? Does the indeterminacy of our knowledge of the irrational sequence undermine our determiniate knowledge of the rational calculation that generates it? Or must we assume that behind the apparent irrationality of pi there is a larger, wholly determinate rationality that we simply have not yet grasped, and that "randomness" and "chance" are therefore only names for our own ignorance of a predetermined truth?

For the French mathematician René Thom, such questions are of crucial importance if scientific inquiry is to proceed with any coherence into the next century. "Is the world subject to a rigorous determinism," Thom asks, "or is there a 'chance' that is irreducible to any description? Posed in such a manner," Thom continues, "obviously, the problem is of a metaphysical nature and only an equally metaphysical option is capable of deciding the issue":

As a philosopher, the scholar can leave the question open; but as a scholar, it is for him an obligation of principle—under pain of internal contradiction—to adopt an optimistic position and to postulate that nothing, in nature, is unknowable *a priori*. [Thom 1983:11–12]

To choose the opposing option, Thom believes, to "assert that 'chance exists' is therefore to take the ontological position which consists in affirming that there are natural phenomena which we shall never be able to describe, therefore never understand" (1983:11). The latter choice, Thom believes, has been made by such exponents of "the popular French epistemology" as Jacques Monod, Edgar Morin, Henri Atlan, and Ilya Prigogine, all of whom, Thom declares, "outrageously glorify chance, noise, fluctuation" (1983:11). Thom further insists that this (apparent) celebration of chance simply "revives the famous *Ignorabimus* of Du Bois-Reymond," resuscitating "the wave of irrationalism and anti-scientism of the 1880's, the waves of the apostles of the 'crisis of science': the Boutroux, the Le Roys" (1983:11). Chance, Thom concludes, is essentially "an entirely empty, negative concept, therefore without scientific interest. Determinism, on the contrary, is a source of fascination—for the one who knows how to scrutinize it" (1983:19).

Interestingly enough, however, many of the scientists whom Thom so categorically numbers among the indeterminists refuse both to regard themselves as indeterminists and to see the issue in such either/or terms. "It is traditional to set the deterministic and random schemata against each other," Ilya Prigogine responds to Thom's attack, "whence, moreover, the possibility for two opposing dogmatisms: that of chance, from which Monod was not exempt, and the dogmatism of determinism with which the expose of René Thom is larded. Now," Prigogine continues, "if there is a surprise in this domain of the sciences, it is that these two views on nature complement each other to a much greater extent than they conflict" (Prigogine 1983:39). So "why choose?" Henri Atlan asks:

Who forces us to take a position on a reality which, by definition, whether momentarily or definitively, eludes our knowledge? Since the stake is to preserve a maximum of options for the process of our knowledge, why not do so directly and operationally, rather than indirectly, through the bias of metaphysical postulates that are only so many traps? All it takes is to select simultaneously from the two postulates that which implies an opening towards knowledge.... This attitude thus amounts to refusing a choice between such postulates insofar as they imply closure: no negation of time and of the new as implied by the postulate of chance through ignorance and no *a priori* limitation of the field of knowledge as implied by the postulate of essential chance. [Atlan 1983:45]

But how are we to embrace both the postulate of chance and the postulate of necessity without contradiction? To choose both chance and necessity appears to preserve the very metaphysical opposition that both Prigogine and Atlan seek to escape—unless the complementarity of chance and necessity is a physical, or natural, fact rather than a mere gesture of our metaphysical understanding. In other words, is it not possible that our contemporary understanding of a world that is at once determinate and indeterminate in a decidable and calculable relation is grounded in the real behavior of nature itself and not simply in the figures of our metaphysics? For Edgar Morin it is not only possible: it is precisely the case.

To start with, Morin believes that Thom has invented "out of nowhere a common trait fundamental to the 'underlying philosophies' of Monod, Atlan, Prigogine . . . [and] myself" in his insistence that the French all "'outrageously glorify chance, noise, fluctuations, all make randomness responsible, either for the origin of the world . . . or for the emergence of life and thought on earth.' Now," Morin continues:

each of the authors singled out tries to conceptualize the association and cooperation of randomness and determinism: each, in his own way, brings out the importance of factors of order that intervene in any birth, constancy and consistency of organization. As far as I am concerned, I write (thus differentiating myself from Michael Serres's adventurous exclamation: "Yes, disorder precedes order and only the first is real"), "What is real is the conjunction of order and disorder," and I say that the problem of all modern knowledge is to conceive this conjunction. [Morin 1983:23]

Thom's error, Morin says, consists not only in his misinterpretation of the ideas of those whom he attacks but equally in his tendency to regard determinism as "a self-evident reality and not a philosophical category," as "a clear and simple concept, and not a notion whose acceptations have been variable and whose meaning has evolved ... from the absolute mechanical determinism of Laplace to the probability theory of today." For

> let us not forget that the problem of determinism has changed over the course of a century.... In place of the idea of sovereign, anonymous, permanent laws directing all things in nature there has been substituted the idea of laws of interaction, that is, laws depending on the interactions between physical bodies that depend on these laws. Thus, gravitation does not govern material bodies: it governs the *relationships* between material bodies, and, without physical bodies, or before their formation, there are no laws of gravity. There is more: the problem of determinism has become that of the order of the universe. Order means that there are other things besides "laws:" that there are constraints, invariances, regularities in our universe.... Thus, in place of the homogenizing and anonymous view of the old determinism, there has been substituted a diversifying and evolutive view of *determinations*. The order of the universe is self-produced at the same time that this universe is self-produced starting from physical interactions: thus, it was not possible for there to have been electromagnetic, gravitational, nuclear interactions before the appearance of particles. But from then on, in and by these interactions, there come to be constituted organizational determinations *proper to* the structure of given systems ... that is, determinations *which do not exist outside these organizations*. [1983:24–25]

What Morin is suggesting is that to say there is order in the universe is not to make an appeal to some transcendental presence that must determine this order from the outside, beyond the play of universal becoming. The order of a system is itself a part of that system (just as, we might note, Aristotelian "form" composes itself with the material substance that it organizes without appearing apart from that substance). Determinations, as Morin puts it, are "proper to" the structures of specific material systems, and this propriety is a function of the evolutionary history of the universe itself. The physicist does not have to look outside the structure of a system for its structural principle or order: that order is specific to the structure in question without requiring a transcending or universalising genus of its own. The order of a system, Morin intimates, is real, but not in the sense of traditional realism, for its reality inheres only with respect to the system of which it is an essential part. In ontological terms, there is no separation, no difference, between the "order" and the material system that is ordered.

But the reality of order does not negate thereby the reality of disorder. For, as Morin continues, "we also have to see that if order develops at the same time as the organizations, the latter (nuclei, atoms, molecules, suns, living organizations) are formed with the cooperation of disorder, disturbance, random encounters" (1983:25). But here, Morin continues, "it is necessary to define this idea of disorder, which, to my way of thinking, is richer than that of chance":

> Just as order is not identified with the determinism of general laws governing nature, disorder, though it still includes it, is not identified with randomness or chance. Disorder is not a notion symmetric to order. It is a macroconcept which, while still containing the idea of randomness, can include sometimes the ideas of disturbance and dispersion, sometimes the ideas of perturbation or accident (relative to a functioning operation, an organization), and, when it is a matter of an informational communicational/machine (such as the living machine), the ideas of noise and error. [1983:25–26]

Morin, however, is not setting up a symmetrical opposition between order and disorder that would be universally true for every system. He is not saying that the irreducible possibility for accident is equal in every case to the potentially regular behavior of a system. What is more, he is not suggesting that the reality of accident must undermine our confidence in the reality of order. The one term is not really in opposition to the other, is not in competition, so to speak, is not engaged in a "speed race" with its "metaphysical" other. Morin, in other words, is not deconstructing the order/disorder relation. He is neither raising one (suppressed) term over the other (e.g., championing the historically slighted concept of chance) nor preserving the old opposition to suspend the relationship of its terms. Rather, Morin writes, "we need to leave behind the ontological opposition between chance/necessity and consider their copresence":

> As a result, the search for determinacies, and the consideration of random occurrences, accidents, disorders, are each necessary and fruitful. But any deification/reification of Determinism or of Chance is impoverished and sterile. A totally determined universe is a universe where nothing new can transpire and where the observing human mind could not be introduced. A universe at the mercy of chance would be nothing but noise and fury. So then, for us, the universe is at once order, organization, noise and fury. [1983:28]

Thus, we may apprehend a scientific ontology that reconciles both Einstein and Nietzsche. God gets to play a little dice, we might say, but there is still more to the universe than "the iron hand of necessity shaking the dice box of chance." The universe produces its own constraints, but the evolution of its self-ordering is never entirely predictable. Its observer cannot be certain just which new forms the universe may generate, but he or she can apprehend a universal order that "is not only the producer . . . of organizational phenomena" but "is simultaneously the product, and it increases, develops with the development of organization" (Morin 1983:25). There is novelty in this generation. There is difference and there is change, but the generation of the new is not simply an effect of differences: it is also an effect of structural regularities whose probable development can be calculated to a practical level of precision.

Still the fact remains that we can be "certain" only of the *probable* course of phenomenal development, thus introducing an apparently inescapable component of subjective indeterminacy into our knowledge of "reality."[1] As a physicist, for example, measures the behavior of a subatomic particle or a light photon, his or her knowledge of that behavior can only be expressed statistically, that is, as a subjective calculation of the probable state of the particle at a given time and place. This apparent superimposition of probabilistic knowledge and interpretation over direct empirical observation and prediction has caused a number of twentieth-century physicists to conclude not only that our measurements of the behavior of elemental matter are subjectively indeterminate but that "reality" itself has evaporated in the face of quantum interpretation. Such scientists believe that physicists study not objective nature but only their own subjective calculations. They can never break out of their own interpretational systems into the "reality" beyond.

In essence, this tendency toward scientific skepticism, or subjectivism, closely resembles the antirealism of literary and linguistic deconstruction, and it is partly what René Thom has in mind when he refers to "the popular French epistemology." But as we have seen, to opt for an objectivistic determinism in the face of such an epistemology can oversimplify the entire ontological situation. "Reality," if we may believe Morin, Atlan, and Prigogine, is simultaneously determinate and indeterminate. So here we might turn to Karl Popper, for in his own passionate defense of scientific realism against positivism, idealism, or subjectivism, we may discover a metaphysical paradigm that is explicitly antideterministic, but which, in its proposed "propensity interpretation" of the quantum atom, is not precisely indeterministic either.

Popper's defense of realism is especially pertinent to our purpose here because it refers explicitly both to Aristotle's metaphysics and to a nuclear reality that has made the defense of realism morally as well as politically necessary. We may find Popper writing accordingly in *Quantum Theory and the Schism in Physics*:

I have argued in favour of realism in various places. My arguments are partly rational, partly *ad hominem*, and partly even ethical. It seems to me that the attack on realism, though intellectually interesting and important, is quite unacceptable, especially after two world wars and the real suffering—avoidable suffering—that was wantonly produced by them; and that any argument against realism which is based on modern atomic theory—on quantum mechanics—ought to be silenced by the memory of the reality of the events of Hiroshima and Nagasaki. [1982a:2]

For Popper, "realism" does not constitute a belief in transcendental universals, nor does Popper oppose realism to philosophical nominalism as such. Rather, Popperian realism simply opposes the epistemological position "that takes our subjective experiences—especially our perceptions, our observations—as more secure, more certainly real, than the physical reality, which, positivism alleges, is merely our mental construction" (1982a:2–3). For Popper, in short, the "world exists independently of ourselves" (1982a:2). Popper does not deny that our conjectures about the nature of this reality are inherently subjective, nor does he believe that any conjecture can ever be conclusive. But he does hold that our subjective conjectures, or theories, can be tested objectively, subjected to an experimental scrutiny that would not be possible without the objective existence of a reality that is beyond our conjectures.

But in referring to the events of Hiroshima and Nagasaki in the context of a defense of realism, Popper raises a difficulty. For as we have seen Derrida point out, there is a difference between the events of Hiroshima and Nagasaki and a nuclear war that has not happened yet. How could we possibly test our conjectures about a "nuclear" future? Is there not only one test, and is that one not the absolutely wrong one? In other words, Popper's defense of scientific realism would have to defend the objective reality of potentialities as well as of accomplished actualities if it were to be adequate for an analysis of the nuclear referent as such. And it would have to do this without lapsing into a predictive determinism, because Popper's philosophy is as rigorously antideterministic as it is passionately realistic. Indeed, as W. W. Bartley explains:

> In *The Open Universe: An Argument for Indeterminism*, Popper presents a critique of both 'scientific' and metaphysical forms of determinism, and argues that classical physics does not, contrary to common opinion, presuppose or imply determinism any more than quantum physics does. Yet he finds that metaphysical determinism continues to underlie the work of many contemporary quantum theorists, opponents of determinism included. Popper traces the continuing role played within physics by subjective interpretations of probability to these metaphysical deterministic presuppositions. [See Popper 1982a:xii]

Popper's philosophy, I believe, is adequate to an analysis of the nuclear referent not in spite of the fact but precisely because it is antideterminist. For while it does not attempt to provide a deterministic scenario for what *must* happen in the world, it does help to define the terms by which realism can anticipate what *may happen*, what may *potentially* be, through a probabilistic mediation between objective reality and subjective knowledge.

We may find these terms developed in the course of Popper's three- volume *Postscript to the Logic of Scientific Discovery*, of which *Quantum Theory and the Schism in Physics* is the concluding volume. This volume contains Popper's detailed response to the "crisis" of contemporary physics, which is "due" as Popper writes, "to two things: (a) the intrusion of subjectivism into physics; and (b) the victory of the idea that quantum theory has reached complete and final truth" (1982a:1). Actually, as Popper himself observes, the second of these two events is no longer particularly critical. That is, the "idea that quantum theory has reached complete and final truth" and an "end of the road" is "a claim that may have been forgotten by now," Popper concedes (1982a:6). But its formulation as an idea is historically connected to the first of the two critical events Popper cites, viz., "the intrusion of subjectivism into physics," for it was this intrusion that first prompted physicists to believe that quantum theory could advance no further and that "reality" itself had disappeared.

This belief, the "end of the road" hypothesis, was a result of the so-called "Copenhagen interpretation" of quantum theory, particularly as it came to be formulated by Werner Heisenberg's famous "uncertainty principle" and by Niels Bohr's less known (at least to nonphysicists) "principle of complementarity" (1982a:6–10). The quantitative factors involved in the Copenhagen interpretation are largely beyond the scope of this book, but its qualitative nature can be stated succinctly:

> In brief, it says that *'objective reality has evaporated,'* and that *quantum mechanics does not represent particles, but rather our knowledge, our observations, or our consciousness, of particles.* [1982a:35]

What caused reality to "evaporate" was the discovery that if we attempt to "measure an elementary particle, we disturb it or interfere with it" (1982a:17). Thus we can never precisely determine the exact location and momentum of an atomic particle experimentally, because our experiment gets in the way. As Heisenberg put it: "The traditional requirement of science ... permits a division of the world into subject and object (observer and observed). . . . This assumption is not permissible in atomic physics; the interaction between observer and object causes uncontrollable large changes in the system being observed, because of the discontinuous changes characteristic of the atomic processes" (quoted in Popper 1982a:40–41). Bohr himself writes that "the *finite interaction between object and measuring agencies* ... entails the necessity of a final renunciation of the classical ideal ... and a radical revision of our attitude towards the problem of physical reality" (quoted in Popper 1982a:40).

Such observations led Heisenberg to propose his famous "uncertainty relations," which argue, essentially, that the *narrower* the range we might experimentally determine for the position of an atomic particle, the *greater* will be the range of its momentum, and vice versa (see Popper 1982a: 16–17). In other words, the closer we might come to measuring the position of a particle, the more distant we would be from measuring its movement. This runs counter to an entire tradition of classical physics, which assumed that both the position and the momentum of a particle could be calculated simultaneously, and thus the future state of the particle as well. As Bohr has characterized this tradition:

In Newton's principles, the foundation was laid of a deterministic description permitting, from the knowledge of the state of a physical system at a given moment, prediction of its state at any subsequent time. [Bohr 1958:84]

But in the quantum age, such precision is no longer possible. The physicist cannot determine a precise measurement of both the positions and the momenta of particles. And it was this loss of classical certainty that caused Heisenberg and Bohr to conclude that since reality had ceased to be scientifically measurable, it had in some sense "evaporated." All the physicist ever really has is a subjective set of probability equations for the positions and momenta of particles, never those positions and momenta, as objective realities, themselves.

The quantum atom has thus taken on a wholly different "appearance" from the neat "solar systems" of earlier atomic hypotheses. Instead of the tidy orbital schemes of early atomic representation, the quantum atom presents us only with probability "clouds." In fact, the orbital "pictures" reproduced in quantum physics textbooks are not, properly speaking, representations of the atom at all: they are representations of the physicist's probability calculus for where an electron *might be* found, not pictures of the precise orbit of an electron itself.

A second, and related, factor in the "crisis" of physics can be found in the apparently "'schizophrenic' character of light" (Bernstein 1983:161). Newton believed that light was particulate (or material) in nature and thus was propagated across space "mechanically." But by the end of the nineteenth century, James Maxwell's equations had convinced the scientific world that light was wavelike (or formal) in nature, not particulate. To be propagated across empty space it thus required a mysteriously substantial "ether" to project its undulations. Einstein's special theory of relativity (1905) more or less did away with the ether, however, and at about the same time (1900) Max Planck's breakthroughs in spectral analysis led to a proposal of light "quanta," according to which each light "unit" or "photon" exhibits *both* the discontinuous behavior of discrete matter and the formally radiating behavior of waves (see Bernstein 1983:153-63 and passim for further discussion of this history).

By the 1920s experimental evidence increasingly suggested, in Jeremy Bernstein's words, "that not only is light schizophrenic—exhibiting both wave and particle aspects—but 'particles' such as the electron are equally schizophrenic. Under suitable circumstances electrons act like 'waves,' i.e., beams of electrons can interfere like interfering beams of light waves" (1983:174). For example:

> If a light ray is sent through a small aperture, because of the interference effects, a diffraction pattern will be formed on a screen at the other side of the aperture . . . the same experiment can be performed by sending light quanta, one at a time, through the aperture. Each light quantum will pass through and hit some point on the screen. According to the Born-Jordan interpretation one cannot predict with certainty what an individual light quantum will do when it arrives at the aperture. One can state only what it is *most likely* to do—something that is determined by the Schrödinger wave function. [1983:175]

In other words, while an experimenter might project either particulate electrons or discrete light quanta (light in its particulate form) through an aperture of some kind, the physicist's prediction of where the particle might end up must be expressed by a wave equation (the equations for wave behavior developed by Erwin Schrödinger), whose functional effect, as Max Born argued, is probabilistic rather than deterministic. Heisenberg, as we have already seen, took all this a step further by suggesting that "the particle-wave duality was not an incidental feature of atomic physics, but was, rather, a basic fact about nature that could be traced back to a careful analysis of the meaning of 'measurement' on the atomic scale, which . . . [he] expressed in terms of his 'uncertainty principle'" (Bernstein 1983:175). That is, since we cannot precisely measure the position of a particle but can only plot its *probable* location in space, the idea that we might someday construct a wholly objective representation of atomic reality is an empty one. Our pictures are only of our own statistical approximations. Physics can advance no further into "reality."

While Popper himself accepts all of the experimental evidence that led to Heisenberg's uncertainty principle, he does not agree with Heisenberg's (at least apparently) skeptical interpretation of the evidence. Heisenberg, Popper writes, "tried to *explain* the limitations which his interpretation imposed on all possible measurements by pointing out that if we measure an elementary particle, we disturb or interfere with it," but an earlier version of Heisenberg's interpretation nonetheless "implied that the particle *had* a sharp position *and* momentum; but owing to our interfering with it, we could never measure both sharply" (1982a:17). Popper concedes that the situation "was changed after Schrödinger suggested that a particle may be represented by a wave packet, or may indeed *be* a wave packet" (1982a:18), thus only increasing, rather than reducing, our uncertainty. But Popper still insists that scientific "reality" does not thereby evaporate. "Admittedly," he writes, "many experimental tests now have a largely statistical character, but this makes them no less 'objective': their statistical character . . . has nothing to do with the alleged instrusion of the observer, of the subject, or of consciousness, into physics. By contrast, the preparation or setting up of an experiment always has had, and continues to have, a great deal to do with our changing knowledge: *it depends on theory*" (1982a:41).

Popper's point is this: it is true that in such experiments as described above a researcher must design his or her experiment to test a theory (and thus become involved in the "objects" he or she wishes to examine), but this does not mean that our experiments and our interpretations are merely subjective reflections upon our own theoretical speculations. "Our *theories* which guide us in setting up our experiments and in the interpretation of their results," Popper writes, "have of course always been our inventions.... But that has nothing to do with the scientific status of our theories which depends on factors such as their simplicity, symmetry, and explanatory power, and on the way they have stood up to critical discussion and to crucial experimental tests; and on their truth (correspondence to reality), or nearness to truth" (1982a:41).

What makes a theory scientific rather than subjective, however, is not a function of inductive reasoning. In fact, Popper argues that the scientific method has never been inductive at all, has never worked from from innocent observations to theoretical conclusions. Rather, for Popper, the scientist always begins with a theoretical conjecture so that he or she may systematize the particularity of past observations. To put this another way, a scientist explains the known by the unknown rather than the other way around. That is, Popper's "conjectural" scientist begins with a subjective hypothesis whose scientific status is unknown before it is tested. The scientist then tests this conjecture through objective experimentation, thus introducing new observational particulars into the history of the problem being investigated. Since theoretical conjectures can always be refuted by the experiments the scientist develops to test them, they are not entirely subjective: an objective reality always remains as a sort of foil to the wildest speculations.

What matters for Popper, then, is the *potential* success of the theory, not its actual success, because no theory can ever be permanently verified. In his lecture "Truth, Rationality, and the Growth of Knowledge," Popper accordingly argues "that we have a criterion of relative *potential* satisfactoriness, or of *potential* progressiveness, which can be applied to a theory even before we know whether or not it will turn out":

> This criterion of relative potential satisfactoriness . . . is extremely simple and intuitive. It characterizes as preferable the theory which tells us more; that is to say, the theory which contains the greater amount of empirical information or *content*; which is logically stronger; which has the greater explanatory and predictive power; and which can therefore be *more severely tested* by comparing predicted facts with observations. [Popper 1968:217]

The key word in Popper's defense of objective theory is "potential." Popper is not arguing that every theory is *actually* an attempt to put a cap on all further conjecture (such an argument, in fact, is one of the reasons he so rigorously opposes the "end of the road" declaration of the Copenhagen interpretation). Rather, the "better" theory is the one that has the most potential to explain past experiences and to predict future ones. If some new experiment (which has been designed to test the theory and is thus predicated upon it) fails to corroborate the theory, then we have learned something. The theory may need to be modified or rejected. For this reason Popper prefers "an interesting, daring, and highly informative theory to a trivial one" (Popper 1968:217).

But the inherently *statistical* nature of quantum theory still presents a particular challenge to Popper's defense of objective realism. After all, the orbital "clouds" in the textbook representations of electron behavior are "pictures" not of electrons but of the statistical results of the Schrödinger wave equations. Does this mean that such pictures are, after all, simply representations of our own subjectivity? Popper obviously believes not, and in *Quantum Theory and the Schism in Physics* he presents "thirteen theses" to defend his position. I will not reproduce all thirteen theses here, because much of the presentation is too technical for the present purpose. But by displaying the more qualitative arguments of the theses, I will present Popper's defense of theoretical objectivity-in-subjectivity and of "reality" itself in the face of Heisenberg's uncertainty principle.

Popper's first thesis is based on his conviction that any given theory must be evaluated according to "the kind of *problems* which the theory is supposed to solve" (1982a:47). In the case of quantum theory these problems evolved into what were "essentially *statistical problems*" (1982a:47). That is to say, the quantum hypothesis arose from such observations as Einstein's that light appears to be "emitted and absorbed in the form of 'particles' or 'light quanta' or 'photons' " but appears to be "*propagated* like waves" (1982a:48). To determine the "density (that is, the statistical probability) of the photons," one must calculate the square of the amplitude of their waves; and "the amplitude of the waves at the place where an atom . . . is located determines the probability of the absorption of a photon" (1982a:48). Schrödinger later developed these observations into his wave equations, and Max Born applied "to this new wave mechanics the statistical interpretation of the relationship between photons and light waves which we owe to Einstein" (1982a:48). But Popper's point is that quantum theory after Born came to be expressed in statistical terms and that "*statistical questions demand, essentially, statistical answers*" (1982a:49).

In other words, it is not the case that photons, say, are not real or, to put it another way, are merely statistics. Rather, when we attempt to measure their probable states, we have already involved ourselves in a statistical analysis. Quantum theory represents the historical development of these analyses, constituting a search for statistical *techniques* not for statistical *entities*. Given the experimental data that demonstrated the particle-wave "schizophrenia" of light, quantum theory thus evolved as a probabilistic enterprise bent on measuring the statistical probabilities for the behavior of the photon, not on determining whether there were any such phenomena to measure.

Still, the fact remains that quantum theory has developed a powerful formalism of its own that itself requires interpretation. That is, if the quantum theoretic has been a statistical or probabilistic enterprise, then one must accordingly interpret "probability" itself. Thus, our interpretation of physical reality leads us to the philosophical problem of interpreting our interpretations. In other words, the one inquiry cannot be separated from the other, for while the statistical predictions of the quantum equations are "real," the realist still must interpret them. Are they as "real," we must ask, as the objects whose behavior they interpret?

Sensitive to such questions as these, Popper accordingly proposes in his "eighth thesis" that *"the interpretation of the formalism of quantum mechanics is closely related to the interpretation of the calculus of probability"* (1982a:64). The calculus of probability, Popper points out, has endured "a great variety of interpretations, which may be divided into two main groups: the *subjective* and the *objective* interpretations." The subjective interpretation of the probability calculus argues, essentially, that our confidence in the probability that event *a* will follow from condition *b* is nothing more than a "belief." The argument here is more mathematically technical than Hume's famous attack on certainty, but its conclusions resemble it. Popper, it is perhaps needless to say, rejects this interpretation. Thus the question becomes: What might constitute a valid *objective* interpretation of the probability calculus? Popper presents three such possibilities (in a highly condensed demonstration), but only the third interpretation concerns us here. This is what Popper calls "the *propensity interpretation of probability"* (1982a:68ff.).

Popper's propensity interpretation constitutes a refinement of the so-called "classical" interpretation of probability. Now, the classical interpretation asserts that the probability of event *a*'s following from condition *b* can be calculated as "the proportion of equally possible cases compatible with the event *b* which are also favourable to the event *a*" (1982a:67). This can be best explained by example. If we "let *a* be the event 'at the next throw of this die 5 will turn up' and take *b* to be the assumption '6 will *not* turn up' (or 'only throws other than 6 will be considered as throws'); then $p(a,b)$ [or the probability of *a* given *b*] = 1/5" (1982a:67). In other words, since the probability of a die cast turning up "5" is, under normal conditions, one in six, if we restrict the conditions for the toss (i.e., posit *b*), then we will proportionately affect the total probability relations of the situation. If we posit a *c*, for example, as the favorable condition "1, 2, 3, 4, and 6 will *not* turn up," then $p(a,c)$ will equal one in one. We can best achieve such conditions, of course, by loading, or weighting, the die, and this is essentially what Popper does in his own reformulation of the classical probability calculus.

Popper's reformulation appears as follows: "The formula $p(a,b)$, or 'the probability (or propensity) of *a* given *b*,' may be interpreted as 'the sum of the weights of the possible cases that satisfy the condition *b* which are also favorable to *a*, divided by the sum of the weights of the possible cases that satisfy *b*'" (1982a:70). Again, this can be best clarified by example. Imagine that "we have a large die containing a piece of lead whose position is adjustable" (1982a:70). Now, "we may *conjecture* (for reasons of symmetry) that the weights (that is, the propensities) of the six possibilities are *equal* as long as the centre of gravity is kept equidistant from the six sides, and that they become *unequal* if we shift the centre of gravity from this position. For example, we may increase the *weight of the possibility* of 6 turning up by moving the centre of gravity away from the side showing the figure '6'" (1982a:70). Our *conjecture*, then, is that the *propensity* (or weight) for any particular number to turn up in a *virtual* sequence of experiments (tosses of the die) will be equal to the propensities of all of the other numbers as long as the lead is equidistant from all sides, and that this propensity will become unequal if the die is loaded. This conjecture, which is as yet untested because the die has not yet been cast, constitutes our *probability statement* for the relative frequency of any given number's appearances in a series of repeated experiments. Once we start actually experimenting to test our probability conjecture (i.e., start tossing the die), we will obtain certain statistical results about the actual frequency of any given number's turning up in a series of experiments. On the basis of these statistical results we can then formulate a *statistical statement*, which may or may not corroborate our probability statement.

If we then change condition b (i.e., shift the center of gravity in the die), we thereby change the objective situation of the die and thus the conjectural weights or propensities that are related to this situation. And if we are really sharp, we can arrange condition b so that we can conjecture that only "6" (a) has any chance of turning up in our loaded die: i.e., $p(a,b) = 1/1$. This again is our *probability statement*, constituting our conjecture about the virtual propensities of the system. We obtain our *statistical statement* by actually throwing the die a number of times.

Popper summarizes his thesis thus:

> In proposing the propensity interpretation I propose to look upon *probability statements* as statements about some measure of a property (a physical property, comparable to symmetry or asymmetry) of the *whole repeatable experimental arrangement*; a measure, more precisely, of a *virtual frequency*; and I propose to look upon the corresponding *statistical statements* as statements about the corresponding *actual frequency*. [1982a:71]

The referent of a probability statement, in other words, is not simply a subjective calculation but a real property that we may conjecture as belonging to the total relational economy of an experimental situation. Accordingly, Popper writes, "we can look upon probability as a *real physical property of any concrete unique physical situation, and therefore also of the single physical experiment.* . . . A propensity is thus a somewhat abstract kind of physical property; nevertheless it is a real physical property. To use Landé's terminology, *it can be kicked, and it can kick back"* (1982a:72).

Popper realizes that his proposal may have a rather mysterious ring to it, but his intention is not to imply that experimental situations are inhabited by a sort of anthropomorphic "consciousness" or Schopenhauerian "will." Rather, for Popper an experimental propensity or "disposition" constitutes "a kind of generalization of—or perhaps alternative to—the idea of force, mainly because the idea of force was also first viewed with suspicion by rationalist physicists who rightly viewed it as occult and metaphysical. But since then we have learned (or so I hope)," Popper adds,

that physical science explains the known by the unknown, and the visible world by a hypothetical invisible world; and we have got used to the idea of forces. (Newton was never quite happy about the idea of an attractive force; Heinrich Hertz tried to do without it; and so did Einstein.) Thus, we may likewise get used to that of propensities. [1982b:95]

Popper's "propensity interpretation" of the probabilistic results of quantum mechanics, then, represents his refutation of the inductivist interpretation of natural law. A natural law, inductively considered, determinately universalizes particular events. A conjectured propensity, on the other hand, only lays claim to a probabilistic knowledge of the predictability of related events. In other words, while a faith in the inductive certainty of our knowledge can enable us to calculate determinately what will happen in a future experiment, a conjectured propensity only predicts what is most likely to happen in an experiment, what is probable or potential.

Still, while the propensity interpretation may appear to undermine the possibility for objective knowledge, it is important to recall that our conjectures about a situational propensity can be objectively tested. What is more, given a history of such tests, we may calculate the probable results of experiments of the same type. As Popper puts it, "Propensity statements in physics describe properties of the situation and are testable if the situation is typical, that is, if it repeats itself" (1982a:80). Electron behavior, for example, can be typed experimentally (i.e., we can repeat the same experiment by which we test our conjectures about the electron), and while the actual behavior of an individual electron in a specific experiment cannot be inductively determined, its potential or probable behavior can be statistically represented by a wave equation that refers to the objective propensities of the experimental arrangement. The probability or propensity "fields" that the wave equations determine for the behavior of subatomic particles are therefore as "real" as our knowledge that "5" has a propensity of one in six in any virtual experimental die cast, according to Popper's interpretation. And this propensity can be regarded as a "physical," if invisible, property of experimentation itself.

But since this may imply a certain dualism between the particle under observation in a given experimental arrangement and its "real" probability field (its propensity to be in any given location), Popper takes care to point out, in his eleventh thesis, that

> even though both the particles and the probability fields are real, it is misleading . . . to speak of a "duality" between them: the particles are important *objects* of the experimentation; the probability fields are propensity fields, and are as such in the first instance important *properties of the experimental arrangement* of the specified conditions. [1982a:81]

The propensity of a particle to be in any given place under experimental conditions, in other words, is not separable from the experimental arrangement. The presence of the particle, on the one hand, and the statistical representation of its potentiality, on the other, are not two entirely separate phenomena. The relation between the particle and its probability field can best be illustrated by Popper's own figure:

The propensity or probability is not (like baldness or charge) a property of the member of the population (man, particle) but somewhat more like the popularity (and consequently the sale statistic) of a certain brand of chocolate.... And a wave-like distribution of a probability ... is, indeed, something which cannot be said to be an alternate 'picture' of the member of the population (man; bar of chocolate; particle). It would be awkward to speak of a *'duality'* (a *symmetrical* relation) between a bar of chocolate and the shape of the distribution curve of its propensity to be sold tomorrow. [1982a:82]

In other words, in the relation between a particle and its behavioral propensities we do not find a purely symmetrical (or oppositional) dualism. A particle's probability/propensity field expresses the probable behavior of things of its type. But this behavior is not something symmetrically extrinsic to a particular particle, is not something else. As Popper puts it, "The waves merely determine the probable *states* of the particle, that is to say, the probability or the propensity of the particle's being in a certain place, or possessing a certain momentum" (1982a:141). In a sense, then, we might say that a particle's potential behavior relates to it as the potentiality of an Aristotelian "genus" relates to the actuality of the "this," for a specific particle's calculable propensities also can be said to inhere in something like a generic identity. Our probability statements about a particle, that is to say, refer to its virtual behavior as it may be tested in repeatable experiments involving entities of the same kind, not to the actual behavior of the unique particle in a unique experiment. Individual particles can behave quite otherwise than our probabilistic predictions, but through a course of repeated experiments a generic curve for the propensities of particle behavior can be drawn.

The Aristotelian background to Popper's thinking here is made explicit in Popper's own texts. In *Realism and the Aim of Science*, for example, he observes that like "all dispositional properties, propensities exhibit a certain similarity to Aristotelian potentialities. But there is an important difference," Popper adds, because they cannot, as Aristotelians might be inclined to think, be inherent in the individual *things*. They are not properties inherent in the die or in the penny, but in something a little more abstract, even though physically real: they are relational properties of the total objective situation; hidden properties of a situation whose precise dependence on the situation we can only conjecture. [1983:359]

In other words, as Popper explains in *Quantum Theory and the Schism in Physics*, under the propensity interpretation of probability, the "Aristotelian view of inherent potentialities and their actualization is developed into a *relational* theory in which relational structures, instead of inhering in each material thing, may be characterized by potentialities" (1982a:206). That is, in Popper's modification of Aristotle, a potentiality inheres not in the particular actuality of the "this" but in the structural economy of the system under observation. When we make a conjecture about the future behavior of that system, our conjecture refers not to the differential particularity of some future event but to the systematic potentiality of the present experimental field.

We might say, in other words, that according to Popper's formula it is potentiality that relates present actualities to future states of being or behavior, not sheer incalculable difference. This does not mean that the temporal relations between situational actualities can be experimentally totalized, that our knowledge of a potentiality or propensity is determinate. But it does suggest that a lack of determinate certainty does not necessarily entail an incalculable uncertainty or undecidability, and that while the uncertain and the indeterminate cannot be reduced to determinate certainty, we can have objectively testable knowledge of the probable behavior of things, and this knowledge can be calculated within definable margins of error. To put this another way, the possibility of error, according to the kind of potentialist realism that Popper's thesis implies, does not necessarily lead to *errance*, to the perpetual undermining of our knowledge that an infinite field of differences, or the immaterial play of différance, would entail.

Popper's own recognition of the quasi-Aristotelian "metaphysical programme" that his propensity interpretation implies appears in the conclusion of *Quantum Theory and the Schism in Physics*, where he remarks how the metaphysical implications of his thesis "might be summed up, in the concise language of the Ionian cosmologists, by the statement: 'Everything is a propensity.' Or in the terminology of Aristotle we might say: 'To be is both to be the actualization of a prior propensity to become, and to be a propensity to become'" (1982a:205). In our own terms, we might say that Popper's thesis translates into a metaphysical formula by which present situational configurations might be characterized as a complex composition of "potentiality-*and/also*-actuality." For what actually "is" equally bears a potential temporal relationship to future and to other states of being: it can be reduced neither to its individual actuality alone nor to the pure potentiality of its relationship to the future.

Given Popper's opposition to Heisenberg's stance on the Copenhagen interpretation, it is somewhat surprising that Heisenberg himself has entertained an Aristotelian notion not unlike Popper's. In a relatively late lecture entitled "Planck's Discovery and the Philosophical Problems of Atomic Physics," Heisenberg observed how the "decisive step away from classical physics" that has been effected by quantum analysis

can be interpreted as a quantitative formulation of the concept of *dunamis*, possibility, or in the later Latin version, 'potentia,' in Aristotle's philosophy. The concept that events are not determined in a peremptory manner, but that the possibility or 'tendency' for an event to take place has a kind of reality—a certain intermediate layer of reality, halfway between the massive reality of matter and the intellectual reality of the idea or image—this idea plays a decisive role in Aristotle's philosophy. In modern quantum theory this concept takes on a new form; it is formulated quantitatively as probability and subjected to mathematically expressible laws of nature. The laws of nature formulated in mathematical terms no longer determine the phenomena themselves, but the possibility of happening, the probability that something will happen. [1961:9–10]

Even in the face of quantum uncertainty, then, Heisenberg modifies the classical understanding of natural law to preserve its trust in the regularity or coherence of phenomenal behavior and in the capacity of the physicist to quantify the probabilities of natural becoming. And he does so in the name of the metaphysics of *dunamis*, of real, rather than speculative, potentiality. Indeed, we might say that Heisenberg's remarks also constitute an economical expression of a potentialist metaphysics or potentialist realism, by which the probabilities and potentialities of quantum-era science can be interpreted objectively, as realities that science discovers in nature rather than imposes upon it.

But what critical role, finally, might a potentialist metaphysics play in an analysis of what we have called the nuclear referent? What relevance, for instance, has Popper's propensity interpretation in such a context? Does it offer an alternative to the post-structural approach? It must be conceded that in one sense it does not. For Popper's overall conception of scientific method might be seen to place us in precisely the predicament in the face of the nuclear referent that Derrida describes in "No Apocalypse, Not Now" (1984:20–31). That is, our conjectures about the truth of the situation known as the "nuclear age" cannot be tested without destroying the basis of the conjectures. We cannot absolutely test, for example, a conjecture that the world would suffer a devastating "nuclear winter" in the aftermath of a total nuclear war. And we cannot absolutely test a conjecture that civilization could survive such a war through adequate civil-defense planning. Each conjecture, in Derrida's terms, is only a belief until it is tested, and the whole point of the matter is that such tests must not occur.

Still, we may look at the issue from another perspective. The uncertainty, the absolute undecidability, the destinerrance described in Derrida's essay tend to exclude the probabilistic method of contemporary scientific projection and prediction. Science makes no claim to certainty, but it tests conjectures against the background of reality, not discourse. Computer simulations, for example, are often used to test hypotheses about future states of being, and while the simulation, or simulacra, is not the future itself, we can view it, rather than as as a representational substitution for an absent event, as a testing of conjectured propensities or potentialities.

If we look at the nuclear present as a situational configuration of actual scientific and historical conditions whose relation to the future can be found in their real propensities for becoming, then we can make conjectures about these propensities and test them as best we can. In this view the present can appear as a dynamically developing situation rather than as a "presence" that has been differentially undermined by an absent future. Between the actualities of the present and the actualities of the future, in other words, is a relation constituted not by differential alterity but by potential capacities, by real propensities whose existence can be defended in the terms of Karl Popper's own version of a potentialist realism.

In itself, of course, Popper's propensity thesis refers explicitly to an interpretation of subatomic behavior, but its purpose is broader than that. Popper's thesis is not a theory of history, and, in fact, he formulated it precisely to refute "historicist" (in Popper's sense of the term) visions of historical determination. But as a defense of realism it can be used to justify a scientific distinction between competing conjectures. Sometimes we may be able to test our conjectures only through computer simulation, but as Walter J. Ong has written, while a "computer cannot tell us everything we need to know to make a decision . . . it is good to have it tell us all that it feasibly can" (1971:7).

What is more, conjectures such as those characterized by the prediction of a postwar nuclear winter are not apocalyptic in the sense that Derrida suggests. That is, they are not simply predicated on archival metaphors, for until recently no one could have even dreamed of such a thing. The prediction of a nuclear winter is predicated upon the results of recent meteorological, geological, and paleohistorical research, upon the computer-simulated study of the "greenhouse effect" and the mechanics of glacial history, not upon figures drawn from the archive.

To accept the objective ground for conjectural speculation does not grant us certainty in the face of the nuclear referent. But even so the relative, rather than absolute, uncertainty that a potentialist realism proposes can have certain practical critical benefits. First of all, it can justify the probabilistic ranking of beliefs in the nuclear era. How probable are the predictions, say, of the Union of Concerned Scientists, on the one hand, and the Civil Defense Administration, on the other? To what kind of tests can they be subjected? To what kind of tests *have* they been subjected and how severely? The tests enacted will not prove anything, but they can establish a pattern of typical causal relations, of propensities that can help us choose between conjectures at a time when practical action is still possible. For if no choice is taken, if one remains suspended between contradictory alternatives with no basis for distinguishing between them, then no action can be taken either.

This raises a second practical point. There are really very few courses of action open to anyone in the nuclear age, and none of them is certain of success. To hold out for certainty in such a case can lead only to inaction at a time when inaction seems particularly dangerous. On the one hand, for example, to refuse to negotiate arms limitations without a pledge of absolute verifiability of treaties can only prolong the destabilizing effects of the arms race. On the other hand, however, to hold out for a treaty banning all nuclear weapons (which, were it possible, would grant absolute certainty) can also only delay practical action (as was the effect of the failure of the 1986 Reykjavik summit). But to insist upon the absolute undecidability between courses of action, to suspend all decision in the face of the nuclear referent, is equally to preserve the status quo. My point here is that while criticism cannot offer any new solutions to what might be called, from both sides of the controversy in America, "the present danger," it can point out that while nothing is certain, things are not absolutely uncertain either. Our beliefs, as long as we are willing to grant the objective reality of empirical potentialities and propensities, can be supported by objective tests, and it is on the basis of such supports that we can justify our decisions. We need not, in other words, inscribe the nuclear referent wholly in an intertextual archive of subjective speculations.

It would seem that criticism hardly needs to make such an argument, that all this is simply common sense. But at a time when not only post-structural critics but philosophers and historians of science as well (Paul Feyerabend comes particularly to mind here) are vigorously attacking the rational objectivity of scientific knowledge, it has become important to reconsider the possibilities of realism—particularly when the critical stakes have been raised. If all knowledge is equally subjective, then there is no point in attempting to distinguish between the many speculations offered by the various voices in the nuclear debate. My readings of Aristotle and Popper, then, have been intended primarily to stimulate such a reconsideration.

But I have had a second purpose in these readings not unrelated to the first. While it is not my intention to suggest that criticism must become "scientific," I do mean to suggest that to deconstruct scientific realism, to put its discourse on a par with literary discourse, is little more justifiable than attempting to compete with science. The referent of literary criticism, the nature of its subject matter, is unquestionably indeterminate. No one has ever been able to arrive at a satisfactory definition of literature, and after a period of attempting to emulate scientific method in this regard, criticism has wisely given up the attempt. But while the referent of scientific discourse, as we have seen, is also indeterminate, it is not indeterminate in the same way. Its indeterminacy is extratextual rather than intertextual and is expressible in the calculable terms of probability. By insisting that science is trapped inside its own governing tropes, criticism has become imperial in a way that may be self-defeating at a time when it is looking away from the aesthetics of the word to the politics of the world. I do not mean to imply that criticism should ignore extratextual phenomena. I only wish to suggest that critical techniques derived for the purposes of aesthetic inquiry can be inappropriate when addressed to such nonaesthetic phenomena as the nuclear referent. My readings of Popper and Aristotle have been aimed, then, at reintroducing to criticism some voices and terms that can help us to "read" the extratextual referent differently than we read the purely aesthetic text.

Still, as Derrida points out, there is a rhetoric, a language, of the nuclear referent as well as a reality, and this rhetoric cannot be ignored by any sort of nuclear criticism. But here too there is a place for a reconsideration of objective realism. For one might say that, in the face of the nuclear referent, it has become essential to distinguish between "mere" rhetoric and "sincere" rhetoric. That is, a politically minded nuclear criticism might set as one of its tasks the job of establishing the critical principles for distinguishing between arguments that are grounded in testable references and those that are indeed referentially empty platitudes. But given the tendency of post-structural criticism to assimilate all speech acts to a nonreferential play of intertextual tropes, such a task might be frustrated from the start. Indeed, in the writings of such contemporary critics as Stanley Fish, not only has the objective reality of the extratextual or extrarhetorical referent been called into question, but the objective reality of the text has been called into question as well. Recent criticism has undermined the reality of both text and referent in such a way that it would be difficult for a critic to justify any judgment regarding the objective validity of any proposal offered within the context of the nuclear debate. To argue, as I have thus far, for a potentialist realism in the face of the nuclear referent accordingly requires a defense of what might be called a potentialist hermeneutics. The purpose of this potentialist hermeneutics would be to explore the ways in which texts might be said to relate to the potentiality of an extratextual world and the ways in which readers might be said to relate to extrasubjective texts. This exploration and defense will be the project of part 3.

PART 3

A POTENTIALIST HERMENEUTICS

CHAPTER 8

A Rhetoric of the Real

"THE WORLDWIDE ORGANIZATION of the human *socius* today hangs by the thread of nuclear rhetoric," Derrida observes. "This is immediately readable in the fact that we use the term 'strategy of deterrence' or 'strategy of dissuasion,' as we say in French, for the overall logic of nuclear politics" (1984:24). To speak thus of the age of mutual assured destruction, however, "is not to say of this absolute *pharmakon* that it is woven with words," Derrida continues, "as if we were saying 'all this horror is nothing but rhetoric.' On the contrary, this allows us to think, retrospectively, the power and the essence of rhetoric; and even of sophistry, which has always been connected, at least since the Trojan War, with rhetoric" (1984:24).

So let us imagine, for a moment, the Trojan War, and the power and essence of its most crucial rhetoric. Before us stands a "mountainous horse," left behind as "an offering for safe return"—or at least that is the Greeks' story (Virgil *Aeneid* 2.22–25). But how are we to interpret this silent figure, and what shall we do with it? Thymoetes advises that the horse be brought within the gates of the city, while Capys "and those with sounder judgment" counsel us "to cast the Greek device into the sea, or to set fire to this suspicious gift, or else to pierce and probe that hollow belly." Quickly, as in so many cases of interpretational difficulty, a "doubting crowd is split into two factions" (2.46–55). And each side consults the evidence. On the one hand, we have the actual state of affairs: the Greeks have taken to their ships and vanished, leaving behind only their mysterious horse and, also,

Sinon, who has some plausible rhetoric of his own. Chosen for sacrifice but having escaped the alter, as his story runs, Sinon appears to be trustworthy, swearing to the gods that he is "no longer bound to obey the laws of my own country" (2.223-24). He says that the horse is indeed an offering to Minerva and must not be harmed. Still, the Trojans waver.

But suddenly, two serpents emerge from the sea to destroy Laocoön and his sons, for Laocoön has consulted a different kind of evidence in his own attempt to interpret the wooden horse. Even before Sinon has woven his net of sophistry, Laocoön has guessed the trick. Referring his interpretation not to the actual appearances of the matter but to the more abstract potentialities of the entire situation, Laocoön asks his fellow citizens if they "think that any Grecian gifts are free of craft? Is this the way Ulysses acts? . . . some trickery is here. Trojans, do not trust in the horse. Whatever it may be, I fear the Greeks, even when they bring gifts"—and then he hurls his spear against the hollow-sounding engine (2.62-75). But the Trojans ignore the echoing sound of the spear, heeding instead only Sinon's rhetoric and the signs sent by the gods. The horse is taken for a sacred offering, the symbol is taken for the substance, and the city falls.

We may take the story of the Trojan horse as an allegory not only of our own nuclear predicament but of the interpretive act itself. As we confront the bellicose rhetoric of the nuclear powers, we too must interpret both the speeches and the actions of the major participants in the nuclear debate. Was the SALT process a Soviet Trojan horse? Is Ronald Reagan's "Star Wars" defense initiative simply an excuse to increase the Pentagon's budget, a story without a referent fashioned not for the Soviets but for the American people? We are surrounded by rhetoric, by a rhetoric of words and by a rhetoric of weapons. But while we dare not attempt to test the palpable "rhetoric" of an ICBM, we can seek to interpret the rhetoric of both sides in the nuclear debate to probe its referential validity. Indeed, as the editors of *Diacritics* have written, "Rhetorical analysis of the forms, the themes, the performance of nuclear political argument as it is presently enacted must begin" (1984:3).

But to what purpose would a nuclear criticism perform its rhetorical analyses? Would it be to assimilate a new body of texts whose rhetoric, like the figures of literary discourse, might be reduced to a self-referring play of metaphors? Or would it be to uncover the real intentions of those who control the nuclear reality as well as the nuclear rhetoric? In other words, is it the purpose of a nuclear criticism to treat the texts of the nuclear debate as literature, or is the purpose of such a critical effort more politically directed, seeking to expose the concealed meanings, the real references, behind the rhetoric that we hear from all sides in the nuclear controversy, just as the Trojans sought to interpret the rhetoric of Sinon?

If the purpose of a nuclear criticism is simply to perform a series of rhetorical analyses of political texts, then no further exploration of the referent is necessary here. The critical tools for rhetorical analysis have been forged already. There is nothing to stop us from treating "the forms, the themes, [and] the performance of nuclear political argument" as a form of literature. But if one defines the purpose of a nuclear criticism as being politically oriented, then a certain amount of critical work remains to be done. For the extratextual referent by which the objective validity of political rhetoric might be tested has been deconstructed as a figure of "metaphysics" (in the bad sense) in recent criticism. Rhetorical analysis, many contemporary critics believe, can have access only to more rhetoric, to an unending play of tropes with no way out of the circle of signs. Indeed, we might see the interference of the gods in the Trojans' interpretation of the wooden horse as a symbol of our own poststructural hermeneutic predicament, for in the Trojans' decision to regard the signs of the gods and the rhetoric of Sinon as more certain indicators of the truth of the wooden horse than the objective evidence demanded by Capys and Laocoön, we may find a figure for our own post-structural disposition to take the sign for the substance, or rather, to deny that there *is* any substance beyond the play of signs. But then, the serpents of the gods might be taken in a second sense as well: as a symbol of the uncertainties inherent in acts of human interpretation. For Laocoön's attempt to delve into the truth of Sinon's story is itself cut short before any objective certainty can be achieved. The substance of the matter, the truth of the Trojan horse, is deferred until it is too late. But while, as Walter J. Ong writes, our practical decisions must often "be made when the grounds for decision are not under full logical control," compelling us, accordingly, "to deal often with probabilities" (1971:6), we are still best advised to work with such probabilities as best we can. In other words, if we seek to interpret the rhetoric of the nuclear age, to reveal the intentions of its speakers and writers, we must learn to deal with probabilities, with the potentialities of a case, just as Laocoön consulted not the rhetoric of Sinon but the typical propensities of Greek behavior. It is the purpose of part 3 to explore the theoretical principles by which such a "potentialist hermeneutics" might be constituted and defended. I shall argue that some of these principles have been established already in the reader-response hermeneutics of Wolfgang Iser. At the same time, I shall review two representative post-structural challenges to the kind of hermeneutic I will propose (i.e., those of Stanley Fish and Paul de Man), both to defend my position and to indicate the practical consequences of post-structural interpretational theory.

A potentialist hermeneutics, then, would begin by defining a text not as a wholly indeterminate and referentless play of endlessly deflective tropes but instead, in Edward Said's words, "as a dynamic field, rather than as a static block, of words," as a field, that is, "with a certain range of reference, a system of tentacles ... partly potential, partly actual: to the author, to the reader, to a historical situation, to other texts, to the past and present" (1983:157). In its use of the concepts of potentiality and actuality, Said's formulation, whether intentionally or unintentionally, refers us back to the Aristotelian metaphysical principles we have already explored.

But if there is a trace of Aristotelianism here that might be developed further into a potentialist hermeneutics, we will not develop it in the manner of the Chicago school of Aristotelian criticism. For the dynamic text, as we will define it, is not one that is, in R. S. Crane's words, "a definite structure of some kind which is determined immediately by its writer's intuition of a form to be achieved in its materials by the right use of his medium" (1971:1087). Rather, the "matter" of the dynamic, or potentialist text, is less determinate than that, constituting a field of potential meanings that the critic actualizes in the forms of his or her interpretation. So regarded, such potential forms do not exist as wholly realized actualities in the text. They are not discoverable as a determinately fixed poetic "shape." To put this another way, Crane's neo-Aristotelian formalism would allow the text's sheer form to overshadow the potentialities of its "matter," the propensities of a virtual textual field. But this does not mean that a text is wholly potential either—which is the implication of certain versions of contemporary reader-response criticism. Rather, a text can be seen as a composition of linguistic actualities and potentialities. The critic's activity is to realize textual potentialities: neither to wholly invent them nor yet to wholly "find" them either. The dynamic field of a text, I shall argue, is in "play," but it is a play of forms, of textual potentialities becoming actual in the mind of their interpreter according to the "material" constraints of a virtual textual situation.

To guide our inquiry into the simultaneous potentialities and actualities of interpretation, we can borrow from avant-garde poet Ron Silliman a figure that appears in a rambling prose poem appropriately entitled *This* (Silliman 1978). This figure appears near the end of the poem, as Silliman considers the image of a "bus route" as if it were "a specific syntax" (1978:88), suggesting thereby a range of possible bus trips that is nevertheless contained within the closure of a specifically defined route. We can take the bus only to its own destinations. We can stop only where the bus stops. But we can choose where to enter and exit. The "syntax" of the route is intersected simultaneously by the objective actuality of the route and the subjective potentiality in our choice of precise destination. The one principle cannot function without the other: we cannot choose where no choice is given, but we must choose our destination once we have agreed to ride. And as we proceed through our analyses of selected versions of reader-response and deconstructive criticism, we will keep this figure of the bus route in mind as a caution against any imbalance in emphasis: whether that imbalance favors textual potency or textual actuality, textual indeterminacy or textual determinacy, textual subjectivity or textual objectivity.

CHAPTER 9

Reader-Response Theory and the Hermeneutics of Potentiality

THE CRITICAL HISTORY out of which the reader-response movement in America emerged is a complex one with no single source. I will not reproduce that history here but will confine myself instead to an analysis of some of its resultant critiques. Still, a few guiding generalizations may be given. In one sense, American reader-response criticism can be seen as the product of a long hermeneutical history that can be traced back to the researches of F. D. E. Schleiermacher and Wilhelm Dilthey up through the twentieth-century hermeneutics of Martin Heidegger and Hans-Georg Gadamer and into the present-day work of the so-called "Konstanz school" of German hermeneuticists.[1] The writers of this tradition stress, according to one emphasis or another, the various roles that the reader plays in the interpretation of a text, the ways in which the reader involves himself or herself more (or less) subjectively in the realization of the objective text. Reading is regarded as a dialogue, a play between the objective reality of the text and the equally essential reality of the reader's subjective response to that text. The two, text and reader, participate in each other. The text questions the reader's pre-understanding of the world, and the reader, in turn, interrogates the text according both to his or her experiential pre-understanding and to his or her search for a new understanding. The two horizons of text and reader thus converge upon a new horizon in which reader and text engage in an extended dialogue from whose dialectical dynamic a given reading may emerge.

For Hans-Georg Gadamer this has meant that no interpretation can be completely without prejudice, and that every reading involves a confrontation between a historically situated reader and a text, whose own alien historicity is itself a productive part of the reading process. Gadamer, then, challenges the classical hermeneutic position of Schleiermacher and Dilthey, which holds, in David Linge's words, that "the knower's own present situation can have only a negative value" in interpretation, which, as "the source of prejudices and distortions that block valid understanding... is precisely what the interpreter must transcend" (Gadamer 1977:xiv). Gadamer instead, Linge continues, "takes the knower's boundness to his present horizon and the temporal gulf separating him from his object to be the productive ground of all understanding rather than negative factors or impediments to be overcome" (Gadamer 1977:xiv). The very act of interpretation is thus, for Gadamer, a historical event that is a part of the life and tradition of the text itself. As Gadamer himself puts it, "Understanding itself is not to be thought of so much as an action of subjectivity, but as the entering into an event of transmission in which past and present are constantly mediated" (Gadamer 1977:xvi). Thus, the pastness of a text can appear to us "as an inexhaustible *source of possibilities of meaning* rather than as a passive object of investigation" (Gadamer 1977:xix). In other words, understanding, Linge writes, "is an event, a movement of history itself in which neither interpreter nor text can be thought of as autonomous parts" (Gadamer 1977:xvi).

Hermeneutic understanding, so conceived, thus directly intersects the phenomenological tradition of criticism. In this context, the response critique bears a debt to such Geneva school critics as Georges Poulet, whose critical method stresses the reader's experience as he or she interiorizes the "transcendental consciousness" behind the text, as well as to those more explicitly phenomenological practices that focus on the temporal unfolding of a text within a reader's consciousness as he or she constitutes the horizons of the text.

The text does not disappear in such an approach, but its full reality requires an intersection of two horizons: that of the text and that of the reader. As we shall see, however, this phenomenological interpretation of the reading experience encounters certain difficulties when it attempts to clarify just what the reader interiorizes in the course of a reading.

The American version of response criticism, while cognizant of the hermeneutic/phenomenological tradition, has emerged all the same in its own specific context. As Jane Tompkins writes in her introduction to *Reader-Response Criticism*: "In the context of Anglo-American criticism, the reader-response movement arises in direct opposition to the New Critical" rejection of affective, or impressionistic, criticism and follows almost as many paths as it has practitioners (1981:ix).[2] In essence it is antiformalistic, where "form" is taken to be an objectively present (or actual) shape in a text, but it is not everywhere equally opposed to "form" as such. Rather, American response criticism finds its forms in the very *activity* of textual interpretation itself and can thus be seen as a variant of American pragmatism. For just as the pragmatist regards the truth of a proposition as being relative to the contingent circumstances of its utterance, so too does response criticism often regard the meaning of a text not as it has been objectively *given* but only as it might be subjectively *constituted* in given discursive contexts. Since it is radically circumstantial, critical pragmatics takes as its point of departure not the objectivity of formal "truth" but the circumstantial conditions under which such "truth" may be constituted.

Teun Van Dijk has characterized this pragmatics of the reading process in conceptualist terms, arguing that the reading, or understanding, of a text

> basically requires that a language user, i.e., a hearer or reader, assigns a semantic structure to the respective units of the text. He thereby gradually constructs a semantic or *conceptual representation* of the text in memory. Thus, the variety of "surface structural," e.g., morphophonological and syntactic, information in the

text is "translated" or "transformed" into meanings which are cognitively represented in terms of "concepts." [1979:145]

In other words, we might say that a reader constitutes the cognitive forms of his or her conceptual understanding of a text out of a textual field that is at once structurally actual with respect to its surface forms and semantically potential with respect to the reader who actuates the potential meanings that the surface structure may bear. The objective information of the text must be cognitively, or subjectively, organized, but that organization does not occur apart from the existence of the surface text. The precise conceptual shape of the potential semantic units of the text, that is to say, may be said to depend upon the reader who is actuating them in the forms of his or her interpretation, but these conceptual forms cannot exist without the "matter" of the potential text.

We can compare Van Dijk's observations with Susan Horton's more hermeneutically determined, but essentially similar, judgment that differing interpretations of texts "result primarily and most often from differing conceptions of what constitutes the 'part' or the unit of interpretation that contributes to the whole during the hermeneutical process," a "unit" that "can be as shifting and various as the word, the line, the sentence, the paragraph, or chapter" (1979:17). To read, that is to say, is to construct a concept, to constitute an *actual* semantic figure out of a *potential* linguistic field. But how, precisely, does a reader determine the "units" of his or her reading? What is the reader's relation to the potentiality of his or her text, and how might that text be said to constrain the possibilities for the reader's conceptual constitutions?

In "The Reading Process: A Phenomenological Approach" (1981:50), Wolfgang Iser proposes an answer to such questions through his analysis of the dialogical relationship between two kinds of text as they bear upon the constitution of the virtuality of the literary work as a whole. The first of these texts, Iser's "artistic text," simply "refers to the text created by the author" (1981:50). But while this text has been composed *by* a given author, it has been written *for* a reader who is implied in the strategies and forms of the artistic text itself. Thus, the artistic text already bears, in potentia, a second, or "esthetic text," that refers to the actual textual "realization accomplished by the reader" (1981:50). Together, the artistic text and the esthetic text dialogically determine the "virtual" reality of the "literary work" as a whole, a reality that seems to hang in the balance between the specificity of artistic and esthetic textuality. The "work," that is to say, represents an unspecifiable composition of actual textual forms and potential textual readings. As Iser puts it:

From this polarity it follows that the literary work cannot be completely identical with the text, or the realization of the text, but in fact must lie halfway between the two. The work is more than the text, for the text only takes on life when it is realized, and furthermore the realization is by no means independent of the individual disposition of the reader—though this in turn is acted upon by the different patterns of the text. The convergence of text and reader brings the literary work into existence, and this convergence can never be precisely pinpointed, but must always remain virtual, as it is not to be identified either with the reality of the text or with the individual disposition of the reader. [1981:50]

The "gestalt" of a literary work, then, involves three essentially interrelated parts. The accomplished artistic text is the source of our own further hermeneutic constructions. The esthetic text constitutes a given reader's actual response to a work; this response is at once subjective (because it is fashioned according to the reader's own "disposition") and objective (because it is guided "by the different patterns of the text"). Finally, the general *virtuality* of the entire literary work, which is identifiable neither with any given reading nor with the written document itself, constitutes a phenomenal identity that is real but never wholly specifiable.

The artistic text, we might say, provides the material for a specific textual realization. A reader constructs the forms of his or her interpretation, in other words, out of the matter that the artistic text presents. This construction of actual hermeneutic units or concepts occurs across the temporal course of a reading process that continually matches the reader's expectations or "pre-intentions" against the actual movement of the text (see Iser 1981:53). When we anticipate what is to come in a literary reading, we involve ourselves in its own unfolding. Our memories of what the text has already told us confront the new information at hand, thereby prompting us to make new textual connections and syntheses that are not, strictly speaking, *in* the text itself. As Iser writes:

> Whatever we have read sinks into our memory and is foreshortened. It may later be evoked again and set against a different background with the result that the reader is enabled to develop hitherto unforeseeable connections.... These connections are the product of the reader's mind working on the raw material of the text, though they are not the text itself—for this consists just of sentences, statements, information, etc. [1981:54]

Iser's artistic text, then, is an *open* text: it exists apart from us, in one sense, but its full reality can be accomplished only insofar as a reader inscribes himself or herself in its interstices, filling in the gaps of what the text does not actually say but potentially accomplishes. Thus, for Iser, the actually written text, as the matter out of which interpretations emerge, is like a "night sky," for just as "two people gazing at the night sky may both be looking at the same collection of stars, but one will see the image of a plough, and the other will make out a dipper," so too are the "'stars' in a literary text . . . fixed," while "the lines that join them are variable" (1981:57).

Each star in the literary night sky, in other words, is like a stop on a bus route: for while we can articulate a figure according to our own decisions (i.e., we can plot our own itinerary), we are limited to our given sky or route (i.e., we can go only where the bus goes). Thus conjoining the objective actuality of an accomplished artistic text with the potential choices inscribable within specific esthetic texts, Iser's phenomenological hermeneutic appears to mediate between subjectivistic and objectivistic theories of interpretation, allowing neither the one pole of the reading process nor the other to assume dominance, but not suspending their relation undecidably either. For between the objectivity of the artistic text and the subjectivity of the esthetic text lies not an uncrossable gap or difference but the real virtuality of the work as a whole.

Roland Barthes has proposed a distinction of his own that is not unlike Iser's—a distinction, that is, between what Barthes calls a "work" and a "text." Barthes's distinction runs as follows:

> The work is concrete, occupying a portion of bookspace (in a library, for example); the Text, on the other hand, is a methodological field. . . . While the work is held in the hand, the text is held in language: it exists only as discourse. . . . In other words, *the Text is experienced only in an activity, a production.* [1979:74–75]

But in spite of the commonsense appeal of such a distinction, there is still a difficulty to be confronted. For once one "opens" the literary text, it is very hard to "close" it again. Once critical subjectivity has been inscribed alongside textual objectivity, the old specter of interpretational relativism raises its head. What is to prevent each particularly realized esthetic text from departing completely from authorial artistic texts? How can we be certain whether a given reader has properly responded to a solicitation from the text or has simply followed his or her own impulses? Under such circumstances any given artistic text can potentially produce as many different esthetic texts as there are readers to produce them; for without a formally self-sufficient work of art before us, what is to limit the range of our interpretational activities?

Such were (and still are) the kinds of questions put to response critics by American New Critical formalists throughout the seventies, thus polarizing American criticism into at least two camps, the one maintaining the interpretational authority of the objective text and the other supporting the claims of the reader. Among the latter group of critics, Stanley Fish has distinguished himself as a leading exponent for response analysis, but his own position, significantly, has evolved. We can follow this evolution through the pages of his collection of essays *Is There a Text in this Class?* (1980), a book in which Fish deliberately redisplays his original critical judgments and his own revisions of them.

Among Fish's earlier reader-response statements, his essay "Literature in the Reader: Affective Stylistics" (1980:21–67) is notable for the breadth of its treatment. In the essay, Fish relentlessly attacks W. K. Wimsatt's and Monroe C. Beardsley's position that a poem, or text, can ever be available to us "as an object of specifically critical judgment" (quoted in Fish 1980:23). Rather, for Fish, a poem "is no longer an object, a thing-in-itself, but an *event*, something that *happens* to, and with the participation of, the reader" (1980:25). Thus, when Fish looks at a given textual statement, he substitutes "for one question—what does this sentence mean?—another, more operational question—what does this sentence do?" (1980:25). For Fish, then, the *meaning* of a text is not its "objective," or semantic, content but what that text *does*, what *happens* to its reader. Meaning is to be found in the temporal experience of readers, not in the spatial fixity of texts.

But while Fish at this point lines up clearly on the side of the reader, he has not yet abandoned the text altogether. The text is "kinetic," something that forces us "to be aware of 'it' as a changing object" and that "makes inescapable the actualizing role of the observer" (1980:43). Thus, at this relatively early stage in his career, Fish does not substantially differ from Iser. In Fish's thinking, as in Iser's, a reader actualizes what is potential in a text through his or her own temporal activities and is guided by what the kinetic text *does*. What is more, to make certain that the reader properly responds to the text's promptings, Fish invents the concept of an "informed reader," who, rather like Iser's abstract "model reader," consciously attempts to learn as much as possible about a poetic text (including knowledge of its "genre, conventions, and intellectual background") to make his or her "mind the repository of the (potential) responses a given text might call out" (1980:49).

Fish's early reader-response analyses, then, are roughly compatible with a potentialist hermeneutics. His kinetic text, like Iser's artistic text, must be realized by a reader's activities, but it is there to be realized, an entity at once actual and potential, objective and subjective. Anticipating a charge of "subjectivism" here, Fish concedes the label but argues that he "would rather have an acknowledged and controlled subjectivity than an objectivity which is finally an illusion" (1980:49). But the situation is not as wholly subjective as Fish himself suggests, because the subjectivity that he concedes is a "controlled subjectivity." That is, while a reader must subjectively actualize a text, that actualization does not occur just anyhow: it is controlled, or guided, by the objective limitations of the text. At this point, we might say, Fish is very much "on the bus."

But Fish altered his position radically as the seventies advanced. While in 1970 he was "asking the question 'Is the reader or the text the source of meaning?' " by 1980 he had begun to question his assumption "that the text and the reader can be distinguished from one another and that they will hold still" (1980:1). Thus, rather than defending the subjective authority of the (informed) reader or attacking the objective authority of the text, Fish, in this later phase, began to look for an alternative authority that would be neither subjective nor objective, but which would make our conceptions of subjectivity and objectivity possible in the first place. He found that authority in a new concept—that of the "interpretive community"—which replaced his earlier notions of the "informed reader."

According to Fish's latest position, the "relationship between interpretation and text is . . . reversed":

> Interpretive strategies are not put into execution after reading; they are the shape of reading, and because they are the shape of reading, they give texts their shape, making them rather than, as is usually assumed, arising from them. [1980:13]

But recognizing that it now "looks as if the text is about to be dislodged as a center of authority in favor of the reader whose interpretive strategy makes it," Fish argues instead "that the strategies in question are not his [the reader's] in the sense that they would make him an independent agent. Rather, they proceed not from him but from the interpretive community of which he is a member; they are, in effect, community property, and insofar as they at once enable and limit the operations of his consciousness, he is too" (1980:13–14). Thus, we now find that

> it is interpretive communities, rather than either the text or the reader, that produce meanings and are responsible for the emergence of formal features. Interpretive communities are made up of those who share interpretive strategies not for reading but for writing texts, for constituting their properties. In other words these strategies exist prior to the act of reading, and therefore determine the shape of what is read rather than, as is usually assumed, the other way around. [1980:14]

Such communities, however, constitute not only the shapes of texts but the very "thoughts an individual can think and the mental operations he can perform . . . he is as much a product of that community (acting as an extension of it) as the meanings it enables him to produce" (1980:14).

Fish's definition of the "interpretive community" may appear to be compatible with a more or less Marxian analysis of the relationship between consciousness and social existence, but there are important differences. For while a Marxist critic might agree with Fish's contention that critical consciousness is socially determined, he or she would miss in Fish's analysis any recognition of the dialectical interplay between material history and the forms of consciousness that it both determines and is determined by. Fish, that is to say, does not account for the constitution of his interpretive communities: they are historical, but they do not seem to have any material links to history. And what is more, Fish's thesis ultimately implies that material history is itself an interpretive construction, a "standard story," "written" within what might be called the "group idiolect" of "interpretive communities." For according to Fish's theory, the conformations, the referents, the "facts" of experience are communally constituted rather than objectively determined. But while Fish's argument might appear to be an expression of philosophical idealism (at least to a scientific realist), it really expresses the logical result of philosophical pragmatism. To see how this is so, we can look at his essay "How To Do Things with Austin and Searle: Speech-Act Theory and Literary Criticism" (1980:197-245).

Fish's critical pragmatism, it appears, derives from an extension of the logical consequences of J. L. Austin's theory of linguistic speech acts. Fish develops this logic as follows:

> In the penultimate chapter of *How To Do Things with Words*, J. L. Austin presents a sentence and asks us to consider it. The sentence is "France is hexagonal," and the question he puts to it is a very familiar one in analytical philosophy: Is it true or false? The answer, however, is not so familiar. It depends, says Austin: "I can see what you mean by saying that it is true for certain intents and purposes. It is good enough for a top-ranking general, perhaps, but not for a geographer.". . . In other words, the truth or falsehood of the sentence is a function of the circumstances within which it is uttered, and since it is always uttered within some set of circumstances or other, it is not in and of itself either true or false, accurate or inaccurate, precise or imprecise. [1980:197]

The consequences of Austin's essential pragmatism, his conviction that the value of a statement is to be found in the circumstances of its production rather than in the nature of its propositional (or semantic) content, can be epistemologically disturbing. For if the authority for the judgment of a proposition is absolutely context-specific, then there appears to be no objective reality against which we might test the truth of our propositions, or, in Popper's sense of the term, our conjectures. The pragmatic approach has thus apparently undermined its own material or objective ground. Accordingly, Fish concludes:

> In the drama of *How To Do Things With Words*, this discussion of France and its hexagonality marks the final overturning of the distinction with which Austin begins, the distinction between constative and performative language. Constative language is language that is, or strives to be, accountable to the real or objective world. It is to constatives—to acts of referring, describing, and stating—that one puts the question "Is it true or false?" in which true and false are understood to be *absolute* judgments, made independently of any particular set of circumstances. Performative language, on the other hand, is circumstantial through and through.... One kind of language is responsible to what John Searle calls brute facts—facts that exist prior to any linguistic report of them—and the other is responsible to institutional facts, facts that are facts only with reference to some social or conventional human practice ... but what Austin discovers at the end of *How To Do Things With Words* is that all utterances are performative—produced and understood within the assumption of some socially conceived dimension of assessment—and that therefore all facts are institutional, are facts only by virtue of the prior institution of some such dimension. This means not only that statements about an object will be assessed ... according to the conditions of their utterance, but that the object itself, in so far as it is available for reference and description, will be a *product* of those conditions. [1980:198]

Thus Fish turns the tables on writers who, like John Searle (1979), have asserted the secondary or "parasitic" nature of literary language, because if even the "facts" of "ordinary" discourse must be determined on the basis of a story (or "standard story") that a given "interpretive community" tells itself, then there can be no difference between "fictional" and "ordinary" uses of language. "What we know is not the world but stories about the world," Fish insists, and thus "no use of language matches reality," but "all uses of language are interpretations of reality" (1980:243). We can be certain, then, only of our own "stories." There is no substantial "what is" before us, only our own "what we say it is." The world itself is text, a constituted field. Nothing is available to us that would be outside the rhetorical configurations of our interpretive communities.

Still, one might reasonably suggest that the Bomb is a rather "brute" fact. Not only can we "kick" it, but it can kick back. But how are we to approach such an entity while arguing that all such "facts" are really the products of a "standard story"? If our "world" is only a configuration of stories, then our knowledge is finally self-reflexive, unable to break out of its own conformations. Of course, Fish's concern is with the social dimensions of hermeneutics, not with global political issues per se, but the implications of his implied epistemology (and ontology) are politically disturbing. And although we cannot expect a critic whose subject is the interpretation of literature to supply a thoroughgoing extratextual ontology, we might request a further discussion of just what it is that readers read or what "interpretive communities" tell themselves stories about. Fish consistently questions the existence of both textual and "brute" facts beyond our institutionally determined constitutions, but he has thereby left himself a yet unanswered ontological question.

Fish, for his part, does acknowledge a certain gap in his theory, recognizing that, having identified the "forms" of a text with a reader's constitutive activity, he still has before him the question: "What is that act an interpretation *of*?" But his answer, while candidly disarming, is hardly reassuring. "I cannot answer that question," he writes, "but neither, I would claim, can anyone else" (1980:165). Should someone suggest that, after all, a critic knows the difference between, say, T. S. Eliot's *The Waste Land* and Milton's *Lycidas* without having to constitute that difference, that they are ontologically different entities, Fish answers that they do not have to be different at all. Indeed, he writes in his essay "Interpreting the Variorum":

If I read *Lycidas* and *The Waste Land* differently (in fact I do not), it will not be because the formal structures of the two poems (to term them thus is an interpretive decision) call forth different interpretive strategies but because my predisposition to execute different interpretive strategies [as determined by a given interpretive community] will *produce* different formal structures. That is, the two poems are different because I have decided that they will be. The proof of this is doing the reverse. . . . That is to say, the answer to the question "why do different texts give rise to different sequences of interpretive acts?" is that *they don't have to*, an answer which strongly implies that "they" don't exist. [1980:169–70]

Such statements have caused a good deal of shouting in the critical community, but Fish has a point. There *is* an active, subjective component in critical interpretation that has often been neglected by critical formalists. The potentialist realism that I have derived thus far from the theories of Karl Popper does not deny this. Where a potentialist realism would disagree with Fish is in his implied denial of the possibility of ever testing our subjective conjectures against an extra-conjectural, or extra-interpretational, reality. "What we say" or conjecture, realism argues, can be tested against a "what is" to which our conjectures refer. But how are we to approach this referential reality without ignoring the modifying and mediating role of the interpreter? Fish, for his part, believes that we can never transcend our linguistic interpretations on behalf of an essential reality beyond our designations. A significant number of contemporary language philosophers, however, can be seen to believe that we can, and while the position of such "analytic" realists might well require a hermeneutic supplementation from Fish's perspective, their program may help us mediate between the ultimate subjectivism of the interpretive community and the naive realism of essentialist objectivism.

CHAPTER 10

Naming and Referring in a Potential World

THE PROBLEM OF LINGUISTIC REFERENTIALITY has for nearly a century dominated the agenda of Anglo-American philosophy, and it is no closer to a conclusion now than is the problem of critical hermeneutics. And just as literary criticism was set adrift earlier in this century by a challenge to its own fundamental axioms (i.e., by the New Critical assault on authorial intentionality), so too has referential theory recently been cut loose from its moorings. We might, for present purposes, identify these moorings with a distinction proposed by John Stuart Mill between linguistic "denotation" and "connotation," a distinction of such commonsense appeal that few nonphilosophers realize that it is no longer philosophically authoritative.

Mill, in short, felt that the use of any single-term expression *denoted*, in John Lyons's words, "a class of individuals of which it was the name" and *connoted*, or implied, "the property or properties by virtue of which individuals were recognized as members of the class in question" (Lyons 1979:176). In other words, when someone uses the term "lemon," he or she at once explicitly designates the class of all existing lemons and implicitly connotes all of the properties that identify lemons (e.g., yellow color, oblong shape, tart taste, and so on). Herbert Hochberg explains that every word so conceived constitutes a "composite sign . . . linked to the complex object it corresponds to since the signs it is composed of refer to the entities the object is composed of" (1970:70). To put it another way, according to Mill's referential analysis, every expression constitutes an implied (or connoted) *description* of the object, or class of objects, that it names. If one knows the name one also knows the description that goes with it.

The German mathematician/philosopher Gottlob Frege later introduced his own referential distinction into the language, but while his opposition of linguistic *Sinn* to linguistic *Bedeutung* is sometimes taken to be equivalent to Mill's connotation/denotation distinction, the equivalence is not at all clear. First of all, we have a confusion within the German terms themselves. *Bedeutung* properly signifies "meaning" in English, but Frege uses the term as if it meant "designation" or "reference." What is more, *Sinn*, properly translated as "sense," also signifies "meaning" to the English ear. "It is unfortunate," Lyons remarks, ". . . that Frege selected 'Bedeutung' as his technical term for what is now generally called reference in English," because, Lyons continues, there is "an alternative technical distinction drawn in German between 'Bedeutung' ('meaning') and 'Bezeichnung' (often translated into English as 'designation')" (1979:199). But Frege's terms specify a distinction between *Sinn* and *Bedeutung*, not between *Bedeutung* and *Bezeichnung*, so we will have to make of these terms what we can.

Early in his essay "Ueber Sinn und Bedeutung" (translated by Peter Geach and Max Black as "On Sense and Meaning," 1980:56–78), Frege attempts to provide a clear definition for his terms before turning to the logical analyses of sentential truth conditions that form most of the paper. Still, while "less than a third of 'On Sense and Reference' concerns proper names, while the rest focuses upon the central thesis that sentences have truth-values as their reference," as Baker and Hacker remark (1984:282), our concern here will be solely with this third, for it is here that *Sinn* and *Bedeutung* are defined. Frege presents this definition in the form of what appears to be a commonplace observation about the nature of a sign:

It is natural, now, to think of there being connected with a sign (name, combination of words, written mark), besides that which the sign designates, which may be called the meaning [*Bedeutung*] of the sign, also what I should like to call the *sense* [*Sinn*] of the sign, wherein the mode of presentation is contained. . . . accordingly, the meaning of the . . . [expression] 'evening star' would be the same as that of 'morning star,' but not the sense. [1980:57]

The definition, at first sight, appears to be fairly straightforward. Every sign, or name, refers to or designates something, and this is its *Bedeutung*. So *Bedeutung* is apparently equivalent to Mill's "denotation," but the equivalence is not precise, for as Lyons reminds us, "denotation" signifies *classes* of things, while *Bedeutung* signifies the designated thing itself (see Lyons 1979:176). Still, a sign's *Bedeutung* does appear to be, in one way or another, its reference. But what is its *Sinn*?

As we see above, Frege equated linguistic *Sinn* with what he called "the mode of presentation" of what a sign designates, but it is not at all clear what he meant by this. As Baker and Hacker explain it: "Frege gave only minimal clarification of the notion of sense, no doubt considering this concept to be primitive and unanalyzable. He simply explained that the sense of an expression is the mode of presentation of the entity designated" (1984:300). Still, Frege's "simple" explanation has a certain intuitive force in the context of the now-classic example that he gives. That is, while we know that the expressions "the morning star" and "the evening star" each refer to the same entity (the planet Venus) and thus have the same "meaning," or *Bedeutung*, we also know that the two *expressions* are different. What is different about them is not, for Frege, the fact that they employ different signs ("morning" vs. "evening") but that our *thoughts* about them are different. Thus, even while knowing that "the morning star" and "the evening star" both refer to the planet Venus and thus "mean" the same thing, we can "sense" an expressive difference. First, of course, we can logically deduce this difference, because a proposition such as "the morning star is the evening star" is synthetically informative, while "the morning star is the morning star" is analytically tautologous. But at the same time, "the morning star" itself seems to suggest different information than does "the evening star." Our associations are different, even though we know that they "mean" the same thing. Somehow each expression contains more than its reference, and Frege called this "something more" the *Sinn* of the signs involved.

The *Sinn* of a sign, then, does appear to bear a certain "connotative" weight as long as we do not press the analogy too closely. But the associated thoughts that comprise the *Sinn* of a sign should not be confused with merely subjective associations. The latter comprise not the *Sinn* of a sign, which is, as Frege puts it, "definite" (1980:58), but rather its *Vorstellung*, or "associated idea" (1980:59). In other words, there is something objective about *Sinn*: it is tied to a "meaning" or "reference." But because our personal ideas (or *Vorstellungen*) can be quite idiosyncratic, they can range far from the "sense" and "meaning" of an expression. As Frege puts it:

> The meaning and sense of a sign are to be distinguished from the associated idea. If what a sign means is an object perceivable by the senses, my idea [*Vorstellung*] of it is an internal image, arising from memories of sense impressions which I have had and acts, both internal and external, which I have performed. [1980:59]

Thus, there is "an essential distinction between the idea and the sign's sense," Frege writes, because the "sense" of a sign "may be the common property of many people, and so is not a part or a mode of the individual mind. For one can hardly deny that mankind has a common store of thoughts which is transmitted from one generation to another" (1980:59). "By a thought," Frege adds, "I understand not the subjective performance of thinking but its objective content, which is capable of being the common property of several thinkers" (1980:62). In other words, while the actual signs that we may use from generation to generation or from language to language may differ, and the subjective ideas we may have about things may vary from individual to individual, some *thoughts* do not differ: if they did, no scientific knowledge would be possible. These thoughts cannot be the same things as signs themselves, because signs change and are arbitrary; nor are these thoughts equivalent to the referents of signs, because thoughts and things are not the same. They are not "ideas," because "ideas" are subjective, while heritable "thoughts" can be objectively shared. Yet they must exist, or no body of knowledge could ever be constituted: we should only have arbitrary signs, actual designations, and subjective ideas without any objective, thoughtfull, mediation. So there must be something else involved with expressions, something Frege called *Sinn*.

But in spite of several attempts to clarify this elusive concept, Frege's thoughts about it remain vague. *Sinn* is neither sign nor object nor subjective idea: it somehow hangs in the balance. Frege writes that the "meaning of a proper name is the object itself which we designate by using it, the idea which we have in that case is wholly subjective; in between lies the sense, which is indeed no longer subjective like the idea, but is yet not the object itself" (1980:60). Struggling for a further clarification, Frege resorts to a metaphor:

> The following analogy will perhaps clarify these relationships. Somebody observes the Moon through a telescope. I compare the Moon itself to the meaning [*Bedeutung*]; it is the object of the observation, mediated by the real image projected by the object glass in the interior of the telescope, and by the retinal image of the observer. The former I compare to the sense [*Sinn*], the latter is like the idea [*Vorstellung*] or experience. [1980:60]

Neither wholly subjective nor wholly objective, *Sinn* thus appears to mediate between the horizons of subjectivity and objectivity. Have we not in this intersection, then, a distinction that is as epistemological as it is logical? Frege distinguished between *Sinn* and *Bedeutung* to facilitate his analyses of propositional truth conditions, but in spite of his wholly logical intentions, Frege does appear to have defined here the terms by which objective reality might be related to subjective knowledge. Between the referent and the idea there lies a mediating "sense:" is it not possible that the opposition between denotation and connotation, and between textual reference and textual interpretation, might be similarly mediated?

But we shall reserve judgment on the matter for the moment, because the very distinction between *Sinn* and *Bedeutung* has recently come into question. In recent years both Mill's distinction between "denotation" and "connotation" and Frege's *Bedeutung/Sinn* demarcation have been challenged by a number of analytic philosophers who have attacked both *Sinn* and "connotation" on the basis of certain "possible worlds" or "counterfactual" logical analyses. And in their challenge, the counterfactualists have shaken referential orthodoxy no less than the New Critics shook philological and historical criticism half a century ago.

The goal of the counterfactual critique is to refute the traditional referential proposition that argues, as we have seen, that a "general term or name refers to whatever fits the characteristics the term or name means" (Schwartz 1977:13). More specifically, the counterfactual logicians question the *necessity* of any given description in the determination of nominal referentiality. Elements of the critique first emerged in the 1950s in such articles as W. V. Quine's "Two Dogmas of Empiricism" (1971:63–81), which questioned the analytic necessity of the connections between words and things under the ever-contingent circumstances of pragmatic experience. The critique was most fully worked out in the 1960s by such modal logicians as Saul Kripke, David Lewis, and Keith Donnellan. What the calculus of the newly developed modal logic consistently implied was that referring expressions *cannot* secure their referents on the bases of connotational descriptions, because under certain logically possible circumstances the description of a referent might change without altering the "rigidity" of the referring act itself. If it is discovered in some "possible world" or "counterfactual" situation, for example, that roses are not really red at all (that they only appear red because of an atmospheric trick) but are absolutely transparent, our exclamation "Oh look another transparent rose!" will still secure a reference even though redness has dropped out of the customary connotative description. How a reference is originally secured, however, is a question that, as we shall see, has been only tenuously developed by the counterfactualists.

Perhaps the most immediate negative source for the counterfactual program can be found in Bertrand Russell's own version of the description theory of linguistic reference. For Russell, that is, there is a difference between a "proper" proper name and a name that really functions as an abbreviated "definite description," a difference, in other words, between "simple symbols" and complex descriptions. Russell defines his distinction in the following terms:

> A name is a simple symbol whose meaning is something that can only occur as [a subject of a proposition].... Thus "Scott" is a simple symbol.... On the other hand, "the author of *Waverley*" is not a simple symbol, because the separate words that compose the phrase are parts which are symbols.... We have, then, two things to compare: (1) a *name*, which is a simple symbol directly designating an individual which is its meaning ... [and] (2) a *description*, which consists of several words, whose meanings are already fixed, and from which results whatever is to be taken as the "meaning" of the description. [1971:170-71]

At this point in his argument, Russell still maintains, as do more recent logicians, a logical distinction between proper names and referring descriptions. Thus, while the proper name "Scott" can be logically substituted for the variable in a proposition of identity "$x = x$" (i.e., "Scott = Scott"), the definite description "the author of *Waverley*" cannot be so substituted because it has no logically necessary referent (Frege's *Bedeutung*). Indeed, Russell's position at this point closely resembles Frege's: i.e., a definite description can be said to have sense (*Sinn*) but no *necessary* reference or meaning (*Bedeutung*), while a name, in Russell's terms, must have both sense *and* reference. For a name to *be* a name, Russell insists, "it *must* name something: what does not name anything is not a name" (1971:174).

This last point rather smacks of Cratylus's position in the Platonic dialogue bearing his name, but its possible dubiousness is not our concern here. The critical point for possible-worlds theory comes when Russell considers those names whose referents are uncertain. Consider "Homer." In such a case, Russell felt, "Homer" is not a name at all. Instead, "when we ask whether Homer existed, we are using the word 'Homer' as an abbreviated description," Russell writes, and "we may replace it by (say) 'the author of the *Iliad* and the *Odyssey*'" (1971:174). But what if there *was* a man named Homer who was not the author of the poems attributed to him? Or, to give a more recent and lively instance, what if William Shakespeare really did not write "the plays of William Shakespeare"? Would these be instances in which Homer was not Homer, or Shakespeare not Shakespeare? This is precisely the kind of question put to Russell's description theory by Saul Kripke (whose work in modal logic has defined the terms for current debate) when he offers the following simple proposition: "Suppose someone uses 'Tully' to refer to the Roman orator who denounced Cataline and uses the name 'Cicero' to refer to the man whose works he had to study in third-year Latin in high school." Then suppose "that Cicero actually did denounce Cataline, but thought that this achievement was so great that he should not bother writing any literary works. Would we say that these would be circumstances under which he would not have been Cicero" (1977:92)?

To so conclude, Kripke believes, would be counterintuitive, so he offers the alternative suggestion that under such possible-world (or counterfactual) conditions we should simply say that Cicero did not produce any literary works.

Thus, while the descriptive property "having produced certain works" may help us to fix a reference for "Cicero," it would not invalidate that reference in some possible world in which Cicero writes nothing at all. The designation "Cicero" is thus "rigid" with respect to all possible referential circumstances.

What Kripke's critique boils down to is a kind of essentialist realism, a conviction that once a name has referentially marked out its object, that object must always be itself. Once we have indexed the man, he stays indexed in spite of any discovery that may alter the description associable to him. But since such a conviction places the primary meaning of a name somewhere beyond hermeneutics (i.e., the name cannot be properly interpreted, only posited), we are faced with the prospect that our securest knowledge is simply deictic.

This situation is exactly the reverse of what we face in Fish's critique, where we have our interpretation but nothing to index it, a "what is said" but no "what is." And the reversal is only accentuated by Kripke's extension of the principle of "rigid designation" to natural kind terms as well—a position Kripke summarizes so well in the third lecture of *Naming and Necessity* that it is well worth quoting at length:

My argument implicitly concludes that certain general terms, those for natural kinds, have a greater kinship with proper names than is generally realized. This conclusion holds for certain various species names, whether they are count nouns, such as 'cat,' 'tiger,' 'chunk of gold,' or mass terms such as 'gold,' 'water,' 'iron pyrites.' It also applies to certain terms for natural phenomena, such as 'heat,' 'light,' 'sound,' 'lightning,' and, presumably, suitably elaborated, to corresponding adjectives—'hot,' 'loud,' 'red.'

Mill, as I have recalled, held that although 'singular names,' the definite descriptions, have both denotation and connotation, others, the genuine proper names, had denotation but not connotation. Mill further maintained that 'general names,' or general terms, had connotation. Such terms as 'cow' or 'human' are defined by the conjunction of certain properties which pick out their extension— a human being, for example, is a rational animal with certain

physical characteristics. The hoary tradition of definition by *genus* and *differentia* is of a piece with such a conception. . . .
The modern logical tradition, as represented by Frege and Russell, disputed Mill on the issue of singular names, but endorsed him on that of general names. Thus *all* terms, both singular and general, have a 'connotation' or Fregean sense. More recent theorists have followed Frege and Russell, modifying their views only by replacing the notion of a sense as given by a particular conjunction of properties with that of a sense given by a 'cluster' of properties, only *enough* of which need apply. The present view, directly reversing Frege and Russell, (more or less) *endorses* Mill's view of *singular* terms, but *disputes* his view of *general* terms. [1980:134–35]

Here we have, in miniature, a general history of referential theory. "The hoary tradition of definition by *genus* and *differentia*" recalls for us Aristotle's metaphysical account, while Kripke's allusion to Mill, whose distinction between connotation and denotation is roughly echoed by Frege's *Sinn/Bedeutung* distinction, brings us up to more modern times. Frege's and Russell's modification of Mill (i.e., their tendency to treat *all* terms as having sense, or connotation) has itself, in turn, been modified by Wittgenstein, whose "cluster" theory of reference holds that a term successfully secures its reference by picking out only a *sufficient* number of properties from a descriptive "cluster" (see Schwartz 1977:19). And finally, what Kripke calls the "present view" refers us to the current state of affairs, according to which even the cluster theory has been rejected, holding that *no* combination of properties is *necessary* to reference.

In short, for Kripke *both* proper names (singular terms) *and* natural kinds (general terms) lack *essential* connotation; or, to put it another way, in both semantic cases Kripke privileges objective denotation to the point of nearly obliterating subjective description. A natural kind, Kripke insists, refers no more upon the basis of a necessary description than does a proper name. But while it seems to be at least empirically possible to go out and find the living referent of a proper name ("that man there"), how do we determine the referent of a natural kind without relying upon a special description? The man himself may be the ontic existence, the "this" itself, that a proper name refers to, but what is the ontic reference of a natural kind? The trouble here is that a natural kind is, by definition, a universal rather than a particular and is thus, according to a strictly Aristotelian reading, the object only of *potential* knowledge. *Actual* knowledge, categorically considered, is of the particular, of the primary substance of "that thing there." Potential knowledge, on the other hand, has to do with the secondary substance of the natural kind or genus. But for Kripke, the "substance," so to speak, of the kind is the same as the "substance" of the individual. The essence of *this* lump of gold, for example, is that of "gold itself:" that is, anything with the atomic number 79. According to Kripke this definition of gold is not simply a contingent description or interpretation: it is the ultimate essence of the kind. Our knowledge of this essence, however, does not constitute an a priori necessity, because it must be empirically discovered; rather, Kripke views such knowledge as an a posteriori necessity, as a knowledge that science can always potentially determine because it is always there to be determined.

Kripke develops his thesis in the following manner. Sometime in history (possible-worlds theorists do not specify when) a certain "original sample" of gold is presented. It is a yellow, ductile metal. On the basis of this description, a natural kind term is circulated through a discursive community in such a way that "many who have seen little or no gold can still use the term" (1980:139). Kripke believes that the term "gold" thus will refer to real gold within this "causal (historical) chain, not by any use of its items"—or properties—but simply according to the genetic "baptism" that took place at some undetermined time. It is logically possible (in some counterfactual or possible-world situation) that a sample of blue gold might be discovered (indeed, we have "red" gold and "white" gold), but while this would alter the connotational description of gold, it would not change the reference. Hilary Putnam explains that when a speaker first says, "with surprise, 'lemons have all turned blue,' lemon will still mean what it means now" (1977:113). In other words, a natural kind has an essential identity (it *is* what it *is*), and our words refer to this identity alone. It is true that in a world where gold turns blue, the connotative meaning of the word "gold" would change (gold would now be a blue, ductile metal), but it would still be "gold" all along. It is as if one were once to have had a taste of coffee and been told that it was tea, and to use thereafter the term "tea" when really thinking of coffee. Coffee will always be coffee no matter what we think about it.

But there is a difficulty here. If a possible world can always be imagined that would counter the "facts" of *our* world, how can we ever be certain that we know what the essential facts, finally, are? Here Kripke places his faith in the a posteriori necessity of scientific discovery. "Scientific investigation," Kripke says, "generally discovers characteristics of . . . [a kind] which are far better than the original set. For example, it turns out that a material object is (pure) gold if and only if the only element contained therein is that with the atomic number 79" (1980:138). Kripke realizes that science may not actually ever determine the essence of a kind, but he does believe that it is always necessarily there to be discovered:

> In general, science attempts, by investigating basic structural traits, to find the nature, and thus the essence (in the philosophical sense) of the kind. . . . The type of property identity used in science seems to be associated with *necessity*, not with a prioricity, or analyticity. . . .
> Note that on the present view, scientific discoveries of species essence do not constitute a 'change of meaning'; the possibility of such discoveries was part of the original enterprise. [1980:138]

But while Kripke's intuitive sense that things, finally, are what they *are* does have a certain commonsense attractiveness, it nonetheless leaves us with certain difficulties. For example, what if we discover that our entire system of atomic nomenclature is wrong and that the essence of gold is not "atomic number 79"? If the meaning of "gold" is a universal denotational essence that has no necessary relation to a contingent interpretative description, then what meaning can the term "gold" have for us before we find the essence? Is the term simply a pointer until certainty has been achieved? And what if we never do achieve scientific certainty? How would we know anyway?

Kripke's extension of the principle of "rigid designation" to natural kind universals, in other words, seems to require a scientific certainty about kind identities that not even scientists believe can be achieved. As we have seen, contemporary science is an interpretatively probabilistic, not a determinate, enterprise. But if we cannot be certain of the identity of a natural kind referent, perhaps we can be certain of the referent for a "proper" proper name—that is, for the particular subject to which the name, say, "Richard Nixon" refers. Surely we can be certain of the identity of this "rigid designation."

Well, "suppose," Stanley Fish replies, "someone with a philosophical turn of mind were to declare that Nixon as a free and independent agent whose actions can be reported and assessed did not exist; that 'in fact' the notion of his agency was a bourgeois myth (one might say a fiction) by means of which a repressive society evaded responsibility for its own crimes and tyrannies. It would follow from such a view," Fish continues,

that any sentence in which the name Nixon were attached to a finite preterite transitive verb (Nixon said, Nixon rejected, Nixon condemned) would be false to the way things really are, would be mistaken; and any evidence brought forward to substantiate Nixon's existence (birth certificate, photographs, witnesses to his actions) would be inadmissible because the rules of evidence (the procedures for its stipulation) were derived from (or constituted by) the same myth. [1980:237]

In other words, our "commonsense" view of the world, according to which we may always be sure of individually existing human agents, is founded, Fish believes, not on indexed "facts" but upon the "standard story" according to which interpretive communities constitute the "facts" of their experience. Fish's version of the referential logic for proper names thus, by reversing the denotation/connotation distinction, essentially deconstructs Kripke's version. Denotative "fact," which for Kripke is always potentially discoverable by empirical science, yields in Fish's analysis to connotative (or interpretational) "fiction." Thus we seem to be at an impasse: counterfactual theory denies the necessity of any connotative *Sinn* when we refer to the world, while reader-response hermeneutics can lead us to a denial that we can ever have anything *but* connotation, even when referring to such "obviously" denotative "facts" as "Richard Nixon." So how, it might now be asked, would a potentialist hermeneutics approach such a difficulty?

Let us look more closely into the case of "Richard Nixon." How do we know who he is anyway? For the majority of us, such information must come from a complex of certain descriptions, since we have never met the man. We might consider here, then, one such definite description. Suppose that someone refers to "the president of the United States in 1970," but finds that Richard Nixon really was not president in 1970. An imposter has been discovered to have seized the Oval Office. According to Kripke's theory of "rigid designation," "Nixon" remains Nixon in spite of the change, and the description ("president of the United States in 1970"), which might stand as a criterion for a "transworld" identification in some other world where the name "Richard Nixon" is not known, must itself be based upon this original, and rigid, identity. "Those who have argued that to make sense of the notion of rigid designator, we must antecedently make sense of a 'criteria of transworld identity' have precisely reversed the cart and the horse," Kripke writes; "it is *because* we can refer (rigidly) to Nixon, and stipulate that we are speaking of what might have happened to *him* (under certain circumstances), that 'transworld identifications' are unproblematic in such cases" (1980:49).

But how do we know, then, that "Nixon" is Nixon? For Fish, this knowledge can come only interpretatively, as part of a communally constituted epistemology on the basis of which individuals can be said to exist. But while Kripke's answer seems to neglect the interpretational implications of communal decisions, he does grant referential knowledge a certain communal foundation. That is, the meaning of a proper name, according to Kripke, is established on the basis of a chain of communications that ultimately stretches back to the actual birth of the referent. For example, a baby boy is born and his parents call him by a certain name:

> They talk about him to their friends. Other people meet him. Through various sorts of talk the name is spread from link to link as if by a chain. A speaker who is on the far end of this chain, who has heard about, say Richard Feynman, in the market place or elsewhere, may be referring to Richard Feynman even though he can't remember from whom he first heard of Feynman or from whom he ever heard of Feynman. He knows that Feynman is a famous physicist. A certain passage of communication reaching ultimately to the man himself does reach the speaker. He then is referring to Feynman even though he can't identify him uniquely. He doesn't know what a Feynman diagram is, he doesn't know what the Feynman theory of pair production and annihilation is. Not only that: he'd have trouble distinguishing between Gell-Mann and Feynman. So he doesn't have to know these things, but, instead, a chain of communication going back to Feynman himself has been established, by virtue of his membership in a community which passed the name on from link to link, not by a ceremony that he makes in private in his study: 'By "Feynman" I shall mean the man who did such and such and such and such.' [1980:91–92]

Thus, for Kripke, the possibility for nominal reference begins in the denotative fact of an actual birth, and it is to this fact that a community's nominal index passively refers. For Fish, the fact that a name must circulate through a community of speakers implies that not only the name but the referent as well is communal, an actively constituted institutional, rather than "brute," fact. In this sense, then, there are no "proper" proper names: all names are "fictions" insofar as they are determined by a nontranscendable "standard story." But is it not possible that the relationship between the subjectivity of the community and the objectivity of the referent cannot be so reduced to one side or the other? That is, could we not say that a "proper" proper name represents an inseparable composition of communal interpretation with the potentially ordered properties of an objective reality that is distinguishable from the "matter" out of which fictional names are constituted?

To explore such a possibility, we can continue with our analysis of that apparently most "proper" of proper names: the name of a child. Let us say that a certain male child is born, prompting his parents to call him by a certain name. Now, that we name this child at all can be taken for granted, but is the situation really so determinant? First of all, there are rules, established not by nature but by social convention, governing the form of the names we give. In America we assign a "first" name, a "middle" name, and a "last" (or family) name. The procedure is, historically, relatively new, and even within our own country it may be further refined. In Christian families, for example, firstborn male offspring are often named after their fathers, while in Jewish families naming may be organized to perpetuate the names (or initials) of the deceased. It appears, then, that culture itself determines in advance the conditions for our own naming, constituting those rules by which naming may not only proceed but actually begin.

And yet, is it not the birth of the child that makes naming possible in the first place? Certainly culture does not govern parturition? No, indeed it does not, but culture still determines just which births are "worthy" of naming. The name we give to a child has its motivation not only in the physical actuality of the child alone but in a social decision about which beings shall be granted proper names. We do not ordinarily assign proper names to inanimate objects or to nondomestic animals. And even our pets are not named as our children are named. All this seems natural enough, obviously determined by circumstances, but consider how a human subject *may be* denied a proper name. What happens when we call a grown man "boy," or refer to individuals solely on the basis of their class identities (*"that* Papist," *"that* Communist," *"that* Jew")? Has not more transpired than the simple denial of a name?

We feel the pain of such denials because to deny a human being a name is to deny his or her humanity. That is, the granting of a proper name implicitly expresses a certain classification of the named individual, an inclusion in the "human family." Both the classification of the individual and the constitution of the class as such may be said to be culturally, and thus subjectively, determined. But is this the only determinant? Do such constitutions take place solely in the mind of an interpretive community, or has some outside pressure been exerted on that mind? Given a long tradition of epistemological subjectivism—a tradition that can be seen to begin in Anglo-American philosophy with the British empiricists and to extend up through Machian positivism into the current school of philosophical pragmatism—it has become difficult to approach such an "outside" objectively. But as we have already seen, it can be approached through an analysis of the objective propensities of things that Karl Popper pursued in opposition to subjective positivism (in Ernst Mach's sense of the term). But how would such an analysis fare in the context of an investigation of special classification? Can things be said to have a "propensity" for certain kinds of conceptual organization?

For John Locke, of course, the species into which we conceptually organize individuals were indeed merely subjective ideas, constituting "nominal" rather than "real" essences. In Locke's philosophy, that is to say, the "real essences" of things, which, as he writes, constitute "their insensible parts; from which flow those sensible qualities, which serve us to distinguish them one from another," are to be distinguished from those "nominal essences" that constitute the "boundaries of species . . . as men, and not as nature, makes them" (quoted in Copi 1976:342, 340). For Locke, then, human beings determine their special classifications not, as Irving Copi puts it, through a disinterested compliance with the way things really are but "for *use*, and different intended uses or interests will determine different [nominal] essences" (1976:340). As such, "nominal essences," the species into which we organize the particulars of our experience, are "real" only as ideas. Whatever "real essences" there may be outside our nominal ideas are unknowable.

"Real essences," the realities of an extranominal world, are unknowable according to Locke, because, as Copi explains, "the only objects of our knowledge are the ideas that we have in our minds" (1976:341), and we cannot form any idea of the insensible nature, or "real essence," of a thing. But while Locke's incipient skepticism here (a skepticism that will be confirmed in Hume) is indeed a logical consequence of his overall investigation into the psychology of human understanding, we may also view it as a more or less contingent reflection of his low opinion of the epistemological validity of experimental observation: that is, "his doctrine that experiment and observation yield only '. . . judgment and opinion, not knowledge' "—a term that, as Copi observes, Locke "reserved for what is *certain*" (1976:341).

But for Copi (and indeed for the potentialist realism that we have explored thus far) to reserve the term "'knowledge' for what is certain . . . has but little to commend it. It is more reasonable," Copi continues, "to accept the results of experimentation and observation, although probable rather than demonstrative, as knowledge nonetheless" (1976:342). Copi concedes that the relatively primitive state of scientific investigation in Locke's day may well have discouraged him from having any confidence in scientific experimentation. But what was invisible, or "insensible," to seventeenth-century science has since become visible to modern science.

What has become visible to contemporary science, in short, is the real existence of dispositional forces or powers, the reality of probabilistic laws. As Copi puts it: "With respect to scientific usage, we can say the following. The real essence of a thing will consist very largely of powers, or, in modern terms, dispositional properties" (1976:346). A scientist, in other words, "desires to know how things behave, and to account for their behavior by means of explanatory hypotheses or theories which permit him to predict what will occur under specified conditions" (1976:343). These theories, Copi continues, refer to the real essences of things, the "general laws to which objects conform, and the causal relations which obtain among them" (1976:343).

For Copi, then, as for a potentialist realism, the "real essence" of a thing inheres in its dispositional powers, its regular capacity for behavior, and it is to these powers or propensities that our "nominal" ideas can be said to refer. "Substances may well have objective properties that nominal essences are ideas *of*, or objective *powers* that correspond to them exactly" (1976:339), Copi writes, and it is these powers, the objective propensities of things themselves, that can be seen to be the objective forces that "pressure" our own classifications of things.

My point here is that even though our classifications of things and the names that we accordingly give them are subjective to a certain extent, they are not necessarily wholly subjective. The phrase "family of man," for example, is in one sense a nominal essence—that is, the name does not refer to any actually existing universal form—but the very fact that we can react with outrage at our own history of denying to other human beings their inclusion in the class suggests that there are shareable properties and powers among those beings that can be potentially included within the species. No single one of these powers would be determinant by itself, but even the most traditional of human properties that have been proposed for the definition of "human beings," i.e., the property of having a "rational soul," or the "logos," can still be seen to have a certain decisiveness. For what if it were finally determined that other species have rational souls, that is, in more modern parlance, that other species have a capacity for language? Would we not begin to treat them differently, as if, that is to say, they belonged to "our" family? While it is true that such a reclassification would be subjective in itself, the property, the power or capacity according to whose determination it might be effected, would not be. To be able to speak is not a subjective property: only the definition of the "family of man" as those beings who have this capacity is subjective.

But if proper names might be said to refer both to the subjective decisions of the classifier and to the objective properties or powers by which individuals having those powers might be grouped together, to what do "properly" fictional names refer? How is, say, "Hamlet" to be considered with respect to, say, "Napoleon"? And what about the instances in which proper names are bestowed upon things that are distinctly not human? We name ships, pets, and Kentucky rifles. Are these, therefore, "human"? Or has some property from human naming been transferred to them? This explanation seems the most likely, for the granting of a proper name to an inanimate object or an animal can be seen to involve a transference of human characteristics to nonhuman subjects that do not objectively bear such properties. This transference can be seen to constitute a "poetic" or "allegorical," rather than a scientific, mode of classification, for as Samuel Levin has written:

> The staple of allegory is personification. By definition personification is a metaphoric, hence mixed, mode—something nonhuman is endowed with human characteristics. This "endowment" results from the transfer of semantic features from a predicate normally associated with humans to a noun (typically functioning as a subject) that designates something nonhuman. [1981:24]

In other words, poetry has the capacity to reclassify things, to shift our conceptual organization of the world in such a way as to remind us that our scientific classifications are not *wholly* objective. As Umberto Eco has put it: "To change semantic systems means *to change the way in which culture 'sees' the world*. Thus, a text of the aesthetic type which was so frequently supposed to be absolutely extraneous to any truth conditions (and to exist at a level on which disbelief is totally 'suspended') arouses the suspicion that the correspondence between the present organization of the content and 'actual' states of the world is neither the best nor the ultimate. The world could be defined and organized (and therefore perceived and known) through other semantic (that is: conceptual) models" (1979b:274).

Still, there is a difference between an aesthetic classification and a scientific one. We can aesthetically rearrange the properties of different species to produce a fictional centaur, but this rearrangement will be wholly subjective because it cannot be tested against anything that subsists outside of our imagination of it. We can name a centaur "Chiron," but this does not mean that "Chiron" refers to any extratextual phenomenon. Similarly, we can name a certain configuration of language "Hamlet," but this does not confer upon "Hamlet" the power to act outside our imagination of "him." If "no one thought about Hamlet," Bertrand Russell has remarked, "there would be nothing left of him," but "if no one had thought about Napoleon, he would have seen to it that someone did" (1971:168).

To return to Frege's analysis of names, we might say that the name "Napoleon" has both a sense (*Sinn*) and a reference (*Bedeutung*), while "Hamlet" has only a conceptual *Sinn* without a *Bedeutung*. As Frege himself writes in "On Sense and Meaning," the "sentence 'Odysseus was set ashore at Ithaca while sound asleep' obviously has a sense. But since it is doubtful whether the name 'Odysseus,' occurring therein, means anything, it is also doubtful whether the whole sentence does" (1980:62). In other words, any sentence predicating something or other of "Odysseus" can make perfect sense without requiring a referent or truth value, if, as Frege continues, "one wanted to go no further than the thought," because the "thought remains the same whether 'Odysseus' means something [i.e., has *Bedeutung*] or not" (1980:62–63). That is, we can conceptually understand such sentences even though their subjects do not "mean," or refer to, anything. But there is a difference between a term bearing only a sense, like "Odysseus," and one, like "Napoleon," that has both sense *and* reference. "It would be desirable," Frege remarks of this logical situation, "to have a special term for signs having only sense" (1980:63).

But let us now take another example. How can we characterize the nominal status of what we have called the nuclear referent? For the name that we might give to such a referent would seem to lie midway between the proper and the fictive. The nuclear referent, in other words, designates no actual "meaning" in the manner that such proper names as "World War I" or "World War II" do. But at the same time, its name would not be comparable to the name of the Trojan War (if we regard this war as a fiction). So what kind of name might the name of the nuclear referent be?

To give a name to the nuclear referent is to attempt to classify it, to include it among things of its kind. Thus, the naming of the nuclear referent is an act of predication. But how can we predicate anything of something that does not exist? Would this be the same thing as naming a centaur? Such a conclusion is counterintuitive. But at the same time, the nuclear referent is not an identity that we can classify in the same way that we can a "Napoleon." We can compare and classify the properties or powers of actual beings, but the problem with the nuclear referent is that there is nothing in our experience to compare it to. So how could we begin to name it except as a sort of fictional arrangement of properties that cannot be experienced outside our speaking of them?

It seems, then, that, even after defending the distinction between proper and fictional names on the basis of the objective reality of the properties that proper names refer to and organize, there is still no place for an analysis of the name of the nuclear referent—and so, as Derrida writes, no place for a nuclear criticism either. Unless there is a third kind of name, a name that might be said to be situated between the proper and the fictive. Let us conjecture that there is such a category of name, a category that can be said to have actual conceptual senses and *potential* referents. The name of the nuclear referent might be one such name, for we can both think about it (it has a sense) and anticipate its potential referential actuation. Such a conjecture cannot be "tested" as such, but it can be critically applied to see what value it might have in a concrete analysis of the rhetoric of the nuclear debate. Let us take as an example, then, a text written by the secretary of defense of the United States during the first term of the Reagan administration.

On August 23, 1982, Caspar Weinberger mailed a letter to about thirty domestic, and forty foreign, publications in an attempt to clear up the misconceptions that he had seen in news accounts portraying the Reagan administration "as planning to wage a protracted nuclear war, or seeking to acquire a nuclear 'war-fighting' capability" (see Draper 1983:34–36). Weinberger declares in his letter that it "is the first and foremost goal of this Adminstration to take every step to ensure that nuclear weapons are never used again, for we do not believe there could be any 'winners' in a nuclear war" (quoted in Draper 1983:34). Weinberger was responding to the uproar created by the leaking to the press of National Security Council documents that spoke of a U.S. "policy to prevail in a protracted nuclear war" (Draper 1983:36). Now, the use of the word "prevail" here implicitly classifies a protracted nuclear war among all the other wars that have ever been fought, because "winning" and "losing" have generally been features of past wars. In a sense, this is to give to the nuclear referent the name of "war" itself, that is, the name of *conventional* war. To speak of "prevailing" in such a war, then, certainly makes *sense* (in both Frege's understanding and the common understanding of this term), but is there any real potentiality for such a war, that is to say, for a protracted nuclear conflict in which one side might "prevail"? In other words, we can predicate to a protracted nuclear conflict a property of conventional warfare, but has that property any referential potentiality beyond our predication of it?

There are a number of people who might want to suggest that a "protracted nuclear war" in which the United States might "prevail" is a kind of centaur. We can understand what Weinberger means, but this does not entail a referent, or rather, there does not appear to be much probability of such a referent. What is interesting about Weinberger's letter, however, is that he makes no attempt to defend the concept of a winnable nuclear war: in fact, he foists such a concept off on the Soviet Union. "Whatever they claim their intentions to be," Weinberger writes, "the fact remains that they are designing their weapons in such a way and in sufficient numbers to indicate to us that they think they could begin, and win, a nuclear war" (quoted in Draper 1983:35).

So, according to Weinberger, a winnable nuclear war is the Soviet's centaur. This may indeed be the case, but this does not make it any less of a centaur. And the problem here is that Weinberger uses the Soviet centaur, so to speak, to justify a U.S. centaur. That is, as Theodore Draper points out in his own response to Weinberger's letter, if the real point of the letter were to explain that it is the Soviet Union and not the United States that "'endorses the concept' of a protracted nuclear war," then, as Draper writes, "we would expect you to go on and tell us what is wrong with the concept and why the United States does not endorse it. What we get," Draper continues, "is something quite different. It is: We must take the steps necessary to match the Soviet Union's greatly improved nuclear capability. But it makes no sense," Draper points out, "to take these 'steps' if we do not also adopt the alleged Soviet 'concept' for which these steps were designed. You insist that the Soviet capability and concept are coordinated; if we match their capability, it can only be, according to your own logic, to carry out the same concept" (1983:39).

Indeed, as Draper reveals in a series of quotations from interviews that Weinberger had given, it appears that the Defense Department was entertaining such a concept, for although Weinberger has declared his disbelief in the possibility of prevailing in a nuclear war, he has also said, "You show me a Secretary of Defense who's planning not to prevail and I'll show you a Secretary of Defense who ought to be impeached" (quoted in Draper 1983:40). And again: "We've said many times that we don't think nuclear war is winnable," Weinberger has declared to the *New York Times*, but when asked "how that differed from prevailing, Mr. Weinberger replied: 'We certainly are planning not to be defeated'" (Draper 1983:40–41). "Humpty Dumpty," Draper sourly remarks, "used words this way" (1983:41).

Such rhetoric from the secretary of defense raises two key points for a nuclear criticism. The first is that the names by which we might predicate our understanding of the nuclear referent are not all equal even though there is no actual referent for the name. A protracted nuclear war in which someone "prevails" has less potential (some would say "no" potential) to be actuated than one in which no one prevails. The predicate "no one prevails" can thus inform a different kind of naming and understanding of the nuclear referent, for it would set it off from the class of conventional wars and establish it as a singular but not inconceivable potentiality. But we can make this distinction only if we are willing to grant to the name of the nuclear referent a real potentiality rather than a completely subjective one, a potentiality that can be tested against what we already know about the explosive power, and the effects of this power, of the weapons that we have made.

But there is a second issue raised by the Weinberger letter and interviews. Language can be used *by those in power* as if it were spoken by Humpty Dumpty. In other words, authority can equivocate just as much as Derrida can, and to a far more dangerous extent. Would not a nuclear criticism, then, seek to establish the terms for sorting out such equivocations to reveal the real intentions behind the duplicity? One might suggest that it would, or even should. But when we look at the techniques that post-structural criticism has devised for the interpretation of the rhetoric of literature, we find declarations of the essential duplicity not only of literary language but of all language as well. To see how this is so, we will look next at an essay by the late Paul de Man, which would in itself apparently deny that there can be any reduction of the duplicitous usage of language, paradoxically affirming instead the universal duplicity of words.

CHAPTER 11

"Necessary Equivocation": An Allegory of Reading

AT THE CONCLUSION of William Butler Yeats's poem "Among School Children," the reader is faced with a certain ambiguous question:

> O chestnut-tree, great-rooted blossomer,
> Are you the leaf, the blossom or the bole?
> O body swayed to music, O brightening glance,
> How can we know the dancer from the dance?
> [1976:117]

Taken out of its context, the final line of this stanza may appear to be asking a simple grammatical question, but when considered both within the stanza and within the context of what a New Critical reader would call the "ironic structure" of the poem as a whole, Yeats's "question" appears not to be a question at all. For in its juxtaposition to such nondifferentiable phenomena as tree, leaf, blossom, and bole, the point of the question appears to be that it is not a question. That is, to ask for the difference between the dancer and the dance seems to constitute a *rhetorical* question, a nonperformative trope rather than a straightforward speech act.

But as Paul de Man remarks in "Semiology and Rhetoric," the inaugural essay of his book *Allegories of Reading*, it "is equally possible, however, to read the last line literally rather than figuratively, as asking with some urgency ... 'Please tell me, how *can* I know the dancer from the dance?'" (1979:11–12). To ask such a question literally, de Man points out, would produce a wholly different reading of the poem, a reading entirely incompatible with one proceeding from a rhetorical interpretation of the question:

The oneness of trunk, leaf, and blossom, for example, that would have appealed to Goethe, would find itself replaced by the much less reassuring Tree of Life from the Mabinogion that appears in the poem "Vacillation," in which the fiery blossom and the earthly leaf are held together, as well as apart, by the crucified and castrated god Attis, of whose body it can hardly be said that it is "not bruised to pleasure soul." This hint should suffice to suggest that two entirely coherent but entirely incompatible readings can be made to hinge on one line whose grammatical structure is devoid of ambiguity but whose rhetorical mode turns the mood as well as the mode of the entire poem upside down. [1979:12]

Were we to look at this equivocal relation between the grammatical performative and the rhetorical trope from the perspective of Stanley Fish, we might say that we ourselves have "written" it through the strategy by which we read/write the poem. But for de Man this fundamental equivocation between a literal and a figurative meaning is, in a sense, objective rather than subjective, and no attempt to reduce it to a specifiable "reading" can ever really succeed. We do not "read" Yeats's poem: we "mis-read" it. We do not interpret it: we "mis-interpret" it in our attempt to reduce it to hermeneutic coherence. Indeed, the critical act itself for de Man constitutes a rhetorical or "allegorical" performance by which the critic displays his or her own uncertainties, the reversals and inversions of his or her own textuality. For as de Man approaches the conclusion of "Among School Children," he finds that he is inscribed within the same webs of rhetorical ambiguity as the poem itself. He writes that any "question about the rhetorical mode of a literary text is always a rhetorical question that does not even know whether it is really questioning. The resulting pathos is an anxiety (or bliss, depending on one's momentary mood or individual temperament) of ignorance, not an anxiety of reference" (1979:19). No use of language is exempt from ambiguity or equivocation, de Man believes. And so, de Man concludes his essay, "literature as well as criticism—the difference between them being delusive—is condemned (or privileged) to be forever the most rigorous and, consequently, the most unreliable language in terms of which man names and modifies himself" (1979:19).

In the fifth chapter of *Allegories of Reading*, de Man provides some of the theoretical foundations for such a belief. De Man finds Nietzsche writing in some early lecture notes: "'No such thing as an unrhetorical, "natural" language exists that could be used as a point of reference.'" Nietzsche continues, "'Language is itself the result of purely rhetorical tricks and devices.... Language is rhetoric, for it intends to convey a *doxa* (opinion), not an *episteme* (truth)'" (1979:105). Thus reversing a linguistic tradition that had rooted the authority of a language "in its adequation to an extra-linguistic referent or meaning" (1979:106), de Man writes, Nietzsche suggests that any search for the "proper," referential "ground" of language can uncover only an illimitable play of intralinguistic rhetorical figures, of metaphors and metonymies that are "not understood aesthetically, as ornament, nor are they understood semantically, as a figurative meaning that derives from literal, proper denomination. Rather," de Man continues, "the reverse is the case. The trope is not a derived, marginal, or aberrant form of language but the linguistic paradigm par excellence. The figurative structure is not one linguistic mode among others but it characterizes language as such" (1979:105).

Language and rhetoric, de Man argues accordingly, are one. All is trope, figure, an endless play of metaphorical substitutions. There is no stability, no privileged linguistic space—not even in the figure of rhetoric itself. For as the conclusion of "Among School Children" seems to demonstrate, rhetoric can always be "grammaticized," transformed into its grammatical "other" and back again. The problem is not simply to determine what kind of question it is that concludes Yeats's poem, in other words, because the tropological play that underlies both grammatical (or literal) and rhetorical (or figural) forms prevents any final decision. As de Man puts it: "Rhetoric radically suspends logic and opens up vertiginous possibilities of referential aberration. And although it would perhaps be somewhat more remote from common usage, I would not hesitate to equate the rhetorical, figurative potentiality with literature itself" (1979:10). It is the purpose of de Man's "Semiology and Rhetoric," then, to point out how recent semiological criticism has failed to recognize the consequences of the essential duplicity of rhetoric. For while conducting a brief survey of contemporary trends in critical semiology in the beginning of his essay, de Man observes how, in their literary projects, "Barthes, Genette, Todorov, Greimas, and their disciples all simplify and regress from Jakobson in letting grammar and rhetoric function in perfect continuity, and in passing from grammatical to rhetorical structures without difficulty or interruption":

> Indeed, as the study of grammatical structures is refined in contemporary theories of generative, transformational, and distributive grammar, the study of tropes and of figures (which is how the term *rhetoric* is used here, and not in the derived sense of comment or of eloquence or persuasion) becomes a mere extension of grammatical models, a particular subset of syntactical relations. [1979:6]

Thus Tzvetan Todorov, de Man writes, has tried to elaborate "a systematic grammar of literary modes, genres, and also of literary figures" without recognizing the potential problems inherent in such a reduction of rhetorical figures to grammatical paradigms. Similarly, de Man continues, Gerard Genette, in *Metaphor and Metonymy in Proust*, has demonstrated "the combined presence, in a wide and astute selection of passages, of paradigmatic, metaphorical figures with syntagmatic, metonymic structures ... without considering the possibility of logical tensions" (1979:6–7). "One can ask," de Man "asks," albeit rhetorically, "whether this reduction of figure to grammar is legitimate" (1979:7).

The heart of the problem, it appears, stems from what de Man views as a misapprehension of the implications of Roman Jakobson's fundamental structural opposition between metaphor (or "rhetoric") and metonymy (or "grammar"). In

Jakobson's analysis, of course, the terms "metaphor" and "metonymy" originally provided labels for certain forms of linguistic dysfunction. "Every form of aphasic disturbance," Jakobson writes in "The Metaphoric and Metonymic Poles," "consists in some impairment, more or less severe, either of the faculty for selection and substitution, or for combination and contexture":

> The former affliction involves a deterioration of metalinguistic operations, while the latter damages the capacity for maintaining the hierarchy of linguistic units. The relation of similarity is suppressed in the former, the relation of contiguity in the latter type of aphasia. Metaphor is alien to the similarity disorder, and metonymy to the contiguity disorder. [1971:1113]

Linguistic competence, that is to say, can be said to be constituted by a binary relation between a capacity to note equivalences between things through their similarities (the metaphoric pole) and a capacity to note phenomenal adjacencies (the metonymic pole). In de Man's reading of this binary relationship, the "vertical," or associative, power of metaphor is equivalent to *rhetorical* paradigmatics, while the "horizontal," or combinatory, power of metonymy is equivalent to *grammatical* syntagmatics. These two polarities, in binary opposition, determine the constitution of linguistic signs. Terence Hawkes explains further:

> Jakobson sees metaphor and metonymy as the characteristic modes of binarily opposed polarities which between them underpin the two-fold process of *selection* and *combination* by which linguistic signs are formed: "the given utterance (message) is a *combination* of constituent parts (sentences, words, phonemes, etc.) *selected* from the repository of all possible constituent parts (the code)." . . . Thus messages are constructed, as Saussure said, by a combination of a "horizontal" movement, which combines words together, and a "vertical" movement, which selects the particular words from the available inventory or "inner storehouse" of the language. The combinative (or syntagmatic) process manifests itself in contiguity (one word being placed next to another) and its mode is *metonymic*. The selective (or associative) process manifests itself in similarity (one word or concept being "like" another) and its mode is *metaphoric*. [1977:77–78]

Where literary semiology has "regressed," then, from Jakobson's original distinction has been in its tendency to treat *rhetoric* (associative metaphor) as a mere "subset" of *grammar* (combinatory syntax)—that is, by treating metaphor not "as a substitution but as a particular type of combination" (de Man 1979:6). Tropology, in semiological analysis, has thus been *superseded* by its grammatical complement; the associative, paradigmatic pole of language has been suppressed by the contiguous, syntagmatic pole.

For de Man, such a suppression constitutes a misunderstanding not only of Jakobson but of the very nature of language itself. Since rhetoric, as de Man believes, is not incidental to language but instead constitutes its fundamental nature, it cannot be reduced to a grammatical logic. But neither can grammar be reduced to rhetoric. Rhetoric rhetoricizes grammar and vice versa. Metaphor and metonymy, grammar and rhetoric, then, subsist together in an irreducible tension, the one "always already" oscillating into the other. But this tropological play does not lead to the constitution of determinable forms (as does the binary play between metaphor and metonymy in Jakobson's analysis of the relationship between romantic symbolism and prose realism); rather, in de Man's reading of the rhetorical essence of language, the play of metaphor and metonymy produces only uncertainty.

That is, whereas in Jakobson's structural semiology linguistic forms are constituted through the structured play between two distinct linguistic poles, in de Man's analysis the two poles can no longer be clearly distinguished. Not only can grammar not be elevated above rhetoric, but rhetoric cannot suppress grammar either—as de Man's subsequent deconstruction of Proust's apparent assertion of "the superiority of metaphor over metonymy" seeks to demonstrate (see de Man 1979:13–19). Indeed, one cannot even be certain just which linguistic category one has encountered in a given situation. The conclusion to Yeats's poem presents us with one such quandary: a question that can be interpreted either as a literal (i.e., grammatical) question or as a figural (i.e, rhetorical) one. For de Man, the result of such an encounter is not a formal determination, a hermeneutic "unit" or concept, but a pure aporia, an anxiety.

In an amusing parallel example, de Man considers a certain episode from the television comedy *All in the Family* in which one character (Edith Bunker) is presented with a problem very much like that which faces the reader of "Among School Children." Edith Bunker too must interpret the relative rhetoricity or grammaticality of an ambiguous question, and in guessing "wrongly," she plunges her husband Archie into a certain anxiety. The episode in question unfolds as follows:

> Asked by his wife whether he wants to have his bowling shoes laced over or laced under, Archie Bunker answers with a question: "What's the difference?" Being a reader of sublime simplicity, his wife replies by patiently explaining the difference between lacing over and lacing under, whatever this may be, but provokes only ire. "What's the difference?" did not ask for difference, but means instead "I don't give a damn what the difference is." The same grammatical pattern engenders two meanings that are mutually exclusive: the literal meaning asks for the concept (difference) whose existence is denied by the figurative meaning. [1979:9]

"As long as we are talking about bowling shoes," de Man continues, "the consequences are relatively trivial" (1979:9). But the ultimate implications of this contretemps are not. For de Man's point is as follows:

> A perfectly clear syntactical paradigm (the question) engenders a sentence that has at least two meanings, one which asserts and the other which denies its own illocutionary mode. It is not that there are simply two meanings, one literal and the other figural, and that we have to decide which one of these meanings is the right one in this particular situation. The confusion can only be cleared up by the intervention of an extratextual intention, such as Archie Bunker setting his wife straight; but the very anger he displays is indicative of more than impatience: it reveals his despair when confronted with a structure of linguistic meaning that he cannot

control and that holds the discouraging prospect of an infinity of similar future confusions, all of them potentially catastrophic in their consequences. [1979:10]

The ambiguity of the situation, then, is not a constituted ambiguity: it is the essential nature of language (literary and otherwise) itself. Grounded in tropology, language is "always already" self-different. Our linguistic apprehension always oscillates between a grammatical and a rhetorical formality that can never be realized one way or the other. Rhetoric overturns grammar, and grammar rhetoric: and no appeal to an "extratextual intention" can resolve this play.

Such are the terms of de Man's radically antiformalist position, a deconstructive position that is finally far more subversive than Fish's. No interpretive community can intervene here since even communal decision has been undermined. As de Man remarks of his deconstruction of Proust, "The deconstruction is not something we have added to the text; it constituted the text in the first place" (1979:17). The equivocation, the duplicity, the irreducible doubling of the text is constituted by the wills of neither individual nor communal speakers: rather, according to de Man, textuality is itself the product of rhetorical equivocation, of the illimitable play of tropological difference.

But let us look for a moment at another instance of a rhetorical question of the kind that de Man deconstructs in "Semiology and Rhetoric." The question I have in mind occurs in a comment made by former U.S. Secretary of State Alexander Haig during the controversy over the "nuclear freeze" movement in the early eighties. "Much of the argumentation for a nuclear freeze," Haig observed, "revolves around the question of how much is enough":

> Each side possesses thousands of deliverable weapons. *Does it then really make any difference who is ahead?* The question itself is misleading, as it assumes that deterrence is simply a matter of numbers of weapons or numbers of casualties. It is not. [quoted in Draper 1983:18; my italics]

Actually, this quotation contains two questions—viz., "How much is enough?" and "Does it then really make any difference who is ahead?"—and Haig, in a certain sense, deconstructs both of them himself. The question for us is: How does he do this, and why?

Let's begin with Haig's second question: "Does it then really make any difference who is ahead?" Now, in the context of this remark, Haig himself is not *using* these words; rather, he is *mentioning* them as the kind of rhetorical question that a proponent of the nuclear freeze movement might ask. But while such an advocate might indeed pose such a question, his or her purpose would not be to get an answer (i.e., to determine what difference it might actually make) but to assert indirectly that it cannot make any difference who is ahead in the context of nuclear deterrence. "Getting ahead" could be of value only if one thought that a nuclear war could be won. For Haig, however, the rhetorical question "Does it then really make any difference who is ahead?" should be taken as a grammatical question that can be answered "Yes, it does." This stance is implied by his rejection of the assumptions behind the rhetorical form of the question and his assertion that deterrence is not a matter of numbers of weapons. The nuclear freeze advocate assumes that "thousands of deliverable weapons" are enough for deterrence. Haig says not. But then one might wish to ask the *grammatical* question, "How much, then, is enough?" Haig, however, treats this grammatical question, which he himself raises, as if it were a rhetorical one by not answering it. That is, he "rhetoricizes" it just as he "grammaticizes" the rhetorical form of the nuclear freeze advocate's question. The implication, as Theodore Draper points out, is that for Haig there is no answer to the question "how much is enough" because, according to the strategic logic that Haig represents, "nothing is ever enough" (see Draper 1983:18). As long as the Soviets continue to build up their defenses, the United States must seek to keep one step ahead—to deter a nuclear war by demonstrating a capacity to fight one as if it were a conventional conflict capable of being won. According to de Man's analyses of mis-reading, such reversals between the rhetorical and the grammatical forms of questions are inevitable results of the nature of language itself. But while it cannot be denied that the potential for the kind of grammatical-rhetorical reversals we find in Haig's remarks subsists within the language he uses, it may be argued that that potential must be actuated by the will of the language user. For example, even as I write these lines, I am faced with the possibility of posing a rhetorical question of my own—viz., "Is it really language that forces equivocation upon us?"—which I know perfectly well could be "grammaticized" by a reader: that is, answered, "Yes, it is." But by deciding to ask the rhetorical question, I would really be making a performative assertion, so I might just as well choose the assertive form instead: "It is not language that forces equivocation upon us but our own desire to equivocate." To "rhetoricize" this assertion would take a certain critical effort. That effort would be undertaken for a reason—which presumably would be to undermine what I am saying. In the context of the argument over the rhetorical status of a question posed in an episode of *All in the Family*, the outcome would indeed be rather trivial. But what I mean to suggest here is that there are certain practical consequences of insisting upon the irreducibly equivocal nature of language. For while post-structural criticism has used this form of analysis as a model for deconstructing the "authoritative language" of those in power, it is important to point out that anyone can play this game. In practical, political terms this could result only in an endless process of deconstructions, of two opponents forever derailing each other's language (just as Haig defers and derails the questions of the freeze movement). But this can only defer the issue, particularly if one might wish to ask both Washington and Moscow, "Just how much do you think is enough?" in the nuclear arms race. If we rhetoricize the question—as both Washington and Moscow can certainly and willfully do—then not only are we not going to get a straight answer, but we are not going to get very far in a political discussion of the issues either.

De Man's own arguments, of course, are theoretical rather than practical. It cannot be helped, he implies; language is like that. You cannot reduce it no matter what the need. Equivocation is "always already" actual in language: the language user does not actuate its duplicitous potential. This in turn suggests that speech acts are determined by language rather than by intention, which, of course, is the argument of structuralist as well as post-structuralist theory. And though de Man himself vigorously rejects the "inside/outside" implications of the structuralists' "prison house of language," we can still find in his argument the traces of the structuralist assumption that parole is determined by langue, that linguistic performance is grounded in a play of uncontrollable differences, not in the will of the performer. That is, even given de Man's deconstruction of structural semiology, he does not challenge the implied privileging of the principle of linguistic difference that structuralism brought to the analysis of the sign. In fact, it might be argued that post-structural language theory owes much—if not all—of its existence to the structuralist deconstruction of both intentionality and the referent on behalf of the play of systematic differences. Thus, any attempted qualification of what might be called the "equivocational imperative" of de Man's implied linguistics would have to include a rereading of semiological theory itself, particularly with respect to the introduction into linguistic analysis of the principle of semiological difference effected by Ferdinand de Saussure. This is the task of part 4, in which I reread Saussurean linguistics in the light of the metaphysical principles that I have developed thus far and redefend those newly developed principles through a reading of Charles Sanders Peirce's semiotic alternative to a differentialist semiology.

PART 4

THE POTENTIAL SIGN

CHAPTER 12

Substance and/or Form: Saussure, Semiology, and Ontology

PAUL DE MAN'S NIETZSCHEAN CONVICTION that "the paradigmatic structure of language is rhetorical rather than representational," as we have seen, ultimately implies that the ground of a language system is to be found in an ungovernable play of differences rather than in any simply identifiable grammatical or even rhetorical substrate. This linguistic argument, however, raises an ontological question that has been implicit in semiological study ever since Ferdinand de Saussure reversed a traditional referent-based linguistics in founding his analyses of linguistic systems on a principle of oppositional difference. For while semiological differences for Saussure were certainly "real," their ontological determination raises a certain difficulty. Because if differences alone constitute the identifiable forms of a language system, would this not imply the "existence" of a preformal, unidentifiable principle prior to language that would motivate the play of differences? And if so, what "name" might we possibly give to a principle (difference) that itself constitutes the naming process in the first place?

Such, of course, are the kinds of questions put to Saussurean semiology by Jacques Derrida's well-known "grammatological" deconstruction of structural linguistics. I will not attempt to defend Saussure from Derrida's deconstruction in this chapter. What I wish to show is that while Saussure's raising of the principle of semiological difference over that of linguistic "substance" indeed leads to its own deconstruction, a potentialist reading of Saussurean semiology produces quite other results.

We first might note how Ferdinand de Saussure's *Cours de linguistique générale* begins with an indirect address to "certain persons" (*certaines personnes*), for whom language is essentially a "nomenclature, that is to say, a list of terms corresponding to as many things" (1978:97; translations my own). Saussure might almost have been addressing the counterfactualists. Scolding those who "suppose that the bond which connects a name with a thing is a very simple operation" (1978:97), he established the foundation for a semiological project that, in many ways, developed into the mirror image of the analytic language philosophy developed simultaneously in England and America throughout the course of the twentieth century: mirrored, that is, because reversed. As analysts like Saul Kripke have toiled to secure the logically rigid referential relations between words and things, semiologists have labored in precisely the opposite direction, regarding language systems instead as self-referring "codes" with no outlet into a world of objective referents. The result of such analyses has been a final cutting loose of the signifier itself, a freeing of the "sign" from the last traces of its referential duty, allowing it to float free without any bond to its "signifieds."

It is little wonder, then, that analysts and semiologists have so much trouble understanding each other. Having secured the referential logic of "rigid designation," analytic philosophy could hardly be expected to embrace the "floating signifier." Conversely, the concept of "rigid designation" can make little sense to post-structural semiology. For where analytic philosophy explores the modal relations between words and things, semiology concerns itself with relationships that are more psychological than logical. That is, when Saussure introduced the terms "signifier" (*signifiant*) and "signified" (*signifié*) into the language, his distinction was not between a word and an extramental, or denotational, individual or natural kind; it was not even primarily a distinction between phonetic sounds and their meanings. Rather, in the *Cours* we can read how a "linguistic sign does not unite a thing and a name, but a concept and an acoustic image":

> The latter is not the material sound, which is a purely physical entity, but the psychological imprint of this sound, the representation that is given us by our sensory impressions. It is sensorial, and if we happen to call it "material," it is solely in this sense and by way of opposition to the other term of the association, the concept, which is generally more abstract. [1978:98][1]

In other words, the Saussurean sign (*signe*) is wholly a datum for consciousness; it unites, in the mind, a conceptual signification and a sensory impression. But because the usage current at Saussure's time generally associated the term "sign" with the acoustic image alone ("for example a word"), Saussure felt that he had to introduce some new terms. Thus, Saussure proposes "to conserve the word *sign* [*signe*] in order to designate the total relation, and to replace *concept* and *acoustic image* with *signified* [*signifié*] and *signifier* [*signifiant*] respectively" (1978:99).

There are at least two major consequences implicit in this redirectioning of linguistic inquiry. The first involves Saussure's conviction that the "bond uniting the signifier to its signified is arbitrary" (1978:100), and the second (which, as we shall see, has been more telling in the recent history of structural and post-structural language theory) proceeds from Saussure's exclusion of the referent. It should be noted, however, that Saussure's celebrated declaration of the arbitrariness of the signifier was nothing terribly new to linguistic analysis when the *Cours* appeared. "The principle of the arbitrariness of the sign," Saussure himself remarks, "is contested by no one" (1978:100). Certainly such symbolist poets as Arthur Rimbaud and Stéphane Mallarmé had sought for a natural connection between sounds and signifieds, but their experiments failed. Indeed, the quarrel between linguistic naturalists and conventionalists is at least as old as Plato's *Cratylus*. For more than two thousand years students of language have suspected, or believed, that our natural languages, as systems of sounds, are arbitrary conventions. Saussure takes some care to point out that this arbitrariness is socially determined and not at the whim of the individual language user (1978:101), but this too is really nothing revolutionary. Linguistic conventionalism had suggested nothing less.

Jacques Derrida, for his part, points out in his own commentary on the *Cours* how Saussure's "rupture" of the "natural attachment" between signifiers and signifieds "puts in question the idea of naturalness rather than that of attachment" (1980:46) and thus seems to moderate some of his own claims for the indefiniteness of signification (i.e., Derrida seems to leave some room here for attachment, howsoever arbitrary). But even Derrida's reading reveals nothing astonishing in Saussure's stipulation (Derrida, as we shall see in a moment, is more interested in the implications of Saussurean "difference"). The problem of linguistic contingency has haunted us since the myth of Babel first was told.

What *is* startling, however, at least to a referential semanticist, is Saussure's exclusion of the referent. A signified, that is to say, is neither a "thing," as such, nor a class of things; it denotes nothing that is outside the language system in which it appears. For just like the signifier, the signified does not transcend the structural relations of its language system. Both signifier and signified, that is to say, are data for consciousness, produced by systematic differentiation and governed by social practice. What they denote is structure, the structural conformations of a given language system, its codified relations of semiological differences. Semiology, in other words, is not concerned with things or even with classes of things. Semiology is an analysis of conscientious *forms*.

Thus, for Saussure, the study of language is itself a branch of psychology, a study of mind, of consciousness. For this reason, Saussure takes some pains to distinguish between the material, extramental world of performance and reference and the immaterial, psychological realm of semiological structure. Saussure's distinction between the materiality of linguistic performance (parole) and the immateriality of linguistic rule or possibility (langue) is accordingly related both to his separation of material phonology (or phonetics) from the immaterially differential structures of phonemics and to his parallel distinction between linguistic *substance* and linguistic *form*. We might examine these well-known distinctions a little further, both to point to their implications in Derrida's interpretation of the *Cours* and to prepare the way for an interpretation of our own.

"*La langue*," Saussure writes, "is for us language minus performance [parole]. It is the ensemble of linguistic habits which permits one both to understand another subject and to be understood in turn" (1978:112). That is, langue "is at once the product of a social faculty for language and an ensemble of necessary conventions adopted by the social body in order to permit the exercise among individuals of their own linguistic capacity" (1978:25). Parole, on the other hand, "is an individual act of the will and the intelligence" (1978:30); it is the particular linguistic performance and is always individual. What is more, one cannot inductively comprehend langue from the sum of its particular manifestations; for "in separating langue and parole, one is distinguishing at the same time: first, that which is social from that which is individual; and second, that which is essential from that which is accessory and more or less accidental" (1978:30). Langue, then, is greater than the sum of its parts, and it is no less concrete than its performances, because as a system of linguistic associations "ratified by collective consent," it is a psychic reality that has its "seat in the mind" (1978:32).

The study of language, then, is best conducted as a study of the psychological immateriality of langue, Saussure believes. Parole, as an accidental manifestation of langue, is too unsystematic in its material particularity for a systematic study. The semiological study of a language system is a study of langue and is thus a study of *phonemic* immateriality rather than of *phonetic* materiality. So while it is not easy to reconstruct a distinct theory of the phoneme from the *Cours*, phonemics still plays an important role in the reduction of linguistic materiality. As Rulon Wells puts it, "De Saussure nowhere differentiates a specific sub-branch of linguistics dealing with phonemes, as is usual nowadays": he does show, however, "that langue is made up of phonemes and morphemes, both of which form systems" (1970:87). Such systems are not, however, systems of actual sounds, for "phonetics," as Wells continues, "has to do with parole . . . phonemics with langue" (1970:87). In other words, a study of langue is not a study of sounds as such. As Saussure puts it:

> It is impossible that a sound, a material element, can belong by itself to langue. It is only a secondary thing. . . . All conventional values present this character of not being confounded with the tangible elements which serve as their supports. . . . This is truest of the linguistic signifier, which, in its essence, is not at all phonic: it is incorporeal, constituted not by a material substance, but solely by the difference which separates its acoustic image from all the others.
>
> This principle is so essential that it can be applied to all the material elements of langue, including the phonemes. Every idiom composes its words on the basis of a system of sonorous elements by which each form is a clearly defined unity, the number of which is exactly determined. But what such forms characterize are not, as one might believe, positive properties. Rather, the phonemes are distinguished simply by the fact that they are not confused with one another. The phonemes are before anything else oppositional entities, relative and negative. [1978:164]

And so actual sounds, too, are incidental to a study of langue. What is essential is the structure of differential oppositions by which phonemes, as the minimal elements of langue, are constituted, just as acoustic images (signifiers) are constituted according to *their* differences from one another. All this leads to Saussure's often cited slogan that in langue "there are only differences without positive terms" (1978:166). That is, in any language system every signifier, signified, and phoneme is determined solely by its differential relations with every other signifier, signified, and phoneme, respectively, in its system. For whether, Saussure remarks, "one takes the signified or the signifier, langue is composed neither of ideas nor of sounds which preexist the linguistic system, but solely of conceptual differences and phonic differences issued by the system" (1978:166). Thus, the phonetic "substance" of the sound does not enter into langue, does not become meaningful as a signifier, until it has become phonemically determined; and this determination is accomplished by a play of differences, not by the material substance of a phonetic entity.

Saussure illustrates this point by means of a famous analogy. Consider the identity of the 8:45 Geneva-to-Paris express. Now, as Saussure observes, when we consider, say, today's train, we feel that it is the same one that arrived at 8:45 yesterday. And yet, every material component of the train—locomotive, cars, personnel, etc.—may be quite different from yesterday's. So how can we say that it is the "same" train? How can we recognize it as a repetition of the same? We can do so, Saussure says, because "the entity that constitutes it is not purely material; it is founded upon certain conditions from which its matter is occasionally estranged, for example, its situation relative to others" (1978:151). In other words, the identity of today's 8:45 express inheres not in the material components of the train itself but in the relational circumstances of the train's placement in a schedule, or system, of other trains.

So it is with the phoneme, Saussure suggests. Later developments in structural linguistics have defined more fully this distinction between phonetic substance and phonemic difference, demonstrating thereby how the phonetic sound, say *b*, becomes phonemic, or meaningful, in English, solely on the basis of its binary opposition with, say, *p*. While this is not completely worked out in Saussure's *Cours*, the rudiments are found there. Sounds become meaningful only by virtue of the systems of difference that can be found in langue. Formalizing difference is primary; substantial sound is secondary. Thus, Saussure can remark, in another famous phrase, "langue is a form and not a substance" (1978:169). It is a form in the social mind, a form that is "real" and that is motivated by differences. Material substance enters into the equation only in actual performance, in parole, as an "accident."

From such passages as these Derrida has drawn the conclusion that "the most evident significance of the appeal to difference as the reduction of phonic substance" is that "the phonic element, the term, the plenitude that is called sensible, would not appear as such without the difference or opposition which gives them *form*." But here, Derrida continues, "the appearing and functioning of difference presupposes an originary synthesis not preceded by any absolute simplicity. Such would be the originary trace":

> Without a retention in the minimal unit of temporal experience, without a trace retaining the other as other in the same, no difference would do its work and no meaning would appear. It is not the question of a constituted difference here, but rather, before all determination of the content, of the *pure* movement which produces differences. *The pure trace is differance.* It does not depend on any sensible plenitude, audible or visible, phonic or graphic. It is, on the contrary, the condition of such a plenitude. Although it *does not exist*, although it is never a *being-present* outside of all plenitude, its possibility is by rights anterior to all that one calls sign. [1980:62]

That is, if difference alone is responsible for the constitution of the essential elements of a language system, then the ontological ground of language is not in some differential "substance" or even "form" but can consist only of a pre-ontological, pre-metaphysical *producer* of differences that Derrida alternately calls the "trace," "differance," or "writing" (among other such differing/deferring "names"). But the movement of such a play of differences cannot be enclosed within a given language system, Derrida argues. All that this movement of the trace can "produce" is its own infinite repetition, its own ceaseless iteration of differences, of the play of the other-in-the-same. For Derrida views the iterability of the sign, the semiological capacity for repetition that makes language recognition possible in the first place, as an iter-ability, as a play of the *itara*, of the differential otherness that is "always already" at work in a language system. The sign, accordingly, is "always already" exposed to its own deconstruction by another sign in an infinite play of substitutions that can never be contained within the terms of some master code that would finally transcend the play of iterative difference (see 1982b:315ff.).

In other words, Saussure's deconstruction of the principle of linguistic "substance" on behalf of the principle of differential "form" leads to a deconstruction of "form" itself, because the forms of our languages cannot be systematically enclosed when there can always be another form to "supplement" those that have already been identified. There is no limit to a linguistic structure grounded in difference rather than in reference. But if our knowledge of things, even of languages themselves, can be constituted only according to the terms of nonreferring, ever-playing differential codes, then it seems that we can never transcend the "code," can never define a master code or metalanguage that would enable us to secure any measure of epistemological "truth." It is in this sense, then, that Derrida inscribes "reality" inside an untranscendable "archive" of writings, of traces whose differential play might be halted only in the face of such an absolute referent, or absolute trace, that a total destruction of the archive would effect. For Derrida, then, the nuclear referent, representing here the total destruction of the archive, constitutes the only possible referent that might transcend the play of archival difference. But until the archive, *écriture*, is destroyed, our signifiers and the knowledge that they signify can refer only to the play of signification, not to an extra-archival "reality."

To attempt to transcend the play of the trace, then, to determine a referent outside our signifying systems, is in vain, Derrida suggests, a mere metaphysical gesture, an attempt to speak what cannot be spoken. "There is nothing outside the text," he writes, meaning by this not the simple reduction of the world to ink and paper but the inclusion of all of our knowledge inside a "writing" that can never "write" its own outside, its own referential "origin," because such an origin would exceed the reach of metaphysics itself. For if, as Derrida writes, "differences appear among the elements [of a language system] or rather produce them, make them emerge as such and constitute the *texts*, the chains, and the systems of traces," then whatever it "is" that produces these differences must always exceed the capacity of the language of metaphysics to define it. In other words:

The trace is in fact the absolute origin of sense in general. Which amounts to saying once again that there is no absolute origin of sense in general. The trace is the differance which opens appearance ... and no concept of metaphysics can describe it. [1980:65]

We shall return in chapter 14 to a further consideration of the trace, of differance, but before proceeding to that discussion, we will present an alternative interpretation of the implications of Saussure's apparent reduction of phonic materiality or linguistic "substance" in language study through his privileging of the principle of differential "form." For in employing such metaphysically charged terms as "form" and "substance," Saussure invites an ontological reappraisal of his definitions that might be conducted along the lines of the Aristotelian metaphysical principles that we explored earlier.

To begin with, we might note that the "Saussurean concept of substance," as John Lyons has put it, "is very close to the Aristotelian and scholastic concept of matter." For while, as Lyons continues, in "modern scientific and colloquial usage 'matter' denotes something with spatio-temporal extension," we need to "abstract from this more particular implication of the term in our interpretation of the Saussurean concept of substance":

> To take a traditional example: when a sculptor carves a statue out of a block of marble he takes something which, for the present purpose, we may think of as being shapeless and internally undifferentiated and gives to it, by the process of sculpting, a definite or distinctive shape.... The marble, considered as substance, is potentially many things, but in actuality it is none; it becomes one thing rather than another by the imposition of one structure rather than another on the undifferentiated substratum.
>
> So it is, says Saussure, with language. But languages result from the imposition of structure on two kinds of substance: sound and thought. The phonological composition of a word-form is a complex of phonemes, each of which ... derives its essence and its existence from the structure imposed by the language system upon the continuum (i.e., substance) of sound. The meaning of a lexeme derives from the imposition of structure on the otherwise nebulous and inchoate continuum of thought. [1979:239-40]

According to this interpretation, the sign might be characterized as a form *and* a substance, that is to say, as the actuation of the "material" potentiality of thought and sound. These two principles may be separated for the purposes of linguistic analysis—just as Aristotle prescinds the formal from the material principle for the purposes of a metaphysical analysis—but this does not mean that they are separable in reality. Rather, the implication is that neither the "substance" nor the "form" of a sign can be "accidental," that each is essential to the structuring of a language system. Saussure himself does not neglect phonological materiality in the *Cours*, but his often overt privileging of the formal principle of linguistic difference has had the effect, as we have seen, of throwing the ontology of the sign into an abyss that Saussure apparently did not foresee. By treating the "matter" of the sign as an "accident," as a nonessential linguistic principle, Saussure leads us to the anti-ontology of the trace, of differance, of a linguistic essence or identity that is without essence or existence.

But if we view language as the actuation of a "substantial," though unextended, psychological and phonic potentiality, capacity, or power, then language need not be thrown into an abyss of immaterial differences. Differences alone, we might say, do not constitute the essence of the sign. To see what does, we might return to Saussure's analysis of the differential identity of the phoneme. For Saussure, of course, the identity of the phoneme inheres in its difference from every other phoneme in the language system to which it belongs. As long as it is not confused with any other phoneme in its system, it can be repeated indefinitely. What matters in the recognition of the phoneme is not its material or substantial identity but rather the systematic circumstances through which one phonemic entity can be distinguished from another. We recall the 8:45 Geneva-to-Paris express.

But let us look at the 8:45 again. It is true that we do not ordinarily identify the train on the basis of its material components, because we normally are not concerned with that. Rather, we are usually more concerned with its formal identity, with its schedule and route. But when we consult a train schedule, with what are we primarily concerned? Say that we want to find a train that leaves at 8:45. Do we not look first to see whether there is a train that leaves at that time? And if we find one, do we normally stop to compare it with every other scheduled disembarkation, or are we satisfied with the *typical* identity of the class of trains that leaves at 8:45? In other words, is not our knowledge of the 8:45 primarily a knowledge of its generic identity, so to speak, rather than of its difference from every other train on the schedule? And would this not be the case for phonemic identification as well?

What I am suggesting is that we may view the "matter" of the sign both in the sense of its substrate (voice, thought) and in the sense of the unextended phonemic and morphemic classes to which individual phonemes and morphemes belong. In the *Metaphysics*, Aristotle pursues a parallel semiotic logic in his own analysis of the principles that make possible the iterative recognition of linguistic signs. Seeking to refute the necessity of transcendental universals, or Forms, to enable our knowledge of particular entities, Aristotle remarks that if, "as for example in the case of the elements of speech, nothing prevents the existence of many A's and B's even if there is no A-Itself and no B-Itself apart from the many A's and B's, then in view of this there can be an infinite number of similar syllables":

... For "knowledge," like "*knowing*," has two meanings, one exists in potentiality, and the other in *actuality*. Potentiality, like matter, being universal and indefinite, is concerned with the universal and the indefinite, but *actuality*, being definite and a *this*, is concerned with some definite thing and some *this*. [*Metaphysics* 1979:1087a8–20]

Thus "*this* A, which the grammarian investigates, is an A," Aristotle continues (*Metaphysics* 1979:1087a22), an actual, definite instance of the potential, but indefinite, class of A's. To know *this* A, in other words, is to apprehend an empirical particular whose identity is at once actual, in the form of the *this*, and potential, in the "material" class to which it belongs. Our knowledge of the particular, then, is at once definite and indefinite, actual and potential. As Joseph Owens puts it: "Knowledge (and the act of knowing) is definite. But since this definite knowledge of the form is able to be applied indefinitely to singulars of the same species, it is potentially indefinite and universal. As such it can be regarded as matter for each new actual cognition of a singular" (1978:429).

The iterability of our knowledge of the sign, we might say, according to such an interpretation, is made possible not by a pure movement of the *iter*, of the other-in-the-same that the principle of semiological difference implies, but rather is motivated by the nondifferentiable relation between an actual entity and the unextended potentiality of the class to which it belongs. To put this another way, semiotic structures do not emerge purely from other semiotic structures or differences but also in relation to their own "material" identities. The phoneme /a/, for instance, constitutes an actuation of the indefinite potentiality for specific actuation that subsists within the class of phonemes to which it belongs. Only after we have identified it as "*an* /a/" can we differentiate it from another phoneme within its language system.

The semiotic logic that I am suggesting may appear peculiar to both structural and post-structural semiologists. But this relationship between the particularity of the individual sign and the semiotic class to which it belongs should not be unfamiliar to a Peircean semiotician, for it anticipates the relationship between a semiotic "token" and a semiotic "type," which Peirce explored as a part of his overall investigation into the Firstness, Secondness, and Thirdness of semiotic and of extrasemiotic phenomena. By turning our attention to Peirce's semiotic at this point, we can explore further a nondifferential ontology of the sign—an ontology that can ultimately reintroduce into semiotic analysis not only the extrasemiotic referent but the communal consciousness that determines its signs rather than being determined by them.

CHAPTER 13

Producing the Referent:
C. S. Peirce's Semiotic Realism

IN 1867, Charles Sanders Peirce, then twenty-eight years of age, published a brief paper in the *Proceedings of the American Academy of Arts and Sciences* with the purpose of presenting the phenomenological groundwork for a new list of categories (1931–66:1.545–59).[1] The impetus for this paper, Peirce later wrote, came from his realization "that Kant's list of categories might be a part of a larger system of conceptions":

For instance, the categories of relation—reaction, causality and subsistence—are so many different modes of *necessity*, which is a category of modality; and in like manner, the categories of quality—negation, qualification, degree, and intrinsic attribution—are so many relations of inherence, which is a category of relation. Thus, as the categories of the third group are to those of the fourth, so are those of the second to the third; and I fancied, at least, that the categories of quantity, unity, plurality, totality, were, in like manner, different intrinsic attributions of quality. [1931–66:1.563]

The point of Peirce's rather torturous analysis here is that Kant's twelve categories of the understanding might be reduced to a more logically rigorous set of fundamental conceptions whose purpose it would be "to reduce the manifold of sensuous impressions to unity" (1931–66:1.545). The purpose of a categorical conception, in other words, is to explain how the apparently diverse phenomena of our experience (which include both the differences between things as such and the differences between a thing and its own predicational qualities—e.g., a stove and its color) can be unified in coherent epistemological forms. Without such categories the "manifold of sensuous impressions" (including our impressions of ourselves as conscientious individuals) would appear solely in the (non)form of an infinite play of differences, of causeless particulars that cannot be contained within the closure of conceptual "knowledge." And these particulars themselves would endlessly fissure through differential division after differential division, because there would be no privileged point from which knowledge might begin to draw its lines around the "forms" of experience. This, of course, is precisely Derrida's point as he pursues his relentless deconstruction of a "logocentric" history. As I am arguing here, however, Derrida's deconstructions of categorical thinking raise practical and theoretical problems of their own, and at a time when some degree of objective knowledge has become essential to the humanities as well as to the technical sciences, it is not inappropriate that we should reapproach such thought to see what it still might teach us.

For Peirce, at any rate, the key to the solution of the puzzle of empirical-diversity-in-unity appeared to him early in his career in the promise of logical analysis. As he puts it, "After trying to solve the puzzle in a direct speculative, a physical, a historical, and a psychological manner, I finally concluded the only way was to attack it as Kant had done from the side of formal logic" (1931–66: 1.563). Now, "since there were ultimately only three modes of logical combination," as Thomas Goudge explains, it occurred to Peirce that "the number of categories could not exceed three" (Goudge 1969:83), and so Kant's twelve appeared to be far too many. In his 1867 essay "On a New List of Categories," Peirce accordingly attempts to lay the groundwork for a categorical reduction and correction. In this early paper, however, Peirce describes not three but five fundamental categories, which include "*Being*," "Quality," "Relation," "Representation," and "*Substance*" (1931–66: 1.555). In his later writings Peirce dropped the first and the last of these categories because of his mature conviction that phenomenology properly could be concerned only with empirical phenomena and thus could not "have any traffic with such ontological notions as 'being' and 'substance'" (Goudge 1969:83). But before looking more closely at Peirce's mature doctrine, we might first examine his earlier speculations, from the 1867 essay, to see how they anticipate and help explain his later work.

Peirce commences his phenomenological analysis of the first of his irreducible conceptions, or categories, in a rather Hegelian fashion. That is, where Hegel begins his inquiry into the phenomenology of consciousness with the absolute immediacy of sense-certain experience, Peirce begins with an appeal to that "universal conception which is nearest to sense... *the present, in general*" (1931–66:1.547). And also like Hegel's "sense-certainty," Peirce's notion of "the present in general" is a product not of cognition but simply of pure *attention*. It is a conception that "has no connotation at all, but is the pure denotative power of the mind, that is to say, the power which directs the mind to an object, in contradistinction to the power of thinking any predicate of that object—so the conception of *what is present in general*, which is nothing but the general recognition of what is contained in attention, has no connotation, and therefore no proper unity" (1931–66:1.547). In other words, like Hegel's sense-certain "this," the "present in general" is seized before it can be compared to anything else; and before its cognitive discrimination, it "must have been recognized as such, as *it*" (1931–66:1.547). And since "*it* is thus neither predicated of a subject, nor in a subject," Peirce concludes, it "accordingly is identical with the conception of substance" (1931–66:1.547).

Peirce's first category, then, as the "present in general," or "substance," roughly corresponds to the "substance" of Aristotle's *Categories*, for Peirce's *it*, like Aristotle's *ti esti*, is taken without predicational qualification. In this sense, Peirce believes, it is "therefore no proper unity" (1931–66:1.547). To achieve unity within the understanding, *it* must be predicatively distinguished. The "unity to which the understanding reduces impressions," Peirce writes, "is the unity of a proposition," a unity that "consists in the connection of the predicate with the subject."

For example, Peirce continues, if "we say 'The stove is black,' the stove is the *substance*, from which its blackness has not been differentiated, and the *is*, while it leaves the substance just as it was seen, explains its confusedness, by the application to it of *blackness* as a predicate" (1931–66:1.548). In other words, an undiscriminated "substance" achieves its discrimination through its connection to a predicational quality, but this, in turn, implies that between the "quality" and the "substance" there must be a copula, an unqualified, substanceless connector that enables their articulation. Since it is this articulation that "completes the work of conceptions of reducing the manifold to unity," Peirce reasons, the conception of "being" that "is implied in the copula" must have a categorical status of its own (1931–66:1.548). But it is an entirely empty category, for the "conception of *being* contains only that junction of predicate to subject wherein the two verbs agree. The conception of being, therefore, plainly has no content" (1931–66:1.548).

Thus, *it*, the substance of our immediate attention, is simply an indefinite feeling or impression as long as nothing is predicated of it. We may have a vague sense that the stove in front of us is black, but we cannot *know* this without the articulation of the "is." *It*, then, remains indefinite, an object only of potential knowledge, until it can become the subject of the proposition "*it is* ... such and such." Together, *substance* (i.e., *it*) and *being* (as introduced by the propositional copula) constitute a unity of objective conception that *substance* alone leaves unrealized, and therefore they comprise "the beginning and end of all conception" (1931–66:1.548).

But still to be considered is the categorical status of the predicative "quality," of the "such and such" that the "is" articulates with a substance. For while, as Peirce writes, the "conception of *being* arises upon the formation of a proposition," a "proposition always has, besides a term to express the substance, another to express the quality of that substance. . . . Quality, therefore, in its very widest sense, is the first conception in order in passing from being to substance" (1931–66: 1.551).

A "quality," then, is a predicational property, the completion of the proposition "*it* is . . . such and such." Peirce recognizes that this "quality" (say, the stove's *blackness*) might be taken "to be given in the impression" of *substance* itself and thus might be rendered unnecessary among the least conceptions. But he argues instead that since a "proposition asserts the applicability of a mediate conception to a more immediate one . . . the more mediate conception is clearly regarded independently of this circumstance, for otherwise the two conceptions would not be distinguished, but one would be thought through the other, without this latter being an object of thought, at all" (1931–66: 1.551). In other words, when we look at a stove, our immediate conception is of *this stove* and not of its blackness. But to predicate the mediate *quality* of blackness to the stove, we must have a certain immediate conception of blackness as well, which, while being merely mediate with respect to the *substance* of the stove, must nonetheless "be discriminated from it and considered *in itself*, not as applied to an object, but simply as embodying a quality, *blackness*" (1931–66: 1.551).

Peirce, however, is in some danger here of contradicting himself, because once we regard a quality *in-itself*, we have begun to treat it rather like an immediate substance, that is, as the subject of a proposition, say, "blackness is . . . such and such." So here once more is the intractable problem of the universal. Does "blackness" exist? To avoid the transcendental implications of Plato's affirmative answer to such a question, Aristotle carefully categorized such predicates under the category of "quality"—as does Peirce in his 1867 essay. But there is a difference between the two categorizations, for Peirce insists that a quality is "entirely hypothetical," a pure abstraction that is conceptually necessary all the same, "because we cannot comprehend an agreement of two things, except in some *respect*, and this respect is such a pure abstraction as blackness. Such a pure abstraction," Peirce concludes, "reference to which constitutes a *quality* or general attribute, may be termed a ground" (1931–66:1.551).

But the categorical status of a quality, or ground, raises a fourth categorical candidate. As Peirce writes: "Empirical psychology has established the fact that we can know a quality only by means of its contrast with or similarity to another. By contrast and agreement a thing is referred to a correlate, if this term may be used in a wider sense than usual. The occasion of the introduction of the conception of reference to a ground is the reference to a correlate, and this is, therefore, the next conception in order" (1931–66:1.552). That is, since one quality can be known only with respect to its relation to another one either like or unlike it, there must be another categorical conception to accommodate this fact. Peirce categorizes this conception under the name of "relation."

The category of "relation," by which individual qualities may be epistemologically distinguished, in turn entails the categorization of a fifth, and final, conception, which Peirce terms a "representation" or "interpretant." The necessity for this final category of the understanding inheres in the diversity of our impressions of things, in the apparent confusedness of our experience. That is, as Peirce puts it, "since there is a manifold of impressions, we have a feeling of complication or confusion, which leads us to differentiate this impression from that, and then, having been differentiated, they require to be brought into unity":

> Now they are not brought into unity until we conceive them together as being *ours*, that is, until we refer them to a conception as their interpretant. Thus, the reference to an interpretant arises upon the holding together of diverse impressions, and therefore it

does not join a conception to the substance, as the other two references [i.e., quality and relation] do, but unites directly the manifold of the substance itself. It is, therefore, the last conception in order in passing from being to substance. [1931–66:1.554]

Peirce's intuition of the "interpretant," the conceptual means by which we unify the diversity of our impressions, is still inchoate in his 1867 essay, but we can already see what problems the concept of the "interpretant" was meant to solve and what problems it raises in its turn. The problem it solves is the problem of the empirical manifold, for without some means of conceptually organizing the diversity of our experience, our knowledge would be reduced to an incoherent apprehension of causally discontinuous particulars. Both Kant's and Peirce's categorical systems, in other words, were introduced to explain how the mind conceptually organizes the experiential manifold into causal coherence. And just as Kant refers to the unified phenomena constituted by the categorical understanding out of the diversity of experience as representations (*Vorstellungen*), so too does Peirce, in his modification of the Kantian system, conceive of the unity of our cognitive apprehension as a representational "interpretant."

But if the interpretant is only a representation, must it not therefore remain, like the concepts determined by Kant's categorical understanding, a subjective captive of the mind that conceives it? In other words, it appears that Peirce solves the problem of diversity at the expense of our ever achieving any objective knowledge of what the extra-interpretantial world is "in-itself." The problem that Peirce's system faces here, of course, is similar to that faced by Kant's, for the categorical account of each thinker, different though they may be in detail, finally seems to solve the epistemological puzzle through a paradoxical denial that objective, nonrepresentational knowledge is possible.

That Peirce explores the nature of the interpretant in "representational" terms in his 1867 essay only seems to confirm this implication. For having introduced his concept of the interpretant as that which representationally unifies the diversity of our experience, Peirce proceeds to an analysis of the various kinds of "representation" available to us, anticipating thereby what is perhaps best known in his mature doctrine. The first kind of representations Peirce discusses are those "whose relation to their objects is a mere community in some quality, and these representations may be termed *likenesses*" (1931–66: 1.558). In later writings this "likeness" becomes Peirce's semiotic "icon," which is a sign, like a map, that bears a resemblance to what it represents. The second kind of representation detailed in the 1867 essay includes "*indices* or *signs*" whose "relation to their objects consists in a correspondence in fact" (1931–66: 1.558). These later became Peirce's "indexical" signs, which might be exemplified by a pointer. Finally there are those representations "the ground of whose relation to their objects is an imputed character, which are the same as *general signs*, and these may be termed *symbols*" (1931–66: 1.558)—in other words, the linguistic sign proper.

Now, Peirce's semiotic conception of the interpretant (in at least one of its many senses) has prompted Derrida to cite with approval Peirce's own reference to the sign as "*anything which determines something else (its interpretant) to refer to an object to which itself refers (its object) in the same way, this interpretant becoming in turn a sign, and so on ad infinitum*" (see Derrida 1980:50). The implication of Peirce's own statement here, of course, is that even the object that a semiotic interpretant representationally brings to unity is itself a sign, and that we can never break out of the circle of interpretantial representation to "place a reassuring end to the reference from sign to sign," as Derrida puts it (1980:49). In other words, it appears that even Peirce's semiotic also finally excludes the referent or, rather, defers it in an endless play of interpretantial signs and conceptions.

But it is important to note that there is finally a crucial difference between Kant's categorical account and Peirce's. For while the Kantian categories are indeed limited to a causally constitutive understanding that can only constitute *phenomenal* knowledge in the face of *noumenal* unknowability, Peirce's interpretant (which, as we shall see, has a number of senses and is not only a sign) belongs to the objective world just as it does to conception. Nature itself, in Peirce's overall phenomenology, has its own unifying principles, which correspond to those of conceptual understanding. And by exploring Peirce's further, and finally ontological, senses of the interpretant, we can find how the referent can be restored to semiotic analysis even where it appears to have been lost once more.

This further exploration of the interpretant and its place in Peirce's general philosophy must be conducted through an analysis of his later writings, for his thought in the 1867 essay, while rich in anticipations of what is to come, is still inchoate. But we might conclude our look at "On a New List of Categories" by noting some of the difficulties inherent in the fivefold categorical schematization that Peirce presents near the conclusion of his essay. The five categories are:

Being
   Quality (reference to a ground)
   Relation (reference to a correlate)
   Representation (reference to an interpretant)
Substance

In the 1867 essay Peirce regarded the categories of *Being* and *Substance* as the most essential of the five, while the "three intermediate conceptions may be termed accidents" (1931–66:1.555). But Peirce later abandoned what were here his most essential categories and spent the greater part of his career trying to clarify precisely what he meant by the remaining three. This is just as well, because Peirce's projection of the category of *Being* out of the English-language grammatical copula threatens to confuse grammar with ontology. The fact, that is to say, that the grammatical copula of the English language inflects in its participial form into "being" does not in itself demonstrate that there is any ontological referent for the grammatical term.[2] At the same time, Peirce's distinction between a quality and a *Substance* causes ontological difficulties of its own, for, as we have seen, the need to distinguish between the two compelled Peirce to claim that qualities have no real existence and are merely "abstractions" of the understanding. What ontological status, then, can such an abstraction have? Is it wholly conceptual, a nominalistic invention? And if it were, would this not contradict Peirce's essential realism?

Rather than either defending or criticizing Peirce's early categorization of *Being* and *Substance* further, however, we will instead accept his own abandonment of them and examine his torturous lifelong inquiry into the nature of the remaining categories of "quality," "relation," and "representation." These terms themselves were destined to undergo a number of terminological mutations in Peirce's work until he finally settled on the connotatively neutral "Firstness," "Secondness," and "Thirdness" by which the three are best known today (see Goudge 1969:83). But while Peirce's understanding of his own terms remained incomplete at his death, it is still both possible and instructive to consider a general description of the essential triadic logic of his philosophy. For it is through Peirce's fundamental intuition of the "Thirdness" of phenomena (semiotic and extrasemiotic) that we may find the terms for a semiotic realism that can break the circle of signs after all.

Nearly thirty years after publishing his essay "On A New List of Categories," Peirce wrote a second, rather poignantly entitled, paper called "The List of Categories: A Second Essay" (ca. 1894; vide 1931–66: 1.passim). In the "Second Essay," Peirce explored his conceptions of phenomenal Firstness, Secondness, and Thirdness according to his division of "all objects into monads, dyads, and triads" (1931–66:1.293). The monadic character of an object, Peirce explains, is its Firstness, that is, that conception which "is predominant in the ideas of freshness, life, freedom" (1931–66:1.302). The First, or the "free," in other words, much like the "substance" of the 1867 essay, "is that which has not another idea behind it, determining its actions":

> In the idea of being, Firstness is predominant, not necessarily on account of the abstractness of that idea, but on account of its self-containedness. It is not in being separated from qualities that Firstness is most predominant, but in being something peculiar and idiosyncratic. The first is predominant in feeling, as distinguished from objective perception, will, and thought. [1931–66:1.302]

The idea of the First, Peirce continues, "is not that of an object," for an object is something that is "dyadically" "over against" one (1931–66:1.303), something that resists us in the definite forms of perception, will, and thought. But while the idea of a First constitutes only an indeterminate impression or feeling of presence rather than a determinate experience of an objective "dyad" or fact, there "must be some determination, or suchness," Peirce reasons, "otherwise we shall think nothing at all" (1931–66:1.303).

The indefinite "suchness" of the First, then, expresses our apprehension of the "being of a monadic quality [that] is a mere potentiality, without [actual or objective] existence." Objective existence itself, the thing that is over against us, as Peirce defines it, "is purely dyadic" (1931–66:1.328). When we experience something as *that thing over there*, our experience is not the impression of a First, or monad, but the cognition of an actually existing Second, the "reality" of the dyad. Peirce writes that, in "the idea of reality, Secondness is predominant; for the real is that which insists upon forcing its way to recognition as something *other* than the mind's creation.... The real is active; we acknowledge it, in calling it the *actual*. (This word is due to Aristotle's use of *energeia*, action, to mean existence, as opposed to a mere germinal state)" (1931–66:1.325). The "dyad," or "Second," accordingly, "is an individual fact, as it existentially is; and it has no generality in it" (1931–66:1.328).

Peirce's allusion to Aristotelian *energeia* here is instructive, though it does invert Aristotle's own metaphysical priorities. For Aristotle, the *this*, or individual objective substance, constituted a composition of an actual form (*energeia*) and a potential substrate (*dunamis*), in which, to a certain extent, the form came first. In Peirce's analysis, potential presence constitutes a First, while actual existence is a Second. But we might note that in both Peirce's and Aristotle's formulations, the potential principle and the actual are only prescindable for theoretical purposes. There can be no empirical *this* without the potentiality of matter and the actuality of form, while the actuality of the Second requires the indefinite "suchness" of the potential First. The Second, in its turn, constitutes potential presence as actual fact.

But taken as such, the Second still "has no generality in it." It is a pure particular, incapable, in itself, of cognitive conceptualization. Thus, Peirce reasoned, there must be a Third principle by which the particularity of the Second (both as sign and object) might be iteratively and conceptually generalized. Peirce categorized this universalizing principle under the general heading of phenomenological Thirdness, "law," or "habit," whose relation to the potentiality of the First and the actuality of the Second can be summarized as follows:

> The first is a positive qualitative possibility, in itself nothing more. The second is an existent thing without any mode of being less than existence, but determined by that first. A *third* has a mode of being which consists in the Secondness that it determines, the mode of being a law, or concept. [1931–66:1.536]

Peirce offers a refreshingly concrete example of this categorical relationship between Firstness, Secondness, and Thirdness in his illustration of the process involved in baking an apple pie. Consider, then, a cook as she prepares to bake. Her object, of course, is to bake a particular pie that can be set on the table, but as she begins to bake, Peirce writes, she "has no particular apple pie she particularly prefers to serve" (1931–66:1.341). Rather, the cook consults a recipe book, which presents "a collection of rules" for the production of a typical apple pie. Fetching her materials (apples, flour, sugar, and so on), the cook begins to bake according to instruction. Now, as Peirce explains:

> Throughout her whole proceedings she pursues an idea or dream without any particular thisness or thatness—or, as we say, *hecceity*—to it, but this dream she wishes to realize in connection with an object of experience, which, as such does possess hecceity. . . . The dream itself has no prominant thirdness; it is, on the contrary, utterly irresponsible; it is whatever it pleases. The object of experience as a reality is a second. But the desire in seeking to attach the one to the other is a third, or medium.
> So it is with any law of nature. Were it but a mere idea unrealized—and it is of the nature of an idea—it would be a pure first. The cases to which it applies, are seconds. [1931–66:1.342–43]

In such a manner a pie comes to be baked and served. As such, it is a particular dyadic reality, or Second, that has actualized the potential Firstness of the baker's "dream," but it could not have been actualized without a set of regular rules for its production, without the Thirdness of a generalizable knowledge of the "law," the habitual course of behavior, of particular things.

The Peircean triad of potential Firstness, actual Secondness, and "legal" Thirdness applies to all phenomena, including the phenomenon of conceptual thought itself. For while, in one sense, a thought is already a Third (since it conceptually determines a generalizable meaning for a particular Second), it also has its own Firstness, Secondness, and Thirdness: First "in its capacity as a mere possibility"; Second as an "event . . . of *experience* or *information*"; and Third "in its role as governing Secondness" (1931–66:1.537). In other words, thoughts themselves have their own indefinite potentiality, particular actuality, and governing generality—and so, Peirce believes, do the signs that represent them.

For a sign too has its own Firstness, Secondness, and Thirdness. Since the Firstness of a sign can be analyzed into a further triad, as can its Secondness and Thirdness, Peirce's resulting analysis presents us with a dizzying and unwieldy panorama of semiotic trichotomies defining some sixty-six classes of signs. The practical value of such an array of semiotic definitions is accordingly rather limited, but by focusing our attention on Peirce's "first trichotomy" of the sign, we may find what is indeed a practical theoretical alternative to the differential paradigm of structural semiology—an alternative that grounds the sign not in an abstract play of differences but in the conscious decisions of language users themselves, as well as in an extrasemiotic "dynamic" reality against which the truth of a sign may be tested.

Peirce defines his first trichotomy of the sign in the following terms:

According to the first division a Sign may be termed a *Qualisign*, a *Sinsign*, or a *Legisign*.
A *Qualisign* is a quality which is a sign. It cannot actually act as a sign until it is embodied; but the embodiment has nothing to do with its character as a sign.
A *Sinsign* (where the syllable *sin* is taken as meaning "being only once," as in *single, simple*, Latin *semel*, etc.) is an actual existent thing or event which is a sign. It can only be so through its qualities; so that it involves a qualisign, or, rather, several qualisigns....
A *Legisign* is a law that is a Sign. This law is usually established by men. Every conventional sign is a legisign [but not conversely]. It is not a single object but a general type which, it has been agreed, shall be significant. Every legisign signifies through an instance of its application, which may be termed a *Replica* of it. Thus, the word "the" will usually occur from fifteen to twenty-five times on a page. It is in all these occurrences one and the same word, the same legisign. Each single instance of it is a Replica. The Replica is a Sinsign. Thus, every Legisign requires Sinsigns. [1931–66: 2.243–46; brackets in original]

In 4.537, Peirce refers to the qualisign, sinsign, and legisign, respectively, as a "tone," a "token," and a "type," but whichever terms we employ here, we can see how Peirce's first semiotic trichotomy expresses the fundamental potentiality, actuality, and law of the sign in itself. For as a "tone," or "qualisign," a sign subsists as a positive but indefinite possibility for semiotic formation. As such, the Firstness of the sign constitutes a semiotic grounding in the principle of potentiality rather than that of difference. Representing the "suchness" behind the actually appearing sinsign, the abstract potentiality of the qualisign can in fact be seen to precede the differential particularity of the semiotic Second, or token. Without this potentiality, or, we might say, power, for sign constitution, the differential particularity of the sinsign could not appear, but at the same time the qualisign remains an abstraction until it is differentially embodied in the sinsign. Might we not regard the relation between the semiotic First and Second, tone and token, qualisign and sinsign, as an essential relation between a certain power and its actualizing difference? A relation of power-*and*-difference?

The relation I am suggesting here is intended to recall the Aristotelian metaphysics that Peirce's semiotic, as I believe, ultimately develops. A sign in itself, according to Peirce's formula, requires both a potential substrate, or First, and an actual differentiated form, or Second. But this raises the question of the iterability of the Second, for as Derrida points out in "Signature Event Context," a sign that cannot be iteratively recognized is not a sign (see 1982:315). For Derrida, as we have seen, this recognizability is a function of the *iter* in iterability, of the differential otherness that structural semiology posits as the essential motivation for the sign. Aristotle, on the other hand, accounts for the iterability of the particular in terms of its epistemological potentiality, that is, of our potential ability to recognize *this* particular form at another time. This potentiality, in turn, inheres in the material universality of the "genus" to which the particular belongs. But while Peirce's own solution to the problem of particular iterability, as expressed in his positing of the Thirdness of the legisign, or type, introduces a concept that is not present in Aristotle's metaphysics, it can be seen to develop what is essentially an Aristotelian intuition.

For what enables the recognizability of the differentiated token is itself a kind of "genus" or unextended class: viz., the semiotic type. This class is determined by the active decisions, the semiotic legislations, of a language community. The type, or legisign, that is to say, conventionalizes a "habitual" meaning for the token, and the origin of these habits is social rather than metaphysically differential. Indeed, Peirce's solution to the problem of semiotic iterability is finally far less metaphysical than Saussure's, for rather than requiring the positing of a pre-social, pre-empirical, essentially a priori principle of semiological difference to account for the formal iterability of the sign, the principle of the semiotic Third, or legisign, grounds the iterative identity of the sign in the concreteness of social consciousness.

My point here is that in Peirce's semiotic we can find an alternative interpretation of the sign by which signs may be seen as the product of social classification and convention, not of sheer differences. This does not mean that difference (or otherness) plays no role in a sign system—that it simply can be repressed or ignored—for we may find the principle of difference inscribed in the Secondness, or actuality, of the sinsign. But it does suggest that differences do not subsist apart from actual phenomena, do not sublate semiotic materiality and intentional consciousness through a finally uncontainable play of essential otherness, do not lead to an abyss of necessary equivocations. For while a sinsign, for example, differs in its actual Secondness from other sinsigns, its differential identity is not prescindable from the Firstness of its positive potentiality in the qualisign and the Thirdness of the legisign, or type, that establishes its habitual iterability. Its difference, that is to say, is not separable from its "legislated" identity. Indeed, as Peirce puts it more generally, "Otherness belongs to hecceities. It is the inseparable spouse of identity" (1931–66: 1.566).

But the regularizing and identifying Thirdness of a linguistic class or type still presents the realist with a certain difficulty. For if the value of a sign is "legislated" by speaking communities, it appears that that value is wholly subjective. Peirce's "pragmaticism," in other words, might appear to anticipate Stanley Fish's pragmatism: the position that our signs mean only what we want them to mean and cannot be grounded in anything outside the "standard story" by which we "legislate" reality. Post-structural critics, in fact, have often noted Peirce's own apprehension that semiotic representation, the Thirdness of the sign, ultimately involves us in "an endless series of representations, each representing the one behind it" (1931–66:1.339). But while such a vision of an antirealistic "unlimited semiosis" does appear in Peirce's papers, we may also find a conviction that "sign interpretation," as Michael Shapiro puts it, is "an essentially teleological, hence, self-corrective process" (1983:66). This "self-corrective" capacity inheres in Peirce's apprehension of an independently existing "dynamic" reality against which our own "immediate" semiotic representations may be tested.

Peirce describes his distinction between the "immediate" sign, as such, and the "dynamic" reality to which it might be said to refer as follows:

I have already noted that a Sign has an Object and an Interpretant, the latter being that which the Sign produces in the Quasi-mind that is the Interpreter by determining the latter to a feeling, to an exertion, or to a Sign, which determination is the Interpretant. But it remains to point out that there are usually two Objects.... Namely, we have to distinguish the Immediate Object, which is the Object as the Sign itself represents it, and whose being is thus dependent upon the Representation of it in the Sign, from the Dynamical Object, which is the Reality which by some means contrives to determine the Sign to its Representation. [1931–66:4.536]

The "Immediate Object" of a sign, in other words, constitutes an interpretational representation of an extrasemiotic reality (or, we might say, referent) that, as Peirce puts it, "the Sign *cannot* express, which it can only *indicate* and leave the interpreter to find out by collateral experience" (1931–66:8.314). Now, if Peirce's semiotic stopped at the Immediate Object, then it would indeed be "pragmatic" in Fish's sense of pragmatism, for the object of such a sign is an interpretively constituted entity that has no direct referential correlation. But the constitution of the Immediate Object of the sign is performed with a purpose, for while it cannot, in itself, grant its interpreter a direct acquaintance with an independently existing "Dynamic Object," the sign prompts us to refer it to some "collateral experience," by which, as Shapiro explains, "Peirce means 'previous acquaintance with what the sign denotes'" (1983:36). That is, as Umberto Eco has written, while there is "a difference between the *object of which a sign is a sign* and the *object of a sign*" (i.e., between a Dynamic Object and an Immediate Object), the Dynamic Object nevertheless constitutes, "from an ontological point of view, the concrete object of a possible experience" (1979a:193)—a potential experience to which a sign can guide us. Thus, although a sign "cannot give us a direct acquaintance with objects," it can still "prescribe to us what to do in order to achieve this acquaintance" (Eco 1979a:193).

For example, as Peirce writes, if "you look into a textbook of chemistry for a definition of *lithium*, you may be told that it is that element whose atomic weight is 7 very nearly":

> But if the author has a more logical turn of mind he will tell you that if you search among minerals that are vitreous, translucent, grey or white, very hard, brittle, and insoluble . . . this mineral being titrated with lime . . . and then fused, can be partly dissolved in muriatic acid; and if the solution be evaporated, and the residue extracted with sulphuric acid, it can be converted by ordinary methods into a chloride, which being obtained in the solid state, fused, and electrolyzed . . . will yield a globule of a pinkish silvery metal . . . and the material of *that* is a specimen of lithium. [1931–66:2.330]

As a rule for the production of lithium, our textbook formula constitutes what Peirce calls a "logical interpretant," that is, a "habit of action which has a verbal analogue or correspondent" (Shapiro 1983:52). Such a rule, or habit, as Shapiro puts it, is "future-directed, being potentially repeatable without end" (1983:52). This iterative, habitual, potential, Peirce believed, inheres not only in the signs by which we represent a rule but in the "laws," habits, or regularities demonstrated in the behavior of things themselves, that is, in the "tendencies, propensities, and dispositions to act regularly in certain ways" that Peirce posited as the Thirdness of the Dynamic Object (see Shapiro 1983:37).

Now, Peirce himself was well aware of that "strong tendency of us all to be skeptical about there being any real meaning or law in things" (1931-66:1.344). But he rejected such nominalistic skepticism on behalf of a pragmatic realism that closely resembles the realism of Karl Popper, for in each writer's system the real is defined as a regular power or propensity that we can test through our own subjective conjectures. "Is the present existence of a power," Peirce asks accordingly, "anything in the world but a regularity in future events relating to a certain thing regarded as an element that is to be taken into account of beforehand, in the conception of that thing?" (see Weinsheimer 1983:254 and Peirce 1931-66:8.12). Such a regularity enables us to establish a conjectural rule, or "logical interpretant," that can in its turn be tested against the behavior of a "dynamic" reality. The goal, or tendency, of semiosis, then, is not the production of another sign but the extension of our knowledge in an evolving dialectic between the subjective sign and the objective dynamics, the habitual propensities, of the real. As Joel Weinsheimer has put it: "The real is the final cause of knowledge. It is the power that effects belief.... [It] ultimately regulates thought, controls it, and gives it rules, and if this is so, it is because the real is itself regular. Such is the case not only of thought but of the most inanimate matter. As true thought is conventional, so also is the mere stuff of the world" (1983:254-55).

Such conventions may appear to be metaphysical in a sense that the legisign is not, because they are determined by extrasemiotic determinants. But like a Popperian propensity, a natural "habit" is an empirical, rather than a transcendental, phenomenon. It belongs to the actuality, the hecceity, of concrete things, expressing the Thirdness of their habitual potential. We represent this Thirdness to ourselves in a sign, but the sign ultimately refers to a "habit" in nature itself. Thus, the end of interpretation, its goal and purpose, is an empirical test, a self-correcting of knowledge through objective experimentation. Eco has written that since "there are general principles [in reality], the ultimate meaning (or the final interpretant) of a sign can be conceived as the general rule permitting us to test or produce that habit" (1979a:194). And it is this rule, habit, or regularity, one might say, that constitutes the dynamic referent of the sign, a referent that is not statically totalized but which, as an extrasemiotic propensity that can be tested experimentally, can be located outside the play of signs.

Of course, my brief sketch of the general logic of Peirce's thought cannot do justice to the bewildering complexity of the analyses undertaken in the sometimes chaotic texture of his *Collected Papers*, but it is not my purpose to present a textbook analysis of Peirce's doctrine. Rather, I mean to indicate that even in the face of the post-structural appropriation of Peirce's work, there is a strong current of realism in his speculations all the same. Peirce's realism itself is a part of his essential pragmatism, but his pragmatism, or "pragmaticism," has an objective, or referentialist, strain that the more recent varieties of pragmatic thought lack. For according to Peirce's pragmatic realism the sign never stops at itself: it "grows" as our knowledge, our "collateral experience," grows. The Peircean sign, in other words, is not self-reflexive, does not refer solely to a system of signs. Its referent is never absolute, but it does have a referent, a referent that can be found in the Thirdness of the sign's potential as a rule-giving "logical interpretant" that can produce actual objects. A sign system that can produce its own extrasemiotic referents is something more than a code, more than an archive. Opposed to the self-reflexive implications of a differential semiology, Peirce's semiotic offers a self-testing logic that anticipates Karl Popper's own theory of a science of conjecture and refutation. Neither Peirce nor Popper argues that we can attain absolute knowledge,[3] but each represents an acceptance of a dynamic reality against which we can test our interpretations.

Through Peirce, then, we may find a semiotic equivalent to the Popperian realism upon which I have partly grounded my own proposals for a potentialist realism. The theoretical necessity for such an alternative to Saussurean semiology can be found in the influentially antirealistic tendencies of structuralist thought, for there is no place for referential realism as long as the sign is conceived differentially, as a nonreferential "trace" in an illimitable play of nonreferential traces. The necessity for a theory, of course, does not prove its truth, and I do not claim that a Peircean semiotic can simply rout its opponents. But I do believe that we can compare the one theory with the other with respect to practical problems. For this reason I have chosen to keep what I have called the nuclear referent in the background of my defense of referential realism, for it is through such phenomena that we may test the practical efficacy of a given theory. At this point, then, we might look to see which interpretation of the sign yields the more useful results when seeking to analyze the nuclear referent.

We can do this by recalling Derrida's citation of the problematic opposition between the discontinuous novelty of the nuclear era and the continuity of historical experience and precedent. As Peirceans, we might say that such a binary opposition is not really an opposition at all, for while the weapons that distinguish the nuclear era from any other are indeed novel introductions both to our knowledge and to our history, their introduction was made possible by a continuous process of "collateral experience," by which the signs of the known grew to include a further knowledge of the technical potentiality of a dynamic reality that had hitherto been unknown. Nuclear technology, that is to say, emerged from a long history of experimental trial and error, from a testing of symbolic formulations whose purpose was to discover something about a reality beyond the symbol. The sign of the nuclear is new, but it is also continuous with an evolving history of knowledge, and while it has added knowledge that was not there before, it has not, at least from this perspective, constituted a rupturing of epistemological history.

A Peircean epistemology, we might say, is an epistemology that respects historical process, the developmental nature of human knowledge and scientific change. Such an epistemology, of course, does not in itself solve any of the political issues involved with the problem of the nuclear referent, but it can enable us to approach a nuclear present historically, that is, as a historical situation that we can refer to our collateral experiences in history to help guide and correct our understanding of it and thus reduce the paralyzing uncertainties of the age.

Were we to approach the nuclear referent from a Saussurean perspective, however, such a collateral comparison would not be possible. First of all, we should have to regard the introduction of the nuclear referent into our system of signs as a discontinuous novelty that would constitute a break from any preexisting sign system. Refering not to a continuous history of semiotic and extrasemiotic experience but to a conceptual signified that signifies only within what might be called a "nuclear system" of signs, the nuclear referent could be approached structurally only as a signifier within a code, as an archival figure without extra-archival reference. In this sense, then, we would view the nuclear referent as a kind of rent in the fabric of history, something that would have nothing in common with anything that we have experienced before, and which we would be unable to understand in historical terms. In the face of the nuclear referent, in other words, we would be cut off from the historical experience that might otherwise be used to guide us through the perplexities of this at once novel and yet precedented crisis in human history.

Derrida, in fact, has noted precisely this ahistorical tendency of structuralist thought in his observation that "the respect for structurality" in the work of such structuralists as Lévi-Strauss "compels a neutralization of time and history. For example," Derrida continues, "the appearance of a new structure, of an original system, always comes about . . . by a rupture with its past, its origin, and its cause. One can therefore describe what is peculiar to the structural organization only by not taking into account, in the very moment of this description, its past conditions: by failing to pose the problem of the passage from one structure to another, by putting history into parentheses" (1972:263). Thus, where a Peircean semiotic does take into account the historicity of the self-correcting, self-testing semiotic process by which human knowledge grows, a semiologically based structural epistemology regards the course of scientific change as a series of paradigm-shattering events that divides the history of knowledge into incommensurable epistemological epochs with no ground for the continuity of historical understanding.[4]

But where we might oppose a developmental Peircean historicism to the ahistoricism that Derrida has located within the structuralist project, we cannot equally line up Derrida's post-structural critique on the side of historical continuity. For Derrida's critique of structural ahistoricism is accompanied by a simultaneous critique of the historical concept by which "history is always the unity of a becoming, as tradition of truth or development of science or knowledge oriented toward the appropriation of truth in presence and self-presence" (1972:262). Derrida, that is to say, deconstructs both structuralist ahistoricism and the developmental historicism that we may find in a Peircean semiotic, lingering instead in the interstice between the two positions, analyzing the difference, as differance, that makes the opposition possible in the first place. Here both positions are upset, neither is privileged, and before we can even begin to approach the nuclear referent, we find ourselves already suspended between the poles of structural discontinuity and historical continuity. Rather than restoring history, then, Derrida's deconstruction of structural ahistoricism only defers the historical present . . . indefinitely.

Such a suspension itself requires further analysis. For while differance disrupts rather than privileges the differential principle, its genealogy nevertheless presupposes a certain acceptance of Saussure's differential reduction of material substance. By analyzing the effects of Saussure's isolation of the differential principle, Derrida exposes the logical consequences of this inaugural structuralist gesture. But rather than searching for an alternative, nondifferential model for the sign that would avoid the ahistorical, finally anarchical implications of semiological theory, Derrida instead pursues them further into an analysis of the predifferential, preformal, (non)principle of differance. But this endless pursuit of differences, as we will see in the chapter to follow, has practical and historical consequences of its own. For in the course of Derrida's tracing of the illimitable traces of differences, both history and reality itself are deferred in an endless sequence of suspended decisions that effectively would defer any practical, or material, confrontation with the historical reality of the nuclear referent.

CHAPTER 14

From Difference to Differance: A Derridean Solicitation

"CONSIDER THE HANDLING OF DIFFERENCE," Michel Foucault proposes in the course of a review of Gilles Deleuze's *Différence et répétition*. "It is usually assumed to be a difference *from* or *within* something;" while "behind difference," Foucault continues,

> beyond it—but as its support, its site, its delimitation, and consequently as the source of its mastery—we pose, through the concept, the unity of a group and its breakdown into species in the operation of difference (the organic domination of the Aristotelian concept). Difference is transformed into that which must be specified within a concept, without overstepping its bounds. [1981:181–82]

For Foucault, following Deleuze's lead, such a containment of difference within the generic or material unity of a class or natural kind constitutes a form of epistemological "subjection," a repression, a tyranny. A subjection to what? "To common sense which, turning away from the mad flux and anarchical difference, invariably recognises the identity of things (and this is at all times a general capacity)." Common sense, Foucault continues, "extracts the generality of an object while it simultaneously establishes the universality of the knowing subject through a pact of goodwill" (1981:182). Thus, in opposition to a "scientific" understanding of the classification of individuals according to "real" resemblances, Foucault views the "natural kind" as something of a "fictional kind," a unifying figure determined by an oppressive "pact of goodwill" historically negotiated among those who have been empowered to speak and to classify.

"But what if we gave free rein to ill will?" Foucault asks. "What if thought freed itself from common sense and decided to function only in its extreme singularity? What if it adopted the disreputable bias of the paradox, instead of complacently accepting its citizenship in the *doxa*? What if it conceived of difference differentially, instead of searching out the common elements underlying difference? Then," Foucault concludes, "difference would disappear as a general feature that leads to the generality of the concept, and it would become—a different thought, the thought of difference—a pure event" (1981:181–82).

Thus Foucault endorses a Deleuzean interpretation of the nature of difference, proposing a reading of difference as *pure* difference, as absolute singularity and discontinuity. This interpretation "liberates" difference from those categorical conceptions that "suppress the anarchy of difference, divide differences into zones, delimit their rights, and prescribe their task of specification with respect to individual beings" (1981:186). Calling for the "invention of an acategorical thought" that would enable us to envision "an ontology where being would be expressed in the same fashion for every difference, but could only express differences," Foucault imagines a new kind of ontology, or anti-ontology, in which "being would be expressed in the same fashion for all these differences, and being would no longer be a unity that guides and distributes them, but their repetition as difference" (1981:186–87).

Foucault, of course, writes as a historian, not as an ontologist, and his apparently deconstructive enthusiasm finally has a certain constructive purpose to it. Because in this clearly demarcated opposition between identity and difference a choice has been made, a position taken, as Foucault undertakes his Nietzschean critique of identitarian metaphysics on behalf of a nontraditional but positional "genealogical" historicism that, in direct opposition to the ultimately totalizing historicism of dialectical thinking, "does not pretend to go back in time to restore an unbroken continuity that operates beyond the dispersion of forgotten things" but rather seeks "to follow the complex course of descent . . . [by maintaining] passing events in their proper dispersion" (1981:146). The genealogist, that is to say, searches not for principles of historical continuity and identity but for the discontinuous emergences of "the accidents, the minute deviations—or conversely, the complete reversals—the errors, the false appraisals, and the faulty calculations that gave birth to those things that continue to exist and have value for us." The task of genealogy, in other words, "is to discover that truth or being do not lie at the root of what we know and what we are, but the exteriority of accidents" (1981:146).

Thus genealogy eschews the search for historical causation and continuity to analyze instead the sudden and disruptive emergences into history that erupt from an endless conflict between historical forces. "Emergence," Foucault observes, "is always produced through a particular stage of the play of forces." It "is the entry of forces; it is their eruption, the leap from the wings to center stage, each in its youthful strength" (1981:148–50). A genealogical historicism, for example, traces the origin of moral values not to the universality of the "good" but to the "domination of certain men over others," to class domination and *ressentiment*. Similarly, not "truth" but "class domination generates the idea of liberty; and the forceful appropriation of things necessary to survival and the imposition of a duration not intrinsic to them account for the origin of logic" (1981:150). Each historical emergence, each eruption from the play of force and domination, appears by accident, by chance, with no grounding principle by which we might chart what continues throughout history. What is repeated in history, then, is only its accidental singularity. One might say that for the genealogist there are only differences in history, without positive terms.

Still, while Foucault's genealogical method seeks a radical overturning of traditional etiological, axiological, or dialectical historiography, it is quite recognizable *as* a historiography. Deconstructing continuity, Foucault develops discontinuity and analyzes the concrete political forces, the identifiable conflicts between powers, that drive forward the play of history. Whether or not one accepts Foucault's insistence that the course of history is entirely accidental and discontinuous, one can still find in his thesis a sense that historical differences, the accidental singularities of genealogical emergence, could not emerge without a material conflict between identifiable political forces whose historical provenance can be analyzed by a genealogical, or an "archeological," historian. To put this another way, while the historical referent of the genealogist differs from the totalized referent of "metaphysical history," genealogy does have a referent: viz., the material reality of political conflict and struggle.

But by so locating the motivation for historical movement and change in a differential conflict between opposing forces, Foucault opens his critique of historical identity or presence to a further critique not dissimilar to that which can be directed at Saussure's differential semiology. For as Derrida argues in a reference of his own to Nietzsche and Deleuze: "Force itself is never present; it is only a play of differences and quantities. There would be no force in general without the difference between forces" (1982a:17). In other words, if history is constituted by a differential play between opposing forces (just as, in Saussurean semiology, language is constituted by a play of differences), then, Derrida believes, there must be "something" prior to history to "produce" the differential play of force. This principle, Derrida writes in "Force and Signification," "cannot be erased in history, for it is not *in* history. It too," Derrida continues, "in an unexpected sense, is an original structure. *Difference*," that is to say, "does not simply belong either to history or to structure. If we must say, along with Schelling, that 'all is but Dionysus,' we must know ... that, like pure force, Dionysus is worked by difference" (1978:28–29).

To say, then, "that force is the origin of phenomena is to say nothing," Derrida writes. "By its very articulation force becomes a phenomenon" (1978:26–27). For Derrida the very *articulation* of force, of the play of historical dominations, implies a pre-phenomenal "principle" to "work" such articulations, a differance prior to all articulating differences and thus prior to history itself, deferring it through an endless analytical suspension of forces, because each force, held in the tension of its articulating opposition to its other, would bear a trace of that other, thus suspending the propriety of its own identity indefinitely. Foucault's privileging of genealogical difference accordingly leads to a historical suspension parallel to the linguistic suspension that is the logical consequence of Saussure's privileging of semiological difference. Once difference has been posited as the "origin" of a structure, there can be no closure of the structure, no limit to its play, and thus, there can be no structure, no properly identifiable historical conflict at all, as the oppositional forces of genealogical study become metaphysical rather than historical phenomena in a Derridean analysis.

This may lead us to ask: Is there any place for history, for the referential reality of concrete historical and political experience, in a thoroughly deconstructive criticism? What sort of historicity, that is to say, does Derrida endorse? There are no easy answers to such a question, but we may find a certain clue to the puzzle of Derrida's historicity in his observation in the seminal essay "Différance" that if "the word 'history' did not in and of itself convey the motif of a final repression of difference, one could say that only differences can be 'historical' from the outset and in each of their aspects" (1982a:11). Given, for example, Saussure's raising of semiological difference over intentional referentiality in linguistic study, the histories of particular language systems would indeed seem to be a history of differences. That is, as Derrida writes, "since language, which Saussure says is a classification, has not fallen from the sky, its differences have been produced, are produced effects" (1982a:11). But lest we jump to the conclusion that such a production of differences is "historical" in the sense that a Peircean "legislation" of semiotic tokens and types would be historical, Derrida adds that these effects of difference "do not find their cause in a subject or substance, in a thing in general, a being that is somewhere present, thereby eluding the play of *différance*" (1982a:11). Differences, in other words, are not subjectively or substantially motivated. So what does "cause" the historical effects of difference for Derrida? Or, as Derrida himself asks: "What differs? Who differs? What is *différance*?" (1982a:14).

It is the very form of such questions, of course, that differance itself questions, for "if we accepted the form of the question," Derrida writes, ". . . we would have to conclude that *différance* has been derived, has happened, is to be mastered and governed on the point of a present being, which itself could be some thing, a form, a state, a power in the world to which all kinds of names might be given, a *what*, or a present being as a *subject, a who*" (1982a:15). Differance, that is to say, "puts into question the name of the name" itself (1982a:27), disrupting the presence/absence structure of the "classical," or "metaphysical," concept of representation, according to which the name "is usually said to be put in place of the thing itself, the present thing, the 'thing' here standing equally for meaning or referent":

> The sign represents the present in its absence. It takes the place of the present. When we cannot grasp or show the thing, state the present, the being-present, when the present cannot be presented, we signify, we go through the detour of the sign. We take or give signs. We signal. The sign, in this sense, is deferred presence. [1982a:9]

According, then, "to this classical semiology, the substitution of the sign for the thing itself is both *secondary* and *provisional*: secondary due to an original and lost presence from which the sign thus derives; provisional as concerns this final and missing presence toward which the sign in this sense is a movement of mediation" (1982a:9). The trouble with this classical picture, Derrida believes, is that it suppresses the *differences* in language, subordinating them to the self-present totality of the referent. But this is to ignore Saussure, Derrida continues, who "first of all is the thinker who put the *arbitrary character of the sign* and the *differential character* of the sign at the very foundation of semiology, particularly linguistics" (1982a:10). The presence of the referent, that is to say, has suppressed semiological difference or absence, has marginalized it in linguistic discourse. So the first deconstructive step is to reverse this suppression, an inversion of linguistic priorities that Saussure himself performed in his raising of the differentially constituted conceptual "signified" over the substantial materiality of the referent in his semiological analyses. Derrida cites Saussure to this effect at some length, quoting from Saussure's *Cours de linguistique générale*:

"The conceptual side of value is made up solely of relations and differences with respect to the other terms of language, and the same can be said of its material side. . . . Everything that has been said up to this point boils down to this: in language there are only differences. Even more important: a difference generally implies positive terms between which the difference is set up; but in language there are only differences *without positive terms*. Whether we take the signified or the signifier, language has neither ideas nor sounds that existed before the linguistic system, but only conceptual and phonic differences that have issued from the system. The idea or phonic substance that a sign contains is of less importance than the other signs that surround it." [quoted in Derrida 1982a:10–11]

"The first consequence to be drawn from this," Derrida continues, "is that the signified concept is never present in and of itself, in a sufficient presence that would refer only to itself":

Essentially and lawfully, every concept is inscribed in a chain or in a system within which it refers to the other, to other concepts, by means of the systematic play of differences. Such a play, *diffé-*

rance, is thus no longer simply a concept, but rather the possibility of conceptuality, of a conceptual process and system in general." [1982a:11]

Thus, what "is written as *différance* . . . will be the playing movement that 'produces'—by means of something that is not simply an activity—these differences, these effects of difference" (1982a:11). But such a difference, the play of differance, is not an activity that precedes difference "in a simple and unmodified—in-different—present." Differance, rather, "is the non-full, non-simple, structured and differentiating origin of differences" (1982a:11). As such, "*différance is not*, does not exist, is not a present-being (*on*) in any form . . . and consequently it has neither existence nor essence. It derives from no category of being, whether present or absent" (1982a:6).

Constantly differing from and deferring itself in the silent economy of the letter *a*, differance not only names no presence of its own (conceptual or otherwise) but defers all naming, all reference, all presence. It is not that differance *forbids* referentiality, and Derrida warns us against too simple a denial of referential force. But it does undermine the referential ground for linguistic functioning, setting the possible nonreferentiality of discourse against its potential referentiality in an undecidable opposition.

For example, in "Signature Event Context," Derrida observes that if, in answer to some interlocuter, "I say, while looking out the window, 'The sky is blue,' the statement will be intelligible . . . even if the interlocuter does not see the sky; even if I do not see it myself, if I see it poorly, if I am mistaken, or if I wish to trick my interlocuter. Not that it is always thus," Derrida adds, "but the structure of possibility of this statement includes the capability of being formed and as functioning either as an empty reference, or cut off from its referent. Without this possibility," Derrida concludes, "which is also the general, generalizable, and generalizing iteration of every mark, there would be no statements" (1982b:318–19).

Now, by saying "not that it is always thus," Derrida does allow for the possibility of referential success, but in his insistence that it is the possibility of "functioning as an empty reference" that constitutes the "generalizing iteration of every mark," he effectively inverts the reference/nonreference opposition in favor of nonreferentiality. *Not that it is always thus*, and Derrida makes no final choice between the two. But in not doing so, he undermines the possibility for seeing things the other way around: that it is the potential for referential success that constitutes the primary possibility for linguistic iteration, and that without this possibility we could not begin to differentiate between referential and nonreferential statements.

And this is precisely the point of the logic of differance, for it forbids us from finally distinguishing between binary opposites. The one pole has always already oscillated into the other. The possibility of referentiality shades into the possibility of nonreferentiality, and vice versa—just as De Manian rhetoric shades into grammar and back again.

The same would be true for being and not-being, and so Derrida must insist that differance itself names no Being and no beingness, no present concept to which philosophy can refer. Rather, it "is the domination of beings that *différance* everywhere comes to solicit," Derrida writes, "in the sense that *sollicitare* in old Latin, means to shake as a whole, to make tremble in entirety. Therefore," he continues:

it is the determination of Being as presence or as beingness that is interrogated by the thought of *différance*.... First consequence: *différance* is not. It is not a present being, however excellent, unique, principal, or transcendent. It governs nothing, reigns over nothing, and nowhere exercises any authority. It is not announced by any capital letter. Not only is there no kingdom of *différance*, but *différance* instigates the subversion of every kingdom. [1982a:21–22]

Thus, the differing/deferring movement of differance can indicate only the pure play of its own reservation, its own deferral of the "truth" of its presence. Neither present nor absent, differance disturbs the opposition between presence and absence. Differance "exceeds the alternative of presence and absence," Derrida insists, in a movement motivated not by the dynamic propensities of a concretely referential "living present" but by an indefinite "structure of delay" that "in effect forbids that one make of temporalization (temporization) a simple dialectical complication of the living present as an originary and unceasing synthesis—a synthesis constantly directed back on itself and gathering—of retentional traces and protentional openings" (1982a:20–21).

It is in just this respect that we may apprehend the strategy at work in Derrida's lecture "No Apocalypse, Not Now" (1984)—the paradoxical "sermon" upon which this book has been predicated. Disrupting the presence/absence model for historical understanding that the tradition of metaphysical history offers, Derrida deconstructs the presence of a nuclear reality that simultaneously bears the trace of its own absence, its own unactuated future, in the form of a weapons race that has been predicated upon that absence. Neither the concrete actuality of the living present nor its "retentional" and "protentional" references to its own actualized past and potentialized future can be unproblematically apprehended from such a perspective. In the place of a historicity of active subjects, of a "living present" in which, as Marx has said in a famous phrase, "men make their own history" (crucially adding, however, that they make it "not just as they please" but only "under circumstances directly encountered, given and transmitted from the past" [1968:97]), Derrida substitutes the self-erasing movement of the trace, in which "the present becomes the sign of the sign, the trace of the trace" (1982a:24). And it is according to such a reading of the historical present that one might indeed say that "only differences can be 'historical' from the outset and in each of their aspects" (Derrida 1982a:11).

Such a deconstruction of the present, of the dynamic propensities and historical actuations of lived experience, has the practical effect of paralyzing decision in the face of a historical present such as that to which the nuclear referent can be said to refer. Within the historicity of differance, that is to say, there can be no realistic ground for the judgment of conflicting policies, no means by which we might distinguish between competing beliefs. Political judgment and belief, according to such a reading of history, becomes a text, a tissue of "errors" and mis-constructions, because there can be no extratextual reality that might ever be finally constructed. History in such a view is not only without positive terms but without negative terms as well, for Derrida offers no principle by which discrete situations might be formally distinguished from the continuum of time.

Because this deconstruction of the historical present has been made possible partly by Saussure's raising of the principle of linguistic difference to philosophical prominence, I have presented in a strategic manner an alternative interpretation of the sign to show that semiotic study need not necessarily lead to a deconstruction of presence but can instead lead to an apprehension of a dynamic historicity grounded in the dynamic presence of "lived experience." Such a historicity would refer us not to a play of differences but to a dynamic synthesis of situational actualities that bear within themselves a calculable potential for future development. Of course, to oppose a Peircean semiotic realism to structural and post-structural antirealism cannot be decisive in itself, but it does offer an alternative perspective for a criticism intent upon practical action and decision in the nuclear age. This is not to say that differance cannot inspire a political program of its own, for it cannot be denied that its kingdom-shaking logic has already proved attractive to radical political theorists. Indeed, the greatest threat inscribed within the nuclear referent comes from a superpower conflict between competing "kingdoms" intent upon continued arms production and development, and this lends a certain force to the argument that criticism might find a model for resistance to this threat in differance. By actively deconstructing the discourse of each player in the nuclear game, criticism might demonstrate how, within the structure of their "speed race," both "East" and "West" are at once different and the same. Such a project, such a perpetual deconstruction of authority, is often regarded as a revolutionary program, and in other political contexts it may well be. But in the context of the nuclear referent, the differing/deferring logic of differance can be seen to support what is indeed the current status quo, the policy of nuclear deterrence that has governed East-West strategy since the 1950s. For while differance would deter deterrence itself, through its perpetual undermining of every kingdom, of every presence, truth, or being, it would also undermine any contrary evaluation of current policy, suspending all judgment in an irreducible undecidability between competing beliefs—which would effectively leave matters precisely as they now stand. With no theoretical or axiological grounding of his or her own, the prospective deconstructive nuclear critic cannot, at least in principle, establish any positive political alternatives. All he or she can do is expose the metaphysical limitations of every opinion offered in the nuclear debate.

Derrida himself signals such a conclusion in "No Apocalypse, Not Now," observing that, in the face of the "absolute pharmakon" of the nuclear referent, there is no "space for a 'nuclear criticism' strictly speaking" (1984:24), because there is no ground for any sort of "scientific" knowledge in the nuclear age. Without knowledge (*épistémè*) there is only belief (doxa), with no way of distinguishing between beliefs. It is for this reason that a criticism of political realities might look for an alternative to the deconstruction of the living present. For if we regard the undeconstructed immediacy of lived experience as a dynamic field in which active human agents legislate and control their own signs by testing them against the extrasemiotic reality of the "dynamic objects" to which the sign can be said to ultimately refer, then we can approach the historical actualities of the present with a certain ability to evaluate competing beliefs in the nuclear debate. To put this another way, there *would* be room for a nuclear criticism, strictly speaking.

But to appeal to the immediacy of lived experience as the basis of human history requires what might be called an ontological, as well as a semiological, analysis, because the disruption of the living present that differance effects proceeds as much from Martin Heidegger's own de-struction of historical presence (in a materialist sense) as it does from an analysis of the sign. Derrida observes that if "it is the determination of Being as presence or as beingness that is interrogated by the thought of *différance*," such "a question could not emerge and be understood unless the difference between Being and beings were somewhere to be broached" (1982a:21). In other words, just as Derrida has found within the terms of Saussure's semiology the means by which differance might be projected from out of the play of linguistic differences, so too does he find differance inscribed within the "ontico-ontological difference" that Heidegger first began to think for Western philosophy. Thus Heidegger's project also bears a crucial relation to Derrida's, which means that a defense of historical realism, of the material reality and ground of lived experience, in the face of Derrida's deconstructions would do well to confront in its own right Heidegger's de-structive reading of material history. This should be done to see both the consequences that this reading has had for historical understanding and what alternative realistic or materialist interpretations of the living present might be offered. This will be the task of part 5.

PART 5

LIVED EXPERIENCE

CHAPTER 15

Martin Heidegger and Ontological Difference in the Atomic Age

"NOT THROUGH INTROSPECTION but only through history do we come to know ourselves," Wilhelm Dilthey, Martin Heidegger's great predecessor in historical hermeneutics, wrote in the waning years of the nineteenth century (quoted in Palmer 1980:101). Self-knowledge, that is to say, comes to us not through a pure, or idealistic, subjectivity but through the temporal structure of "lived experience" (*Erlebnis*). This experience, as Richard Palmer explains, "is not a static matter," but "on the contrary . . . tends to reach out and encompass both recollection of the past and anticipation of the future in the total context of 'meaning' ":

> Meaning cannot be imagined except in terms of what the future is expected to be, nor can it free itself from dependence upon the materials which the past supplies. The past and the future, then, form a structural unity with the presentness of all experience, and this temporal context is the inescapable horizon within which any perception in the present is interpreted. [1980:109–10]

For example, "Suppose one tries in a reflexive act consciously to grasp the course or progression of one's life" (1980:110); that is, as Dilthey asks:

> What happens when "experience" (*das Erlebnis*) becomes the object of my reflection? I lie awake at night . . . worrying over the possibility of completing in old age the work I have begun; I think over what to do. There is in this "experience" a structural set of relationships: an objective grasping of the situation forms the basis of it, and on this basis a stance . . . as concern-towards and pain-over-the-objectively-grasped fact, along with a striving to go *beyond* the fact. And all this is there-for-me in this its structural context. [1980:110]

In other words, our apprehension of present lived experience constitutes the merging, or synthesis, of three horizons in Dilthey's analysis of lived experience. First, we have our grasp of the present facts of the moment itself, our worry, say, over what we must do next. But this present fact includes both the horizon of what we *have accomplished* to date and the horizon of what we *might yet* accomplish. What we might accomplish in the future, then, is contained in the present in the structure of our own anticipations and expectations. These expectations, however, are not simply abstractions, for in conceiving them we consult the concrete facts of our present situation (how much time we have left, the resources available to us, our own capabilities, and so on), and on such a basis we project ourselves into the future through an objective calculation of what is possible or probable.

Dilthey's hermeneutical historicism, his thesis that we must grasp the living experience of the present in terms of both the past and the future, accordingly can be seen as a practical model for the predicament of a nuclear critic, for such a critic too may be said to confront the objective facts of a present that has been produced by a certain history (the invention of the Bomb, the Cold War rivalry between the superpowers) and that forbodes a certain future. The nuclear critic may also ask: "What must I do to go beyond the present facts?" But in so asking, the critic can ignore neither the palpable reality of those facts nor the concrete history that produced them. The critic cannot wish the Bomb away, cannot erase more than a quarter century of superpower rivalry. Still, he or she may feel that the situation, as it is now constituted, is dangerous. The computerization of nuclear deterrence, he or she may believe, only increases the propensities for an accidental holocaust. Postcolonial international instability, coupled with unchecked nuclear proliferation, seems to magnify the prospects for a nuclear war that might be inaugurated neither in the Kremlin nor in the Pentagon, but almost anywhere. The rhetoric of ideological, rather than simply strategic, confrontation raises the specter of a war fought merely for vaguely worded and undeveloped platitudes. All this, and much more, might be said to constitute the material reality, the facts, of the living present of the nuclear age—a reality that at once synthetically combines its present actualization of past potentialities and its own potentiality for further actuation.

Or so we might say according to a pre-Heideggerian interpretation of the historical nature of *Erlebnis*, for in Martin Heidegger's redirectioning of the philosophy of lived experience, the essential nature of historical being is lifted outside the facts of material experience and carried across into an *ontological* "World" that is higher than and prior to the *ontic* "world" of ordinary life.[1] For, as Richard Palmer writes, "just as Dilthey saw hermeneutics in the horizon of his own project of finding an historically oriented theory of method for the *Geisteswissenschaften*, so Heidegger used the word 'hermeneutics' in the context of his larger quest for a more 'fundamental' ontology. It could be said," Palmer continues, "that Heidegger defended the claims of *Leben* against *Geist* in the tradition of those two great life philosophers, Nietzsche and Dilthey, but in a different mode and on a different level" (Palmer 1980:124). For while Heidegger, in *Being and Time*, quotes "with approval Dilthey's aim of understanding life from out of life itself" (Palmer 1980:124), what Heidegger means by the essence of "life" is not precisely the ontic materiality of the experienced present. Rather, for Heidegger we live in a "World" that "does not mean our environment, objectively considered, the universe as it appears to a scientific gaze" (Palmer 1980:132). "World cannot be described by trying to enumerate the entities within it," Palmer explains, because "in this process [W]orld itself would be passed over, for [W]orld is just what is presupposed in every act of knowing an entity. Every entity in the world is grasped as an entity *in terms of* [W]orld, which is always already there" (Palmer 1980:132).

Heidegger, then, does not reject lived experience in the

present, but he feels that there is an ontologically prior "World" from which ontically present beings have "fallen," and his concern is with this *ontological* "World," not with the *ontic* "world." Thus Heidegger, in Palmer's words, "does not negate Dilthey's experience-oriented view so much as place it in an ontological context" (1980:132). But what are the consequences for historical understanding of this ontologizing of lived experience, and whence has it been derived?

In *Being and Time* (1962), Heidegger traces the phenomenological history of human being-in-the-world (*Dasein*) as it moves from "facticity" (the finite historical situatedness of ontological *Geworfenheit*: "thrownness" into Being) to "existence" (*Dasein* as it projects itself into the future and toward its own Being) to "forfeiture" (*Dasein* as it distracts itself from the quest for Being in its social involvement with *Das Man*: the daily reality of the crowd). But while Heidegger regards human being-in-the-world (*Dasein*) as bearing a "power" or potentiality of its own, the potential to which Heidegger appeals is a finally transcendent one, a "potentiality-for-Being" that is ontologically prior to and higher than the contingent powers of material beings that I have argued for in these pages as a grounding for a potentialist realism. For as Heidegger writes in *Being and Time*:

> The Being-possible which Dasein is existentially in every case, is to be sharply distinguished both from empty logical possibility and from the contingency of something present-at-hand, so far as with the present-at-hand this or that can 'come to pass.' As a modal category of presence-at-hand, possibility signifies what is *not yet* actual and what is *not at any time* necessary. It characterizes the *merely possible*. Ontologically it is on a lower level than actuality and necessity. On the other hand, possibility as an *existentiale* is the most primordial and ultimate positive way in which Dasein is characterized ontologically. As with existentiality in general, we can, in the first instance, only prepare for the problem of possibility. The phenomenal basis for seeing it at all is provided by the understanding as a disclosive potentiality-for-Being. [1962:183]

In other words, while our apprehension of the beings of the everyday world, of what is "present-at-hand," is ontically limited by the contingency of all that is not yet actual in day-to-day life, our *existential* understanding of our own potentiality-for-Being is neither contingent nor merely "possible." Rather, our potential-for-Being is always already *there*, but only insofar as *Dasein* projects itself toward its ontological ground in Being (*Sein*). Such a projection is not at all synonymous with the conjectural speculations of scientific experimentation that plot the empirical probabilities for this or that actualization of this or that propensity, because ontological projection is far more determined, is always already *necessary* insofar as it has already begun. We do not plan our Being in the world through our worldly projects: rather, Being, in a sense, plans *us*. As Heidegger puts it:

Projecting has nothing to do with comporting oneself towards a plan that has been thought out, and in accordance with which Dasein arranges its Being. On the contrary, any Dasein has, as Dasein, already projected itself; and as long as it is, it is projecting. As long as it is, Dasein always has understood itself and always will understand itself in terms of possibilities. Furthermore, the character of understanding as projection is such that the understanding does not grasp thematically that upon which it projects—that is to say, possibilities. Grasping it in such a manner would take away from what is projected in its very character as a possibility, and would reduce it to the given contents which we have in mind. [1962:185]

Thus, ontological projection is somehow prior to ontic projection (just as, incidentally, Derridean differance is somehow prior to ontic differences.) For Heidegger, ontic projection, the conjectural plotting of situational probabilities through the analysis of objective propensities, is mere logic; ontological projection, on the other hand, is always already *determined* in its own possibility and potential-for-Being. To put this another way, Heidegger's ontologizing of lived experience supersedes all "scientific" analysis. From a Heideggerian perspective, science can determine the propensities only for the becoming of *this* world, the world of *Das Man*, of the social horde; in contrast, ontological understanding can lay claim to a "higher" potential or power, a potential-for-Being that is always already determined by Being itself. There is a difference, Heidegger believes, between the contingent potencies of beings and the necessary power of Being, a difference that he inscribes within the "ontico-ontological difference."

But as Joan Stambaugh observes in her introduction to *The End of Philosophy*, Heidegger's distinction between Being and beings, his drawing of the "ontico-ontological difference" as such, is "named but not carried out in *Being and Time*" because it had not yet been fully thought through within the history of Western metaphysics (1973:ix). For in its very inauguration, metaphysical thought necessarily had to forget this difference, losing sight of primordial ontological Being in its exclusive attention to the actual substance (as *ousia*) of ontic beings. To return to Being, Heidegger believed, philosophy had first to remember, to think through, the "ontico-ontological difference" by de-structing itself: that is, by critically overturning but at the same time preserving the "forgotten" insights of its own history. As a properly metaphysical discourse, however, *Being and Time* could not accomplish this de-struction. A new, postmetaphysical project would have to be undertaken.

Thus, after writing *Being and Time*, Heidegger came to the conclusion that philosophy had forgotten the difference between the Being of things and the beings that metaphysics had investigated. To return to the Being that metaphysical analysis had concealed, Heidegger accordingly attempted to think for the first time the *difference* between the Being of things and things themselves, beginning his long, post-*Being and Time* lifework to think the "ontico-ontological difference" as it had never been thought before in Western metaphysics, so that the very "difference" might be de-structed through the de-struction of metaphysics. We shall follow this de-struction through a critical review of Heidegger's "Metaphysics as History of Being" and his *Introduction to Metaphysics*.

"Metaphysics has distinguished for ages between *what* beings are and *that* beings are," Heidegger wrote in his

"Metaphysics as History of Being." "The history of Being as metaphysics begins with this distinction and its preparation" (1973:2). From its very first emergence into *metaphysical* discourse, "Being" has thus been divided at its core into *essentia* (whatness) and *existentia* (thatness), according to Heidegger's reading of Platonic and Aristotelian metaphysics. But while this difference between "essence" and "existence" constitutes a distraction inaugurated in the days of Plato and Aristotle from the "true" path of Being that had been plotted by the pre-Socratics, it nevertheless appears to have been a *necessary* distraction, because the *"division into whatness and thatness does not just contain a doctrine of metaphysical thinking. It points to an event in the history of Being"* (1973:4). Being, in other words, is that which enters into metaphysics only at a certain point in its own extrametaphysical history but which can never be spoken from within metaphysical discourse. Instead, it necessarily assumes its division into whatness and thatness, thus concealing itself at the very moment that it has been revealed to metaphysical speculation. For:

> if it is true that metaphysics accounts for its essence through this difference, obscure in origin, of the what and the that, and grounds its essence thereupon, it can never of itself come to any knowledge of this distinction. It would have to be previously and as such approached by Being which has entered this distinction. But Being refuses this approach, and thus alone makes possible the essential beginning of metaphysics—in the manner of the preparation and development of this distinction. The origin of the distinction of *essentia* and *existentia*, for more so the origin of Being thus divided, remains concealed, expressed in the Greek manner: forgotten. [1973:3]

But while this distinction between essence and existence may conceal Being from us, it can also help us to disturb that concealment. "Being (*einai*) announces itself in a difference," Heidegger writes, but our very recognition of this difference causes us to ask just how Being came to be taken "apart in this distinction?" That is, "What essence of Being reveals itself in this distinction as in the openness of that essence?" (1973:4), Heidegger asks. To answer such questions, Heidegger traces the history of Being as it appears in Greek and Roman philosophy. In so de-structing this history, he means to achieve both the de-struction of metaphysics proper and an elusive return to the pre-Socratic doctrine from which metaphysics has "fallen."

"In the beginning of its history, Being opens itself out as emerging (*physis*) and unconcealment (*aletheia*)," Heidegger writes, thus reproducing the pre-Socratic understanding of Being. But this understanding did not last in Greek philosophy, for "from there . . . [Being] reaches the formulation of presence and permanence in the sense of enduring (*ousia*). Metaphysics proper begins with this" (1973:4). Metaphysics, that is to say, begins at the moment that Being, once conceived in the union (*hen*) of *physis* and *aletheia*, is divided in the doctrine of *ousia*. For Being, taken as *ousia*, comes to be limited to its outward appearance, to its ontic presence in the *tode ti* of substance, to "the this and the that *in each case*" (1973:6). In other words, the eventual result of Aristotle's metaphysical analysis of *ousia* as the *thisness* or *thatness* of particular beings (e.g., *this* house, *that* man), Heidegger believes, was a forgetting of the essence of a being ("what" something is), an overshadowing of essence by existence ("that" something is). As Heidegger puts it:

> Since Aristotle thinks *ousia* (presence) in the primary sense as *energeia* and since this presence means nothing other than what in a changed interpretation is later called *actualitas*, "actuality" and "existence" and "reality," the Aristotelian treatment of the distinction reveals a priority of the later so-called *existentia* over the *essentia*. What Plato thought as the true, and for him sole, beingness (*ousia*) of beings, presence in the manner of *idea* (*eidos*), now moves to the secondary rank within Being. [1973:8]

Aristotle's metaphysics of *ousia*, then, marks a decisive moment in the history of Western philosophy, for it was on the basis of Aristotle that Roman philosophy translated substantial *energeia* (thatness) as *actualitas*, "and this," Heidegger remarks, "becomes actuality" (1973:11). This transformation of *ousia* to *actualitas*, for Heidegger, was profound, constituting not only a shift in the history of philosophy but an entire redirecting of Western history itself:

> When counted in epochs, the determination of Being as *actualitas* thus extends throughout the whole of Western history from the Romans up until the most recent of modern times. Because the essential determination of Being as *actualitas* underlies all history in advance, that is, at the same time the structure of relationships of a certain type of humanity to beings as a whole, all Western history since is in a manifold sense Roman, and never Greek. . . . Ever since the transformation of *energeia* to *actualitas* (reality), the real is truly what is in being and thus decisive for everything possible and necessary. [1973:13]

But with the lifting of existence (thatness) over essence (whatness as *idea*), the latter, too, undergoes a series of transformations, Heidegger observes. In Plato, where *eidos* and "Being" are coincident, "*Idea* as whatness has the character of *aitia*, cause. Origination from its whatness dominates in every coming-to-be of beings. Whatness," Heidegger continues, "is the matter of everything, that is, its cause. Accordingly, Being is in itself causal" (1973:13). But when philosophy limited the analysis of Being to an analysis of "real existence" (*actualitas*), this causal identity was simultaneously shifted from essence to existence, leaving essence with very little to stand on. For if, as Heidegger observes, "*actualitas* . . . is *causalitas*," what need have we for the concept of "essence" at all?

Thus, Plato's *Idea*, as the essence of Being, came to be reduced to the status of a mere "idea:" the mental content of "representational thought" (1973:11). And so, Heidegger continues, representational *thinking* came to be distinguished from *Being*, sundering an original unity that the pre-Socratic philosophers once conceived in its primal conjunction of *noein* and *einai* (roughly "apprehension" and "being"). In the wake of this disjunction, Heidegger believes, the science of logic was born, and with it an entire history of metaphysical thinking for which knowledge would always consist of the accuracy of a thinking subject's rational *representations* of the ontic world, and not in the immediate grasp of ontological Being itself. To escape this history, this "philosophy of mirrors" (in Richard Rorty's phrase), we must think our way back to the moment when thinking and Being were first sundered, Heidegger declares in *An Introduction to Metaphysics*, because that sundering itself "springs from an initial union between thinking and being" (1968:119).

What, then, for Heidegger, were the terms for this "initial union between being and thinking?" Heidegger explores this problem in *An Introduction to Metaphysics* by reconsidering the primal meaning of the *logos*, which, having fallen from its original meaning, has come to signify "language" or "reason." "We must free ourselves from the notion that originally and fundamentally *logos* and *legein* signified thought, understanding, and reason," Heidegger declares, for "as long as we cling to this opinion and even go so far as to interpret *logos* in the light of logic as it later developed, our attempt to rediscover the beginning of Greek philosophy can lead to nothing but absurdities" (1968:123). So, what, Heidegger asks, "do *logos* and *legein* mean if not thought and to think?"

Logos means the word, discourse, and *legein* means to speak, as in dia-logue, mono-logue. But originally *logos* did not mean speech, discourse. Its fundamental meaning stands in no direct relation to language. *Lego, legein*, Latin *legere*, is the same as the German word "lesen"—to gather, collect, read. [1968:124]

Originally, then, *logos* signified not "language" in the sense of rational logic or discourse but rather the ingathering power by which a presubjective being-human (*Dasein*) enables the emerging *physis* of a particular "essent" (or "being") to come to stand in its own presence. Without the *logos*, Heidegger believes, without the poetic apprehension in and through which *Dasein* constitutes its world, nothing can come to be, nothing can stand gathered together in "authentic" being. Thus, Heidegger concludes that, in the light of the Heraclitean doctrine that "everything becomes essent in accordance with ... [the] logos," the following three things can be said about the primal meaning of *logos*:

> 1) permanence and endurance are characteristic of the *logos*; 2) it is togetherness in the essent, the togetherness of all essents, that which gathers; 3) everything that happens, i.e., that comes into being, stands there in accordance with this permanent togetherness; this is the dominant power. [1968:127–28]

But what is this "dominant power?" Does it express the power or potentiality of *dunamis*, of a potentiality visible to the rational gaze of science? Quite obviously not, for the power to which Heidegger refers is an ontologically higher power than that expressed in the material potentiality of ontic *dunamis*, an "uncanny," "overpowering" ontological violence fundamentally related to the violence of that "authentic" act of human apprehension by and through which the "essent" comes to stand in its being (see Heidegger's complex interpretation of the crucial first chorus from Sophocles's *Antigone* [Heidegger 1968:146ff.]). It is this power, this *deinon*, not *dunamis*, to which Heidegger refers, a power that ultimately links the *logos* of "authentic" understanding to the *physis* of emergent being. And so, Heidegger writes, if "*logos* is the steady gathering, the intrinsic togetherness of the essent, i.e., being," then "*kata ton logon* means the same as *kata physin. Physis* and *logos* are the same" (1968:130–31).

Thus, "thinking," or "understanding," and Being, Heidegger believes, are fundamentally one, linked in the ontological dialectic of the *logos*, of the power in and through which *Dasein* constitutes not only its own being but that of the "essent" as a whole. But this power is not something that human beings create. It is not a tool, an instrument of thought. Rather, it is a power as strange and uncanny as are the forces of nature themselves, the power in which we ultimately dwell as in our own pre-rational essence. Parmenides's well-known maxim that "Thinking [*noein*] and being [*einai*] are the same" (*to gar auto noein estin te kai einai*) accordingly requires a retranslation (see 1968:145). What Parmenides is really saying, Heidegger argues, is that "there is a reciprocal bond between apprehension and being." That is, as Heidegger puts it, "*noein* means vernehmen,'to apprehend,' not 'thought.' To apprehend means to accept, to let something (namely that which shows itself, which appears) come to one" (1968:137–38). Thus, *einai* should be read as *physis*: that which stands and appears. "Where this happens, i.e., where being prevails, apprehension prevails and happens with it; the two belong together. Apprehension is the receptive bringing-to-stand of the intrinsically permanent that manifests itself" (1968:139). Thus, it is apprehension that enables Being to emerge, and so, before "falling" out of Being into the world of ontic representation, before being "distracted" by the snares of scientific thought, *Dasein* had a holy place in the scheme of Being, a shepherding role by which Being might emerge into unconcealment.

Thus contrasting representational thought to ontological reception, Heidegger rethinks the nature of understanding as a unity of apprehension and being. Thought, in this sense, does not substitute a simulacrum or linguistic sign for what it apprehends but comes into ontological unity with what it, in fact, brings to unconcealment. Understanding, in other words, does not bring a "subject" to representational knowledge of an "object," for "authentic" understanding is ontologically prior to this epistemological division. Thinking, apprehension, understanding, Heidegger believes, originally proceed not from the subjective consciousness of the knower but from his or her presubjective immersion in the *logos*; for to be human is to understand, to be receptive to the appearing-unconcealing of *physis*, of the truth (*aletheia*) of Being. There is a unity of being and understanding for Heidegger, then, not a representational gap between a "subject" and an "object," a unity that must be understood in Parmenides's sense of the *hen*; that is, as a unity that "is never empty indifference . . . not sameness in the sense of mere equivalence. Unity is the belonging-together of antagonisms. This is original oneness" (1968:138)—a oneness from which we have "fallen," "distracted" from the way of Being by a "metaphysical" infatuation with technological actuality. What has sundered the "original oneness" of thinking and being into a metaphysical opposition between a representing subject and a represented object, then, has been the historical distraction by which we have turned away from the quest for Being toward the lesser quest for scientific knowledge, a knowledge of beings rather than of their ontological ground. We have forgotten not only the quest but the very fact that we ever forgot it. And it is this forgetting that Heidegger seeks to recover through his de-structive reading of the history of Western metaphysics.

Heidegger begins this recovery by analyzing what he calls the "end" of Greek philosophy, the Platonic forgetting of pre-Socratic Being that began with the inauguration of Western metaphysics as such. "What was the relation between *physis* and *logos* . . . in Plato and Aristotle?" Heidegger asks (1968:180). Clearly a disjunctive one, for with Plato's identification of Being with *eidos*, the Idea that appears only to the mind's eye, rather than with *physis*, philosophy paved the way for the representational division between "being" (as appearing actuality) and "knowing" (or subjective ideality) that has plagued it ever since. For Heidegger, then, the inauguration of the "ontico-ontological difference" can be found in Plato's identification of Being with the Idea. As a result of this identification, whatness, the ontological *idea*, became "that which is most beingful in an essent," while the appearing ontic essent becomes almost nothing at all. As Heidegger puts it:

Being as *idea* is exalted, it becomes true being, while being itself, previously dominant [as *physis*, what appears], is degraded to what Plato calls *me on*, what really should not be and really *is* not, because in the realization it always deforms the idea, the pure appearance, by incorporating it in matter. The *idea* now becomes a *paradeigma*, a model. At the same time, the idea necessarily becomes an ideal. The copy actually "is" not; it merely partakes of being, it is a *methexis*. The *chorismos*, the cleft, has opened between the idea as what really is, the prototype and archetype, and what actually is not, the copy and image. [1968:184]

Physis, pre-Socratic Being, accordingly undergoes a profound transformation, for from "the standpoint of the idea, appearing now takes on a new meaning":

> What appears—the phenomenon—is no longer *physis*, the emerging power, nor is it the self-manifestation of the appearance; no, appearing is now the emergence of the copy. Since the copy never equals its prototype, what appears is *mere* appearance, actually an illusion, a deficiency. Now the *on* becomes distinct from the *phainomenon*. And this development brings with it still another vital consequence. Because the actual repository of being is the *idea* and this is the prototype, all disclosure of being must aim at assimilation to the model, accommodation to idea. The truth of *physis*, *aletheia* as the unconcealment that is the essence of the emerging power, now becomes *homoiosis* and *mimesis*, assimilation and accommodation, orientation by . . . it becomes a correctness of vision, of apprehension as representation. [1968:184–85]

With the identification of being and Idea, then, knowledge becomes an attempt to achieve the correct "idea" of an Idea, an attempt that is always already representationally divided from what it would know. For the *logos* in Plato's philosophy no longer bears that essential ontological relation to *physis* which it bore in the pre-Socratic philosophy. It has become the form of rational discourse, a form determined not by Being but by the rules of logical statement. Thus "logos as statement becomes the abode of truth in the sense of correctness. And this process culminates in Aristotle's proposition to the effect that logos as statement is that which can be true or false":

> Logos is now *legein ti kata tinos*, to say something about something. What is spoken of is what in every case underlies the *statement*, what is set before it ready made. . . . From the standpoint of the logos as independent statement, being becomes *this* being-set-before. [1968:186]

And so "Being" and the logically determined language that speaks it (i.e., the language of metaphysics) are unalterably opposed. A difference has been inscribed between Being and language, a difference, Heidegger suggests, over which philosophers ever since "have tormented themselves in vain, seeking by every possible and impossible stratagem to explain the relation between statement (thinking) and being— in vain, because they never again carried the question of being back to its native ground and soil, thence to unfold it" (1968:190–91).

The locus for this ontological torment is the *category*, because it is only through the category that philosophy has tried to speak Being, only categorically does Being emerge into metaphysical discourse. To utter the logos is to stipulate some approximation of what a thing is, and thus, "the underlying essent may be represented in different ways: as having such and such properties, such and such magnitude, such and such relations." Now:

Properties, magnitude, relations are determinations of being. Because, as modes of being-said, they are derived from logos—and because to state is *kategoriein*—the determinations of the being of the essent are called kategoriai, categories. Thus, the doctrine of being and of the determinations of the essent as such becomes a discipline which searches for the categories and their order. The goal of all ontology is a doctrine of categories. [1968:187]

Thus, in Heidegger's de-structive reading of the history of Western metaphysics, the metaphysical category of *ousia*, substance, came to conceal Being itself, coming to be identified with "permanent presence, already-thereness," that which is already there for a scientific scrutiny to discover (see 1968:193). In the course of the metaphysical history to follow, as Heidegger traces it, the being of things was to be defined as having been "created by God, i.e., rationally preconceived," which means that "the being of the essent inevitably becomes thinkable in terms of pure mathematical thought," pure reason, transformed "into what can be mastered by modern, mathematically structured technology"

(1968:193–94). In such a manner, the categorical metaphysics of Aristotle evolved toward the eventual domination of rational representation and mathematical reason in the philosophy of the West, further accentuating the "ontico-ontological difference" by concealing the essential ontological relation between a violently "overpowering" (*deinon*) *physis* and the equally violent apprehension that constitutes "authentic" understanding. The power and potentiality of human technology that are exercised in the "world" of ontic substance have accordingly distracted thought away from the ontological power and violence of that "World" in which Being "shines," concealing itself from the rational scientific gaze, and only glimpsed in the moment of "poetic insight" (see 1968:149).

So metaphysics must forever fail in the quest for Being, must fail to close the "ontico-ontological difference," because the language in which it is written is already metaphysical, having fallen out of its original union with *physis*. *Physis* and *logos* once were "one," now they are divided, and we can neither speak nor write our way back to primordial Being without finding a purer language outside the grasp of metaphysical rationality. The lost unity of *noein*, *physis*, and *legein* has been violently sundered into "thinking," "being," and "language," and we have only our longing to return to what has been lost. We must turn to the poet in the darkness of that sundering. Metaphysics can only mark our destitution.

And here, perhaps, we may find the appeal of Heidegger's complex de-struction of Western metaphysics for literary criticism, for having concluded that traditional philosophy could not speak the Being whose lack he felt in the dark night of twentieth-century destitution, Heidegger came to place his faith in poetry, in the power of poetic language to retrace the track of the vanished gods, of a vanished Being.[2] Thus effacing the distinction between philosophy and literature, Heidegger prepared the way for a new, "poetic" approach to the problems of philosophy, overturning the sway of rational logic in critical discourse.

But while such a turning toward poetic irrationality away from scientific rationality in the discourse of critical theory may indeed have provided a breath of fresh air in the wake of formalist scientism, it can be problematic in the context of historical analysis, for as Theodore Adorno has observed in his *Negative Dialectics*, Heidegger's particular understanding of "historical primacy becomes an ontological precedence of 'Being' pure and simple over all ontical and real things" (1973:67). That is, in raising the ground for "lived experience" to a higher level of Being that transcends the ordinary beings of social experience, Heidegger effectively obscures the historicity of material reality. Indeed, as Georg Lukács has complained, "Heidegger tends to belittle history as 'vulgar'; and his 'authentic' historicity is not distinguished from ahistoricity" (1973:715).

In other words, because the gaze of the "authentic" historian is fixed upon the historicity of a Being that transcends the beings and appearances of material, social reality, the history that he or she writes has little to say about that "familiar" world of daily compromise and coping for which Heidegger expresses such repeated disdain. "Authentic" history, finally, appears to be a history for the superman, the poet-as-hero, not a history for ordinary people. Yet it is this ordinary, "inauthentic" history in which we must live, and by which we are most threatened in the atomic age.

In spite of Heidegger's own appeal to "history," to "lived experience," then, the history he pursues is finally a mysterious, transcendental history. We apprehend Being in the beings of the ordinary world, but as L. M. Vail has written, although "Being is 'common' to all things-which-are, it 'holds back' its identity in any particular situation. Being itself does not become manifest *as* Being but as an emptiness—a nothing. Thus, there is a transcendent side to Being" (1972:23). Perhaps such charges are a little too easy to make, but it is difficult to refrain from them in the light of Heidegger's often expressed contempt for the material historicity of the twentieth century, especially as we can find it expressed in his response to the material being of what we have called the nuclear referent. For writing in *Identity and Difference,* Heidegger is led to remark how:

> It is enough, one would think, to say the words "atomic age" in order to let us experience how Being becomes present to us today in the world of technology. But may we simply equate the world of technology with Being? Obviously not, not even if we imagine this world as the totality in which atomic energy, the calculating plans of man, and automation are conjoined. Why does such a directive concerning the world of technology . . . never let us catch sight of the constellation of Being and man? Because every analysis of the situation falls in its thinking short of the mark, in that the above-mentioned totality of the world of technology is interpreted in advance in terms of man, as being of man's making. Technology . . . is taken for the plan which man projects, the plan which finally compels man to decide whether he will become the servant of his plan or remain its master.
>
> By this conception of the totality of the technological world, we reduce everything down to man, and at best come to the point of calling for an ethics of the technological world. Caught up in this conception, we confirm our own opinion that technology is of man's making alone. We fail to hear the claim of Being which speaks in the essence of technology. [1974:33–34]

Now, it is not difficult to understand why literary critics weary of technological arrogance might be attracted by such a perspective. And in an essential sense Heidegger is certainly right when he says that technology is not of man's making alone, since no technological apparatus can be constructed without there being some extrahuman power or potentiality for it to harness. But the power of Being to which Heidegger appeals here is not a material power, is not an ontic potentiality that science discovers and puts to work. It is a higher power beyond any making that human beings can accomplish. In the context of a world of unchecked technological proliferation, the promise of such a power is not without its attractions, but it is only that, a promise—a promise, what is more, that can only defer a coming-to-grips with the material historical challenge that twentieth-century technology has presented us. Heidegger rather sneeringly refers to a possible "ethics of the technological world," seeking thereby to put in its place the anthropocentric arrogance of technological "progress," and it is hard to dispute this. But the trouble is that in the material immediacy of our present experience, it is precisely an ethics of the technological world that we require—indeed, a decision whether we will become the servant of our technology or will remain its master.[3]

Thus, I shall repeat here a point I made earlier: while there is certainly nothing wrong with pursuing an antirealistic, antirationalist, or antimimetic line of approach when analyzing literature, the extension of antirealistic principles into historical or political discourse has certain practical consequences that should cause us to hesitate before applying such an approach to the analysis of political phenomena. Time and again Heidegger condemns as ignoble any contemplation of the kind of concrete political dilemmas that require negotiation and compromise. This is the way of weakness, of the social horde, of a puling desire for security. The Heideggerian hero, who looks more and more like Nietzsche's superman, rejects all security to open himself to Being, to shatter himself upon the unknown. But we have already done that by opening up the unfamiliar world of the atom. It is now time for the unheroic activity of coping with our own discoveries.

To put this another way, the Heideggerian critique cannot lead us to a realistic political criticism. Poetry is not going to solve the concrete problems of the nuclear age. This does not mean, however, that we must simply deconstruct Heidegger's text, because to dwell upon its moments of metaphysical self-contradiction is to remain within the text without offering any political alternative. Where Derrida, for example, *has* exposed the metaphysical tendencies in Heidegger's text, he does not really oppose that text or attempt to escape it. "What I have attempted to do would not have been possible without the opening of Heidegger's questions," Derrida remarks, ". . . would not have been possible without the attention to what Heidegger calls the difference between Being and beings," but "despite this debt to Heidegger's thought, or rather because of it," he adds, "I attempt to locate in Heidegger's text . . . the sign of a belonging to metaphysics, or to what he calls onto-theology" (1981:9–10).

But rather than pursuing a more concrete approach to history than we may find in Heidegger's "authentic" or onto-theological historicity, Derrida projects differance out of the "ontico-ontological difference," just as he does with Saussurean difference, reinscribing "history" as "writing," as a tissue of differences, of traces leading neither to Being nor to identifiable beings, but only to the ever suspended relation between them. And so the actual beings of history, the material realities of lived experience, are only put off, deferred, as Derrida maintains Heidegger's de-structive attitude only to charge, essentially, that Heidegger, in the end, is insufficiently deconstructive, too "metaphysical," after all.

Derrida's point, of course, is that any attempt to ground history or being in some supreme category or power outside the categories of Western metaphysics is futile. All we can do is repeat the same error (Heidegger's, Saussure's, Husserl's—wherever difference is at once named and repressed), the same text, the same metaphysical gesture. It is difficult to see, however, what such an analysis leads to. For Derrida does not negate or oppose the texts that he deconstructs on behalf of any contrary argument: instead, he preserves the traces of difference, or differance, that he finds in them, thus suspending the possibility for any positive political positioning. This sort of analysis can be extended indefinitely, but while it would certainly defer any theoretical "final solution" to our problems, it would also defer satisfaction with any practical provisional solutions. For how could we proceed with any sort of concrete political proposal when by definition we must have always already oscillated into its opposite?

So, just as with Saussure's reduction of language to a play of differences, we may propose in the face of Heidegger's ontologizing of lived experience an alternative interpretation: that is, rather than suspending the opposition between Being and beings, the "ontico-ontological difference" as such, we might turn instead to an analysis of those "beings" of the ontic world that Heidegger contemns and Derrida defers. We might approach once more the material historicity of lived experience that Heidegger de-structs and that Derrida deconstructs, making our approach here through a reading of the referential realism, or historical materialism, of Marxist discourse.

CHAPTER 16

Marxism and the Categories of Historical Presentation

"ALWAYS HISTORICIZE!" Fredric Jameson exclaims in the Preface to his book *The Political Unconscious*, thus defining "the one absolute and we may even say 'transhistorical' imperative of all dialectical thought" (1981:9). But in spite of Jameson's apparently unambiguous appeal to the referential reality of history as the untranscendable ground of lived experience, key questions for the Marxist critique remain. What, precisely, does it mean to historicize? Is it to refer the meaning of a text or experience to a materially objective, scientifically determinate reality? Or is it, conversely, to limit analysis to an exploration of the archival concepts and categories by which human beings have subjectively interpreted their experience? Indeed, Jameson writes, "the historicizing operation can follow two distinct paths, which only ultimately meet in the same place: the path of the object and the path of the subject, the historical origins of things themselves and that more intangible historicity of the concepts and categories by which we attempt to understand those things" (1981:9). Thus, "to historicize" can mean different things to different theorists. It can mean (1) to take the path of the object, arguing for the determinate reality of an objective historical process; or (2) to take the path of the subject, enclosing analysis within an historically constituted archive of interpretational texts whose intertextual historicity would reduce all extra-archival speculation to the status of "metaphysics"; or (3) to search for that elusive space in which the two paths "ultimately meet in the same place."

For post-structural theory, "to historicize" is essentially

to take the second path, the path of the subject, whether it is mapped according to the metahistorical critique of Hayden White or the so-called "new historicism" of Michel Foucault. In each case "history" becomes a text, inscribed within the intertextual borders of a historical archive. But while, for "better or for worse," Jameson also chooses to follow the "second path" in his analyses of cultural and literary interpretation as conducted in *The Political Unconscious* (see 1981:9), his overall project may be seen as an attempt to map out the third course, to find a space where the "two paths" might meet in a specifically Marxist synthesis of textuality and referentiality, thus reconciling (rather than suspending) the oppositional extremes of historicization. But what, then, are the coordinates for this synthetic historicity? How can the "path of the object" and the "path of the subject" be said "to meet" in the mediating ground of "lived experience?"

As with our earlier analysis of the quarrel between scientific determinists and indeterminists in chapter 7 of this study, we can begin our search for a reconciling mediation between oppositional antagonists by first setting out the positions that such antagonists have taken. And again, we will start with the objectivist position, for just as we were able to find in René Thom a forceful exponent of scientific determinism, so too can we find in V. I. Lenin a similarly assertive exponent of the determinist stance. We may find this position clearly represented in Lenin's eulogy to Frederick Engels, a text in which Lenin succinctly, and rather peremptorily, lays out the "scientific," or orthodox, interpretation of dialectical materialism in his declaration that "Marx and Engels were the first to show that the working class and its demands are a *necessary* outcome of the present economic system, which together with the bourgeoisie *inevitably* creates and organizes the proletariat." Lenin writes that

they showed that it is not the well-meaning efforts of noble-minded individuals, but the class struggle of the organized proletariat that will deliver humanity from the evils which now oppress it. In their scientific works, Marx and Engels were the first to explain that socialism is not the invention of dreamers, but the final aim and *necessary result* of the productive forces in modern society. [1968:15; my italics]

In the same text, Lenin clearly identifies the material ground for his necessitarian interpretation of the dialectic in his categorical exposition of the philosophical relationship between Marx and Hegel. "Hegel's philosophy spoke of the development of the mind and of ideas," Lenin writes accordingly, and as such "it was *idealistic*;" because from "the development of the mind it deduced the development of nature, of man, and of human, social relations" (1968:17). But while Marx and Engels themselves retained "Hegel's idea of the eternal process of development," Lenin continues, they "rejected the preconceived idealist view; turning to life, they saw that it is not the development of mind that explains the development of nature but that, on the contrary, the explanation of the mind must be derived from nature, from matter." In other words:

Unlike Hegel and the other Hegelians, Marx and Engels were materialists. Regarding the world and humanity materialistically, they perceived that just as material causes underlie all natural phenomena, so the development of human society is conditioned by the development of material forces, the productive forces. On the development of the productive forces depend the relations into which men enter with one another in the production of the things required for the satisfaction of human needs. And in these relations lies the explanation of all the phenomena of social life, human aspirations, ideas and laws. [1968:17]

Thus in one small space we find indicated most of the classic categories of Marxist thought: the irreducible priority of social class relations in Marxist political analysis; the "economism" of "base" (as mode of production) and "superstructure" (as the field of social institutions determined by the forces of production); and a baldly *predictive* Marxist science of history grounded in the objective necessity of material development. This is to take the "path of the object" with a vengeance indeed, for in Lenin's deterministic interpretation of Marx's project there is little (if any) room for historical accident. The objectivity of matter, Lenin claims, has a determinate destiny for its own development, and so do the human societies that are based upon material modes of production.

It is precisely this kind of totalizing gesture that Louis Althusser challenged in his own interpretation of historical causality, condemning as either "mechanistic" or "expressivistic" those interpretations of Marxist historicity that rely, in turn, upon either a Newtonian or a Hegelian concept of causation. That is, as Althusser writes, "We can say that classical philosophy . . . had two and only two systems of concepts with which think effectivity." These are, respectively, the "mechanistic system, Cartesian in origin, which reduced causality to a *transitive* and analytical effectivity," and the "Leibnitzian concept of *expression*," which was "conceived precisely in order to deal with the effectivity of a whole on its elements," and which "is the model that dominates all Hegel's thought" (quoted in Jameson 1981:23–24). Now, as Jameson explains, "Althusser's first type of effectivity, that of mechanistic or mechanical causality, exemplified in the billiard-ball model of cause and effect, has long been a familiar exhibit in the history of ideas and in particular the history of science, where it is associated with the Galilean and Newtonian world-view" (1981:25). And this, essentially, is the causal paradigm assumed in Lenin's "mechanistic" interpretation of the determinate relation between the material "base" of a society and its "superstructure," an interpretation that has been largely discredited in the discourse of both critical and structuralist Marxism.

But while the "expressive" interpretation of historical causality is more subtle than that posed in the mechanistic model, it has been equally discredited in the discourse of Western Marxism. As Jameson writes:

[The] fullest form of what Althusser calls "expressive causality" (and of what he calls "historicism") . . . [proves] to be a vast interpretive allegory in which a sequence of historical events or texts and artifacts is rewritten in terms of some deeper, underlying and more "fundamental" narrative, a hidden master narrative which is the allegorical key or figural content of the first sequence of empirical materials. This kind of allegorical master narrative would then include providential histories (such as those of Hegel or Marx), catastrophic visions of history (such as those of Spengler), and cyclical or Viconian theories of history alike. [1981:28]

In other words, if the mechanistic version of historical causality results in a sterile Newtonian determinism, the expressive version leads to metaphysics, that is, to a belief in some overarching plot beyond the only apparent accidents of human history that might be discovered and represented by that historian who has discovered its "key." Condemned as "historicism" by such divergent writers as Althusser and Popper, or as "metaphysics" by Nietzsche, Derrida, and Foucault, the providentialist implications of the "expressive" model for historical causality have accordingly been roundly rejected by both Marxist and non-Marxist thinkers alike.

But if both "mechanical" determinism and "expressive" providentialism have been rejected as adequate models for historical causality, what model might there be left? For post-structural thought in general, of course, there can be no such model—which is precisely the point of both Derrida's and Foucault's otherwise divergent critiques of metaphysical history. There is no historical ur-text, no transcendental signified or referent, for the historian to discover and represent, Derrida argues. Rather, in history there are only signifiers without signifieds, a play of historical traces contained within the indefinite walls of an intertextual archive that can never write its own "outside." It is thus hardly surprising that a "host of contemporary post-structuralisms and post-Marxisms," as Jameson puts it, has assimilated Althusser's "antiteleological formula for history" to their own convictions that "history, in the bad sense—reference to a 'context' or a 'ground,' an external real world of some kind, the reference, in other words to the much-maligned 'referent' itself—is simply one more text among others, something found in history manuals and that chronological presentation of historical sequences so often called 'linear history' " (1981:35).

But while Jameson, for his part, is hardly disposed simply to redeem the "mechanistic" and the "expressive" paradigms for historical causality (though he does defend the "purely local validity in cultural analysis" of "the category of mechanical effectivity" [1981:25]), he is not willing to give up the concept of causation altogether, nor that of the referent either. For if, as we might say, the mechanical causationist goes the way of the object, and the post-structural anticausationist the way of the subject (as inscribed within an intertextual archive), Althusser, as Jameson reads him, offers a third alternative by which the object and the subject, the historical referent and the historian, might be reconciled. This third path has been mapped out in Althusser's concept of history as an "absent cause," in his positing of a "third concept of effectivity: that of structural causality" (see Jameson 1981:24).

This "third concept," Althusser writes, "can be entirely summed up in the concept of 'Darstellung,' the key epistemological concept of the whole Marxist theory of value, the concept whose object is precisely to designate the mode of *presence* of the structure in its *effects*, and therefore to designate structural causality itself" (quoted in Jameson 1981:24). What this implies, Althusser continues, is that a "structure is immanent in its effects," that is, subsists as a cause "in the Spinozist sense of the term" insofar as "the whole existence of the structure consists of its effects." A structure consists, in other words, solely in the "specific combination of its peculiar elements" and "is nothing outside its effects" (quoted in Jameson 1981:24–25). Such a structure constitutes an "absent cause" not in the sense of an actual absence of structural causality and coherence but only in the sense of a transcending "mechanical" or "expressive" force. To put this another way, where in a Newtonian system the action of an object is determined by positive causal forces that transcend it, and in an Hegelian system the destinies of beings are determined by the transcendent design of an overarching Spirit, the causative nature of structural effectivity is immanent in the things that belong to a given structure.

For the purposes of Althusser's critique of the "base/superstructure" model of Marxist orthodoxy, this means that the causal "mode of production" does not subsist outside the actual institutions of society but instead inheres immanently within the structural totality of a society as a whole. In opposition to the vertically reflexive model of a superstructure that architecturally rests upon its base as upon a foundational pedestal, then, Althusser proposes a structured model of radiating institutional vectors (including "culture," "ideology," "the juridical," "the political," "the economic," "relations and forces of production," and so on) that all meet in a point, a point that represents the structural mode of production that immanently informs the relations of each cultural vector to the other in a given social system (see Jameson 1981:32–36). So located at the point of conjuncture of a system of related institutions, such a cause takes on the appearance of a geometrical point: that is, a zero-dimensional node which, in its spatial negativity, grounds the spatial structures that emerge from it. Its "absence," accordingly, is an absence only if one is looking for an external presence behind the immediate beings of history, for a Spirit or Being beyond material things. But if one regards the social interrelatedness of human institutions as bearing its causal integrity as an immanent function of its own structured being, then such a cause is not an absence at all but constitutes instead the dynamic coherence by which specific societies are held together, like a keystone centering the dynamic tensions of a standing arch.

I believe that Althusser's historical projection of "effective causality" bears an essential analogy to the neither deterministic nor indeterministic versions of scientific causality that we have seen in the work of such scientists and philosophers of science as Edgar Morin and Ilya Prigogine. For just as, according to Morin, we may find "organizational determinations *proper to* the structure of given systems . . . that is, determinations *which do not exist outside these organizations*" (1983:25), so too does Althusser's "absent cause" constitute a determination that cannot be found apart from its effects, apart, that is to say, from the structural organization whose coherence it defines. As such, it constitutes a nontranscendental ground for historical structurality, a zero-dimensional signified or referent that organizes a given structure without transcending it in either a mechanical or an expressive manner. Indeed, as Jameson writes, what "Althusser's own insistence on history as an absent cause makes clear, but what is missing from the formula as it is canonically worded, is that he does not at all draw the fashionable conclusion that because history is a text, the 'referent' does not exist. We would therefore propose," Jameson continues, "the following revised formulation: that history is *not* a text, not a narrative master or otherwise, but that, as an absent cause, it is inaccessible to us except in textual form, and our approach to it and to the Real itself necessarily passes through its prior textualization, its narrativization, in the political unconscious" (1981:35).

In other words, since the causal principle of history can never be directly encountered in the reified presence of a universal power or form but instead only appears immanently in the effective structures of social experience, it must be textually mediated or interpreted rather than immediately represented. But where for Heidegger this implies the inscription of an ontico-ontological difference by which the interpreter is condemned to represent a presence (*Sein*) that has always already been lost to language, for Jameson the need to interpret, to "narratize" the "absent cause" of history means that we must look to the nontranscendental reality of a "political unconscious" by which given societies and classes *present* to themselves the meaning of their historical experience. Rather than representing the transcending reality of a mechanical or an expressive historical cause, the political unconscious narrates, or presents, the realities of the social world according to its own ideological categories for narrative interpretation. But even though Jameson intends to find in the figure of narrative presentation, of *Darstellung*, a mediating ground between the referential object that is presented in narrative form and the subjective categories of a political unconscious that determine what we might call the "mode of presentation of the referent," it is possible to argue that such a solution still seems to privilege the "path of the subject"; for the categories of narrative presentation that Jameson proposes are finally rather difficult to distinguish from the ruling tropes of metahistory and would thus seem to reinscribe interpretive *Darstellung* (presentation) back within the archival forms of *Vorstellung* (representation) after all.

That is, while, as Jameson writes in "Science Versus Ideology," Marxism properly should be seen not as "a set of propositions about reality, but a set of categories in terms of which reality is analyzed and interrogated, and a set of essentially 'contested' categories at that" (1983:283), it is not easy to see just how one category might be judged against another and which categories would constitute the most adequate presentations of historical experience. "To see Marxism as a problematic rather than as a system ... means displacing (but not effacing) older notions of orthodoxy, heterodoxy, or revisionism," Jameson concedes, but rather than embracing the categorical pluralism that such a displacement seems to imply, Jameson finds a certain rather pragmatic refuge in his belief that under such circumstances "to be a Marxist in this new sense means to agree that the central categories of Marxism continue to designate the most basic interesting problems to be solved; social class, for example" (1983:283). Jameson certainly does not mean to beg the question here, but it is hard to see what else might be happening in such apparently contradictory assertion/concessions as his proposition that social class "has always, and rightly, been taken to be a fundamental category of Marxist thought; yet one has not abandoned Marxism . . . when one has concluded that this category is contested in our own time (as any intelligent person must surely do) (1983:283).

For if the foundational category of class analysis (which must be listed among the essential forms according to which Marxism has narratized the course of history) can be so easily contested, then what objective claim can the Marxist narrative make upon us? Similarly, if the popular "notion that Marxist 'science of history' is predictive" must be listed among "the most frequent . . . misconceptions about Marxism," as Jameson writes (1983:284), then what distinguishes the Marxist vision from, say, sociology? Indeed, as Jameson himself asks, what "would subsist of Marxism itself if it renounced its claims to grasping the 'motion of history' and contented itself with life in a Nietzschean present?" (1983:284). That is, were Marxism to abandon its traditional "narrative" category of predictive totality, to reduce itself "to some mere *method* of historical analysis . . . [that] does not generate vivid images and projections of an alternate future and an alternate set of social relations" (1983:297), then the very heart and soul of the movement would be taken from it. A "Marxism which can be conceived of in isolation from political action, and which has ceased to be a 'unity of theory and practice'—such a Marxism," Jameson concludes, "is worse than dead, it is worthless" (1983:297). But how can a "critical" Marxism recuperate its protentional, or predictive, identity without falling back into deterministic totalization?

Jameson seeks to resolve this essential dilemma of "critical" Marxism in the course of his essay "Science Versus Ideology" by drawing a distinction between two different kinds of discourse that we may find in the text of Marx which "interfere" with each other but without contradiction. Jameson calls these interfering discourses "the *scientific* and the *pro-*

phetic" (1983:285). He defines the former as being analogous to a kind of "mathematical" semiotic founded not on the traditional disjunction "between words and things" but rather on the disjunction "between axioms and propositions, between a pregiven or constituted 'axiomatic' and the various 'enunciations' logically drawn from those axioms" (1983:288), and the latter as a mode of Utopian projection by which Marx ideologically imagines a revolutionary future. Jameson clarifies his distinction in the following manner.

To begin with Marx's "scientific" discourse: it is well known that mathematical languages are constituted with respect not to actually existing referential entities but rather to certain unproven or pregiven nonreferential axioms on the basis of which all further mathematical demonstration and proof may take place. "It would be tempting," Jameson remarks in this context, "to consider such an axiomatic as a system of 'categories' which are called into play in any particular proposition" (1983:288). For example, Jameson continues, "if one proposes to analyze a given system like Marxism as a scientific system in this sense":

... it would seem enough to isolate the various "fundamental" Marxist categories—the labor theory of value, social class, the mode of production—as so many abstract [or axiomatic] categories, which make no claim on the real, which emit no particular empirical propositions in their own right, but which simply constitute the "code" in terms of which Marxist thinking is done. This is not wrong as far as it goes, but the very concept of an axiomatic is richer and more interesting than this, insofar as its "categories" are also "operations": we here therefore [have] reached a conceptual level in which the opposition of subject and verb is annulled, in which what looks as static as a "concept" or "substance" . . . *has the latent dynamism* of a narrative in its own right. . . . If one grasps the axiomatic in this way, then one can grasp, say, . . . a Marxist axiomatic in terms of a latent "vision of history" or historical "master-narrative," which, however, *as* an axiomatic, does not involve a set of empirical propositions or predictions and is not intended to be either a concrete "history" or a concrete forecast, but merely a mode of exposition of the basic axioms (or categories) themselves. [1983:288–89; my italics]

For example, in Jameson's own "(historicist) periodization of the cultures of capitalism into three distinct moments: those of classical or market capitalism, of the monopoly stage or 'stage of imperialism,' and of present-day 'consumer' or more properly multinational capitalism" (1983:289), we find the narrative working out of such an axiomatic Marxist category as the "mode of production" through the presentational actualization of a certain "latency" or potential for narratization that we may find in the historical experience of the past century. That is, as Jameson puts it, the

conception of an axiomatic ... immediately places the Marxist "eschatology," "vision of history," "historicism" (e.g., the account of various "stages" of the modes of production as they lead towards capitalism and then towards socialism or communism), on a wholly different footing from ideological "philosophies" or "visions" of history. What seems like a representational narrative in handbook accounts of Marxism is therefore not that at all, but rather simply a mode of presentation (*Darstellung*), the exposition of the axiomatic by way of its narrative working out. [1983:290]

But while there is indeed no referential reality behind the axioms of mathematics, there is one behind the axioms of Marxist discourse, and if those axioms fail to correspond to (or, in our own terms, to actualize) a *real latency* (or potentiality) in that reality for a certain kind of axiomatic presentation, then the "narrative working out" of the axiomatic would seem to differ little from what Stanley Fish has called the "standard story" of an "interpretive community." That is, if the axiom is only an axiom, is undemonstrable as such and can be presented only through the course of a narrative, then what surety have we that the narrative has any objective force, any historical validity? Before pursuing such questions, however, we might first turn to Jameson's description of Marx's "prophetic" discourse, because in the essential relation between these two sorts of Marxian language we may find a further demonstration of the importance of referential objectivity in the discourse of history. So granting, for the moment, that "the Marxist 'science of society' shares these key features of scientific or mathematical discourse generally," then, as Jameson puts it, "we may be in a position to move on to the question of the future, of 'law' and predictability, to the vexed issue of historical inevitability raised at the outset, and offer a final set of speculative hypotheses" (1983:290). Jameson's hypothesis here is that there is a difference between a Marxist "science of society," which, "far from being a matter of prediction or making claims about historical inevitability is exclusively a mode of understanding the past" (1983:290), and Marxist "prophecy," which, in its relation to Althusserian "ideology," concerns "'the *imaginary* relationship of the subject to his or her *real* conditions of existence,' a formulation," Jameson further explains, "in which the terms 'imaginary' and 'real' have technical, Lacanian senses, the former alluding to the 'imaginary' or dual, mirror-stage in the formation of the infant's psyche" (1983:298). "Ideology," in other words, refers here not to the content of some political consciousness but rather to that stage in child development in which a certain "Absolute Subject addresses the isolated 'subject' of the individual and by the very operation of naming, and by the offering of a second-person slot, a *you*, in which to insert himself/herself, holds out the consolation of a stable identity" (1983:298). As Althusser has put it:

Ideology 'acts' or 'functions' in such a way that it 'recruits' subjects among ... individuals ... or 'transforms' ... individuals into subjects ... by that very precise operation which I have called *interpellation* or hailing, and which can be imagined along the lines of the most commonplace police (or other) hailing: 'Hey, you there!'

Assuming that the theoretical scene I have imagined takes place in the street, the hailed individual will turn round. By this mere one-hundred-eighty-degree physical conversion, he becomes a *subject*. Why? Because he has recognized that the hail was 'really' addressed to him, and that 'it was *really him* who was hailed' (and not someone else). [1984:48]

In other words, "ideology" is here displaced from its orthodox definition "as having something to do with the 'contents of consciousness,' to one in which ideology is grasped in terms of a communicational process or situation," Jameson writes (1983:299). "Ideology" *communicates* itself to the emerging "subject" as a kind of "Voice of the Other" for which the child has been searching as he or she seeks to define himself or herself in this newly dawning world in which he or she has become a "you" with respect to the "hailing" voice of the Other. At first this "Voice" is the voice of "parental authority," but since it is heard in language, language itself becomes the authoritative Other against and within which the child defines his or her identity (see Jameson 1983:299).

Ideology so conceived can lead to an "ideological discourse," Jameson believes, that "must be identified and specified in a more striking manner, as prophetic discourse proper":

In order to grasp ideology, in other words, in its future-oriented function, and in its indissoluble relationship to social and political praxis, we need an analysis of the discourse of great prophecy, a discourse which, as one might imagine, resonates ever more faintly and feebly within the closure of consumer society, with its historical amnesia. [1983:300]

Ideological, *prophetic*, discourse, then, constitutes the *individual* subject's attempt to define himself or herself in the world not only of the present but also of the future. We project our identities forward, Jameson writes, in the "discourse of great prophecy" according to an impulse that "has elsewhere been called the Utopian impulse" (1983:301). Such projections are neither "scientific" nor precisely class based, but while they are privately originated they can still "produce mobilizing images of a radically and qualitatively different future, 'images' . . . fantasies and narratives . . . without which political activity is itself inconceivable" (1983:301). Such "images," Jameson believes, are precisely the sort that are "prophetically" interpolated in the otherwise "scientific" text of Marx: Utopian fancies that drive us toward *creative* political action even as we "scientifically," or axiomatically, present to ourselves the explanations for how conditions came to be as they are.

Prophetic ideology, then, is not a blueprint for the way the future *must be*; it constitutes a vision of what the future *may be* and a stimulus toward the realization of that future. It does not "predict," but guides. In a certain sense, therefore, "prophetic" discourse and "scientific" discourse can be seen to complement each other in a manner that is not developed in Jameson's essay but is implied there. That is, the "Utopian" visions we may have of the future are constituted out of our own "scientific" understanding of the past and the present. If we axiomatically present the course of human history, for example, as a dialectical process of class oppression, then our "ideological" or "prophetic" vision of a Utopian future will be one in which such class distinctions have finally been eradicated. The axiomatic presentation of the category of class conflict in itself is therefore nonbinding; but the prophetic vision that we constitute on the basis of that axiom (like a proof in a mathematical demonstration) would then seem to have a certain objective force and status in its programmatic projection of revolutionary action.

But what if one believes that not class division but, say, religious, racial, or sexual conflict has been the dominant "category" of human history? Would this not accordingly modify one's "Utopian" vision of the future and the political program by which one might plan to achieve it? Jameson tries to take this problem into account by addressing himself to black and feminist activists with respect to their own claims for the axiomatic "categories" of historical narratization. But while he does not propose any "wide-ranging theoretical proposition about the primacy of class in racial or sexual politics," he does offer a "far more modest" (and apparently self-privileging) proposition concerning "the seeming priority and explanatory power of class *analysis*" in the narrative presentation of history (1983:296). But if Jameson is unable to *demonstrate* this "seeming priority" of one axiom over another (and by his own terms he is inherently unable to do so), then the category of "class analysis" would have to be seen as just one more subjective "code" among a potential infinitude of others, a historical hermeneutic with no inherent superiority over any other. This would effectively wrench Marxism away from the untranscendable horizon of "history" and lodge it quite uncomfortably among an irreducible plurality of interpretations as they may be found in the intertextual webbing of the "archive."

It is at this point that the discourse of realism might intercede, because in his careful attempt to reconcile Marxism with post-structuralism, Jameson simply appears to have given away too much. For if the categories of Marxism are undemonstrable axioms, then they are essentially arbitrary and can make no "historical" claim upon us. This, of course, is not a conclusion that Jameson would endorse or desire, but it is difficult to see how it can be avoided—unless his thesis were modified to argue that, while historical experience can admit a plurality of axiomatic presentations, each axiom has to stand as a kind of analytical conjecture that must be tested against an objectively limiting reality. Such a modification, of course, would seem to make rather strange allies of Karl Popper and Fredric Jameson, but it may not be so outlandish in the light of Jameson's own recognition of a limiting reality grounded in an objective history that "refuses desire and sets inexorable limits to individual as well as collective praxis" (1981:102). For here indeed, in the obdurate reality of historical experience, we may find that which exceeds the archive, setting a bound to subjective textuality and a limit to the "axioms" by which we present the movement of history.

But as Jameson points out, this bound, this "history" that "hurts," "can be apprehended only through its effects, and never directly as some reified force" (1981:102). This does not mean, however, that history is a "text," because the "effects" that we experience constitute real historical phenomena that must be analyzed in the context of specific historical structures or actualities. In other words, the "absent cause" that binds together a given historical situation may be specific to that situation and thus irreducible to any more or less universal axiomatic category.

Such, I believe, is the case of the nuclear referent, which, as we have seen in Derrida's analysis in "No Apocalypse, Not Now" (1984), seems to resist the traditional categories of dialectical thought. For instance, we can scarcely say that the future of a world held hostage by the hair-trigger mechanisms of computer-controlled strategic defense networks can be predicted in strictly dialectical terms. And if we should attempt to "narratize" our current historical predicament according to the axiomatic category of Marxist class analysis, we run into similar difficulties. For while there is something of a class confrontation involved in the rhetoric of the competing superpowers, the actual international circumstances that comprise the political component of the nuclear referent would seem to resist any such reduction. How, for example, could we explain the "proletarian" confrontation along the Sino-Soviet border in the terms of class analysis, not to mention the Polish and Czechoslovakian experiences that have proved so embarrassing in Marxist circles. One could go on, but my purpose here is not to carp. Rather, what I wish to suggest is that even though the traditional categories of Marxist or dialectical thought may have been outmoded by the peculiar circumstances surrounding the nuclear referent, this does not mean that we must give up Jameson's essential proposition that it is history and not the text that constitutes the untranscendable horizon of interpretation, and that it is to the extratextual reality of political experience that our narrative categories for historical presentation ultimately refer.

To put this another way, if we are not to stand helpless before the nuclear referent, inscribing it as an "absolute pharmakon" in the light of our dialectical inability to come to terms with it, then we will have to propose, or conjecture, a nondogmatic set of categories by which its structured effects might be presented in the form of a "scientific" discourse that might ground "prophetic" action. And here we might find the place for an active nuclear criticism, a criticism that would be conjectural by nature rather than programmatic, willing to test its conjectures against the agon of reality rather than inscribing them within the play of a text. A criticism of this kind, of course, would be by nature both pluralistic and interdisciplinary, attempting to constitute what Clifford Geertz, in another sphere, has called a "thick description" of the structure of that complex system of interrelated national and international effects that we include under the umbrella of the nuclear referent. Such a criticism, of course, has already begun, particularly within the scientific community, where conjectures about the probable effects of a nuclear exchange are being modeled in computer simulations and calculations. The purpose of such simulations, however, is to provide a ground for the projection of "prophetic" action in the face of the nuclear referent (as we can see in the activities of the Union of Concerned Scientists), not to substitute a simulacrum for an otherwise absent event. Such work has been undertaken to challenge the often less than convincing reassurances that have been given us by those who manage strategic policy in this country, so I would ask whether it is really either revolutionary or even within the critical interest to attempt to deconstruct such projections?

Thus, I would argue that it is not Marxism that provides the key to the analysis of the immediacy of lived experience (an experience which, for the moment at least, has come to be dominated by the looming figure of the nuclear referent), but historical realism. If this is what Jameson means by "Marxism," then the distinction need not be made. But if Marxism and historical realism are interchangeable terms, they can be so only if we claim no priority for any preexisting historical axiomatic but are willing to test every "axiomatic" conjecture against the specific conditions of the problem at hand. This would mean that we would also have to test the often unanalyzed category of "revolutionary struggle" in the context of the nuclear referent, for while some sort of "prophetic" action seems to be called for in our current historical circumstances, it is not necessarily the case that revolutionary action is the universal solution. Without the category of "revolution," of course, "Marxism" as such might lose its appeal. A historical realism intent upon a course of conjecture and refutation, however, can only answer, "so be it."

In terms of political practice, such a program, by which each historical problem would have to be resolved according to particular analyses specifically pertinent to the challenge at hand, may resemble the political programmatic of Michel Foucault, and in certain ways this is indeed the case. But as I shall argue in my concluding chapter, in Foucault's emphasis upon political "difference" as a kind of axiomatic category of its own, we may find certain difficulties. For while Foucault himself has abandoned the "universal" categories of the Marxist critique, he retains a revolutionary fervor that remains to be analyzed (not deconstructed) in the face of the concrete limitations cast over us by the historical reality of the nuclear referent.

CHAPTER 17

Power and Difference in the Nuclear Era

IN HIS ESSAY "Pascal's Bet, Totalities, and Guerilla Criticism," Robert Maniquis explores the causes of what he perceives as a paralysis among left-wing intellectuals as they labor under the totalizing "sign of the Bomb." For Maniquis, the dilemma of the intellectual in the nuclear age is that he or she faces an up-or-down choice, for or against totality, that effectively reverses the choice proposed by Pascal's famous "wager." Because while Pascal's wager advised seventeenth-century human beings to bet, in their own interest, on the totality of God's existence, contemporary thinkers must bet on just the opposite if they are to function at all, wagering that the totality of a nuclear war will not occur. And so, Maniquis writes:

> Sympathy for Pascal's reluctant gambler should come easy to us, as we wait upon, to use the bureaucrat's phrase, our cosmic throw of the dice. Our gamble will decide, so we think, whether we shall be blown into radioactive matter to leave behind, if anything at all, some grotesque mutation of ourselves. We of course turn Pascal's bet upside down. Most of us bet most of the time not that the explosion will, but that it will *not*, occur, though many analysts and scholars of the game tell us we are playing with dice loaded against us. [1983:257]

Our bet against totality is thus, in this sense, a pragmatic gesture, a decision to resist the paralyzing potential of a life lived under the "sign of the Bomb." But our bet can also be regarded as a deconstructive gesture, that is, as an attack on the very category of "totality" itself, a disruption that, in this post-structuralist, post-Marxist critical era of ours, can be seen at work throughout the contemporary discourse of the human sciences. For, as Maniquis puts it:

> Foucault's analyses of power, Derrida's of logocentrism, Lacan's disassembling of Freud into the linguistic, Althusser's freezing of Marxist historical time into synchronic stasis and historical disruption, Enzenburger's media criticism, Baudrillard's masses carapaced in silence—these formulations are what rests (at least in the West) of a once unbounded Leftist faith in totality. [1983:260]

But in this theoretical rejection of the category of totality, the left-wing intellectual finds only another dilemma, another cause for paralysis. For where a "once unbounded faith in totality" enabled Marxist intellectuals to pursue a definitive political agenda based upon a totalizing historical model, "totality" today, at least in the West, signifies totalitarianism, logocentrism, historicism, indeed, like nuclear war itself, everything that is to be avoided in contemporary thought. But without the concept of totality, without a sense of the direction of history, how is one to act at all? On what basis can one define one's political choices?

Still more troubling for the intellectual activist is that even the category of "revolution" has become circumscribed under the "sign of the Bomb." That is, even if he or she were to shrug off his or her theoretical melancholy to demand revolutionary action, today's left-wing intellectual knows that his or her options are limited. "Peasant bodies piled up in El Salvadoran streets and garbage dumps inevitably enflame international anger and revolutionary response," Maniquis observes (1983:262), but what, precisely, is to be done about it? "Translate that response," Maniquis continues, "... into a drift toward nuclear confrontation, and that drift can dampen, even alter, political will" (1983:262). Simple moral outrage, in other words, can no longer be simply translated into military action. Pre-nuclear strategists on both the Left and the Right could plan and execute military campaigns without risking human extinction, but as is increasingly obvious from the tenor of contemporary global politics, nearly everyone's hands have been tied in the face of the nuclear referent. "It would be self-defeating to exaggerate the weakening of political will under the sign of the Bomb," Maniquis writes, "but it may also be naive to underestimate it" (1983:263).

Maniquis, however, believes that this weakening of political will has, in fact, been orchestrated by the State (East or West) as a screen for its own military adventures. For if, as Maniquis writes, "the State is caught in brutality or extermination it can invoke instead terrorist reasoning by which all exterminations below the final extermination of a country, a region, or (when apocalyptic notions are flying well) everywhere are *necessarily* life-saving." Thus, in "an age of terrorist tactics," Maniquis continues, "wielded by the individual and States with access to the nuclear, the bigger terrorist will usually win" (1983:278). In other words, for Maniquis the Bomb has become a weapon of State terror in its drive to suppress revolutionary action. It accordingly becomes the task of the Left to disrupt such totalizing gestures and to design "achievable goals of liberation, constructing measurable political ends out of the terrorizing and imageless End" (1983:263). But how is the Leftist intellectual to so subvert totality—the totality of the State and the totality of the nuclear referent—without, on the one hand, risking his or her own paralysis, or, on the other, risking a nuclear war?

For Maniquis, a solution to this dilemma of the Left can be found in the figure of what he calls a "guerilla criticism," a criticism, that is to say, by which the intellectual can conduct a guerilla action against totality by identifying himself or herself with the repressed and stigmatized political "margin."[1] For while "marginality," as Maniquis writes, "is the home of the weak and the dispersed," it may also be "consciously taken up as a reasoned political idea and not as the refuge of shrinking political will" (1983:271). In other words, the guerilla critic can seize upon the theoretical and political idea of *difference* as a positive and revolutionary category, finding in the margin not a shelter or place to hide but a ground for positive agitation. And so, while "on the margins it is not easy to find figuration to represent the human agency appropriate to political culture under the sign of the Bomb," the "image," Maniquis continues, that "some Leftists have more or less stumbled upon is implicit in the idea of guerilla criticism" (1983:271).

Thus, in Maniquis's reading of the conditions of present history, the "contemporary political guerilla is produced by the totalizing pressure of mass society, of consumerism, of economic empire, of totalitarian repression, of conventional and massive armed force, of the nuclear" (1983:271). "Guerilla" criticism constitutes a reaction against these forces, a refusal to be coerced, to assent to totality, to suppress difference. But to act in the name of "difference" is, in a certain sense, to act without a name at all, to march under no identifiable banner. For the "Leftist intellectual," as Maniquis puts it, "unlike the military guerilla, rarely has a guiding socialist party" (1983:271). This lack of a universal program, however, presents a peculiar challenge to the nontotalizing activist, who must essentially reconstitute his or her theoretical agenda to suit the differential particularity of each problem that he or she seeks to resolve. What is more, a strategy by which the critic-activist always remains on the margin seems to condemn him or her to a bleak prospect of unceasing marginalization. Indeed, Maniquis observes, the "extent ... to which staying on the margin and in loosely connected forms of political action and thought is a strategy or a desperate scramble is a central problem of academic Leftism" (1983:271).

Perhaps the best way to confront this problem is to consider the actual criticism that has been produced from the "margin," as Maniquis does in his presentation of Michel Foucault and Gilles Deleuze as "two prominent cultural critics who have taken up the figuration of guerilla criticism," referring at some length to "a dialogue they had almost a decade ago," which has been since collected in Foucault's *Language, Counter-Memory, Practice* (1981). In this dialogue ("Intellectuals and Power"), which we might take up now in its own right, Foucault and Deleuze discuss the vexed issue of the actual pertinence of academic, or intellectual, theorizing to concrete political action. Deleuze begins by remarking how "at one time, practice was considered an application of theory, a consequence; at other times, it had an opposite sense and it was thought to inspire theory.... In any event, their relationship was understood in terms of a process of totalization. For us, however," Deleuze continues, "the question is seen in a different light. The relationships between theory and practice are far more partial and fragmentary" (1981:205). For Deleuze, in short, no theory can be totalized in itself; it always runs into certain difficulties, or "obstacles," that "require its relay by another type of discourse" (1981:206). This "relay," or, we might say, "supplement," to theory is practice, for practice "is a set of relays from one theoretical point to another, and theory is a relay from one practice to another" (1981:206). Deleuze offers as an example Foucault's own work in prison reform. Foucault's "work began in the theoretical analysis of the context of confinement, specifically with respect to the psychiatric asylum within a capitalist society in the nineteenth century." But this *theoretical* work made Foucault "aware of the necessity for confined individuals to speak for themselves, to create a relay.... It was on this basis that ... [Foucault] organized the information group for prisons (G.I.P.), the object being to create conditions that permit the prisoners themselves to speak" (1981:206). In Foucault's work, then, theory has been indeed supplemented by practice; and, what is more, the theorist has not arrogated to himself or herself the authority to "represent" the voices of the imprisoned or marginalized but has enabled them to speak for themselves.

Foucault picks up the thread at this point, observing how the "events of May" in France demonstrated "that the masses no longer need ... [the intellectual] to gain knowledge: they *know* perfectly well, without illusion; they know far better than he and they are perfectly capable of expressing themselves" (1981:207). The trouble, then, that the "masses" face is that their expression is consistently blocked by "a system of power" of which intellectuals "are themselves agents" (1981:206). "Power" (which would include university authority) stifles free expression, and if the intellectual is to be of any real service he or she must cease to pretend to *form* consciousness or "to express the stifled truth of the collectivity; rather," Foucault continues, "it is to struggle against the forms of power which transform him into its object and instrument" that constitutes the social duty of the intellectual (1981:207–208). The task of the theorist, that is to say, is to struggle against "power," not *on behalf* of those whom power marginalizes but from within the margin itself.

But this struggle cannot be raised to the level of a universal theory, cannot be categorized in terms that would apply in all cases, because for Foucault every theory "is always local and related to a limited field" (1981:205). Thus, every struggle of theory against power must be "local and regional" (1981:208). For this reason Foucault rejects the totalizing implications of Marxism as well as such "universal" "representative agencies" as the French "Communist Party or the General Workers Union" (1981:212). Rather, for Foucault each "struggle develops around a particular source of power (any of the countless, tiny sources—a small-time boss, the manager of H.L.M., a prison warden, a judge, a union representative, the editor-in-chief of a newspaper)" (1981:214). Every struggle against totalizing power, that is to say, is a particular struggle that determines in its own course its own supplementations of theory and practice. The guerilla theorist, then, operates under no *universal* banner but opposes totalizing power wherever he or she sees it. He or she has no universal vision of the future, but only a sense of the day's specific evil, everywhere resisting identitarian power from within the differential margin.

But in spite of the guerilla critic's categorical rejection of all totalizing categories, he or she has still privileged one last "category:" the category of the "revolutionary margin" itself. For one often misses in Foucault's more "revolutionary" discourse a sensitivity to those instances in which the "revolutionary margin" (whether on the Right or the Left) should indeed remain marginalized, when its revolution, that is to say, is for the worse rather than for the better. And the "masses" themselves, even when they "know" what they want, are not necessarily morally justified in their desire at every moment. "We cannot shut out the screams of the Reich," Deleuze himself remarks; "the masses were not deceived; at a particular time they wanted a fascist regime" (1981:215). It might also be noted in this context that Hitler, too, was a prisoner, and began his rise from the margin of state power precisely through his prison discourse. Is it not possible, then, that to be marginalized is not necessarily equivalent to being victimized, that there are cases in which the power of the state (as represented by, say, the Weimar Republic in Germany or the Spanish Republic in Spain) has greater moral force than its opponents? For Foucault, of course, revolutionary struggle must be one *against* power, not *for* it. For Foucault, power should be opposed not reimposed. But how is a political struggle to be conducted without someone getting power, howsoever one wishes not to have gotten it? Has not Nietzsche himself declared the historical ubiquity of political force and domination?

Maniquis, for his part, realizes what is at stake when the guerilla margin does resort to power tactics. There is a certain complicity, he suggests, between "the terrorist psychologies of both revolutionaries and State powers" (1983:277), for both wield power under the "sign of the Bomb." The State, on the one hand, may justify its limited violence upon "the notion that small bloodbaths always keep the nation and its witnesses from the ultimate bloodbath" (1983:277), while the private terrorist, on the other hand, equally can argue that his or her limited action is better than a total one, and that it is better to kill a few civilians to achieve one's ends than to risk thermonuclear war. What is more, we might add, the private terrorist equally resorts to a kind of nuclear blackmail, acting in the knowledge that no Power would risk nuclear war just to get at him or her. The terrorist's calculation is no less cynical than that of a Superpower agreement to demarcate zones of influence within which the other Superpower need not, and dare not, interfere. Terror is terror, no matter what its source.

In other words, we cannot simply assume that the guerilla margin is morally justifiable—which is essentially what the rhetoric of "difference" often implies. But this does not mean that absolute State power is, in itself, any more morally justifiable on categorical grounds, for the suppression of the margin can lead to a tyranny of the majority in democratic societies and to despotic authoritarianism or sheer totalitarianism in nondemocratic societies. Indeed, it has been just such a fear of totalitarianism that has led to a call for "a new dialectics which will not suppress difference or negation in the name of a formal logic of identity" among poststructural social critics and "critical" Marxists (see Bové 1982–83:165). But some care needs to be taken so that "difference" *alone* is not raised as an idol in place of totality, for as Adorno remarks in his own assault on identitarian totalization in *Negative Dialectics*, "once dialectics has become inescapable . . . it cannot stick to its principle like ontology and transcendental philosophy":

> It cannot be maintained as a structure that will stay basic no matter how it is modified. In criticizing [a totalizing] ontology we do not aim at another ontology, not even one of being non-ontological. If that were our purpose we would be merely positing another downright "first"—not absolute identity this time . . . but non-identity, facticity, entity. [1973:136]

In other words, if we attack the "identity," or totality, of State power in the name of the margin, of the difference that negates totality, we cannot take that negation to be absolute, cannot put it in the place of an identitarian ontology or totalizing power without turning it into an identity itself. Difference itself must be analyzed, undermined, subjected to the same play as identity.

So which is it to be: identitarian "power" or revolutionary "difference?" Whose side are you on? It is at such times that deconstructive criticism appears particularly attractive, because according to a strictly deconstructive perspective we neither need to, nor can, make such a choice. All that we can do is suspend the opposition, "problematize" it and subvert it, finding a trace of "power" in the guerilla margin and the mark of "difference" in a center that must define itself against its own opposition. What is more, deconstruction might tell us, we have no choice but to see the issue in such "metaphysically" oppositional terms. We are in "error" to do so, but it is not anyone's "fault." To err is to wander, to dance in suspension, not to lose the way, because there is no "way" to be lost, no track that is better than any other in the labyrinthine maze of history.

Still, history forces us to make choices anyway: this is why it "hurts," as Jameson puts it, this is how it sets an "inexorable limit" to our desire. And this too is why I have set against criticism the challenging figure of the nuclear referent, for while it is certainly not the only one of its kind (one might, for example, mention the "population referent" or the "ecological referent" as similar challenges), it is one whose peculiarly threatening status is something upon which most of us can agree. But from which side must we approach it: from the side of identitarian power or that of marginalized difference? Partisans for each side can be found—let's say the Greens in Germany or the Freeze Movement in the United States for the differential resistance, and both the Reagan and the Gorbachev regimes for centralized power. To opt for the margin in this case is apparently to opt for powerlessness—as the failure of both the Greens to prevent the deployment of Pershing missiles in Germany and the Freeze Movement in America, in spite of the popular vote it has been able to raise, may indicate. But if one has been made nervous by the prospect of a virtually unchecked strategic arms race, one can hardly side with the State. Is the only answer, then, paralysis after all, an unceasing deferral of decision as we languish in the interstice, the différance, between power and difference? Or might some composition between power and difference still be imagined?

To imagine such a possibility, we might indeed begin by deconstructing the difference between the state and the margin, but this deconstruction would be effected not in the name of the play of difference but rather on behalf of a solution, a compromise. In its own peculiar way, in fact, of all the divisive issues of our time, the nuclear referent seems to offer the clearest possibility for compromise, because it is in no one's interest to fight a nuclear war—no matter which side of the debate one is on. "Compromise," as in "to compromise oneself," has come to connote moral delinquency, but in the face of the nuclear referent, compromise, the reduction or composition of differences, may be the only game in town. What is more, it is a very playable game, particularly at a time when the voice of public opinion has become a key prize for both Washington and Moscow in the East-West confrontation. In such an environment the voice of difference, of the margin that opposes unchecked nuclear proliferation, can indeed be heard by the ear of power, and power can be modified accordingly. This does not mean, however, that difference needs only to speak and power will listen, for if the margin speaks from a position of pure opposition, pure uncompromising difference, then it will destroy in advance its leverage in the overall global politics of the nuclear debate. The critical task of the margin, in other words, and of a nuclear criticism in this sense, will thus be to find the terms by which the margin might be heard, to find, that is to say, a common ground of shared values on the basis of which power might be modified by the force of a marginalized public opinion.

To find such a ground, the lines of communication between power and difference not only must be left open but, under the present circumstances of criticism, must be actively cleared, for communication itself has undergone its own deconstructions. The sort of critical attitude I have in mind has been expressed in Wayne Booth's *Modern Dogma and the Rhetoric of Assent* (1974). In his search for a critical answer both to the student-led challenge to the academy during the Vietnam War and to contemporary axiological skepticism, Booth calls for a universal assent to the proposition that "in a world where many claim that there are no shared values, it is no mean practical result to be able to point to one clear value you and I can share, in full cognitive respectability: It is always good to maintain and improve the quality of our symbolic exchange with our fellow 'selves'— to sharpen our symbolic powers so that we can understand and be understood, 'taking in' other selves and thus expanding our own" (1974:202–203). But such an assent is possible only in a society in which (to follow Booth's allegorical partitioning of contemporary American belief) the believers in science and reason, the worshipers "at the shrine of commercial and industrial progress," and "the irrationalists or romantics" all cease their group tendency to, in Booth's words, "daily say yes to each other only by saying no to the other two" groups (1974:198). In other words, science, industry, and criticism all need to enter into a dialogue in the face of real historical problems such as those the nuclear referent presents, and the dialogue cannot be conducted as long as criticism claims that the only proper sort of discourse is its own: the discourse of poetic ambiguity and uncertainty.

But what Booth could not have foreseen in the early seventies was that criticism, far from turning toward a "rhetoric of assent," would increasingly define itself not only against scientism and commercialism but against any expression of symbolic universality whatsoever. Rather than mediating between the claims of "science" and "opinion," "fact" and "value," "objectivity" and "subjectivity," and so on (see Booth's oppositional "tables" [1974:17–18]), contemporary criticism is openly saying no to both sides of the opposition while quietly privileging the "right-hand" side (i.e., opinion over science, fiction over fact, interpretational subjectivity over objective reality). The result of such a critique, as we have seen, has been the deconstruction of a new crisis in the American academy, a crisis engendered this time not by the actuality of an ongoing military conflict but by the potentiality of a nuclear apocalypse that, at present, may be said to "not now" exist but that may certainly come to pass if we are unable to arrive at any kind of consensus on preventing it.

For this reason, in a critical climate different from the one Booth faced in the Vietnam War era, I have argued for an effective mediation between adversaries, seeking to neglect neither the claims of science nor those of hermeneutics. My desire instead has been to suggest that the "realities" of scientific investigation stand as positive potentialities that, while they must be interpreted, also limit the range of valid interpretation. To defend objective limitation in this regard is not to defend totality, not to privilege the status quo, because it is, I believe, only through some sort of objective demonstration that opinions outside the critical community are likely to be changed. It is worth noting in this regard that the so-called "Silent Majority" of the Nixon years came to heed the call of the antiwar margin only after divisive opinion had come to be replaced by the incontrovertible facts of fifty thousand pine coffins. Similarly, political opinion in this country today (howsoever conservative it may appear to be) is more likely to be swayed by a rhetoric supported by concretely quantifiable calculations than by a "guerilla" resistance to all forms of communicational universality.[2] In other words, in the face of the nuclear referent, difference must speak to power on a common ground if it is to persuade it. I believe that this is precisely what is happening when the Greens enter the Bundestag, when the Freeze Movement lobbies for a nuclear freeze, and when the Union of Concerned Scientists presents quantifiable and testable data. There is a place for critical theory in this dialogue as well if it wishes to enter, but not if it dogmatically asserts the priority of the margin, on the one hand, or simply suspends the relation between power and difference, on the other. The place for criticism, I believe, is the place of realism, a space from which a nuclear criticism could compare and evaluate the various "beliefs" that have been represented in the political debate surrounding the nuclear referent, arguing that not all beliefs are equal and not all possibilities the same, but that one belief can be distinguished from another precisely by the limiting power of reality itself, a power that we can never grasp in a reified presence or form but over which we can conjecture, debate, and maybe even agree.[3]

Notes

CHAPTER 1

1. Included in this issue of *Diacritics* (1984) are Jacques Derrida's "No Apocalypse, Not Now (full speed ahead, seven missiles, seven missives)," Frances Ferguson's "The Nuclear Sublime," Michael McCandles's "Machiavelli and the Paradoxes of Deterrence," Dean MacCannell's "Baltimore in the Morning . . . After . . . : On the Forms of Post Nuclear Leadership," Zoë Sofia's "Exterminating Fetuses: Abortion, Disarmament, and the Sexo-Semiotics of Extraterrestrialism," Derrick de Kerckhove "On Nuclear Communication," and Mary Ann Caws's "Singing in Another Key: Surrealism Through a Feminist Eye."
2. This agenda includes the study of eschatology in its social and textual history; the consideration of the arms race as a "dialectic of mimetic rivalry;" an analysis of the "power of horror;" an evaluation of the concept of "origin" (atomic and otherwise) in our culture; psychological inquiry into the motivation of the (mostly male) arms builders and the (often female) antinuclear activists; a rhetorical analysis of "nukespeak;" an inquiry into the semiotics of arms negotiations; a treatment of the narcotizing effects of the mechanically repetitious representations of nuclear war found both in literature and in the mass media; and a study of the hermeneutics of nuclear intentions (*Diacritics* 1984:2–3). A special issue of the *Northwest Review* (1982) has already devoted itself to such an agenda, particularly with respect to the various ways in which nuclear war has been represented in the popular media. Robert Mielke's "Imaging Nuclear Weaponry: An Ethical Taxonomy of Nuclear Representation" (1982:164–80) and Alexander Hammond's "Rescripting the Nuclear Threat in 1953: The Beast from 20,000 Fathoms" (1982:181–94) are especially noteworthy in this regard.

CHAPTER 4

1. For the Greek text, I have consulted the Loeb Library text of the *Poetics* (1946).
2. This passage is also cited in Vincent Leitch's *Deconstructive Criticism* (1983:126).
3. I wish to thank Professor Jerome McGann for his suggestion that I look

into Thucydides' *History of the Peloponnesian War* for an analog to our own situation as "nuclear" historians. I also owe to Professor McGann a later reference to the poetry of Ron Silliman.

CHAPTER 6

1. Two texts of the *Metaphysics* are used throughout this chapter: the Loeb Library edition (1947), from which all Greek terms are taken, and the translation by Hippocrates G. Apostle (1979).
2. See Hugh Tredennick's Introduction to the *Metaphysics* (1947:xxv).
3. See chapter 15 for a fuller treatment of the relation between Aristotle's metaphysics and Heidegger's de-struction of onto-theologism.
4. The "dispositions" of Aristotelian physics have an organic, vital sense that I would not claim for a contemporary potentialist realism. As I show in chapter 7, however, Aristotle's "dispositional" organicism has since been reinterpreted by both Karl Popper and Werner Heisenberg in a wholly non-organicist, nonanthropomorphic sense.

CHAPTER 7

1. In the context of this discussion I have assumed that there is an analogy between the epistemological opposition of objectivity to subjectivity and the scientific opposition between determinacy and indeterminacy. My assumption here has simply been that if the objective reality of some phenomenon or event could be absolutely proved, then its claim upon our knowledge would be determinate; while as long as the reality of the world remains subject to our own subjective interpretations, then our knowledge of it can be only indeterminate. The argument I am pressing here is that our knowledge of reality is neither wholly determined nor undetermined but represents a probabilistic mediation between these two "poles." Accordingly, as I argue further in the chapter 10, our knowledge is neither wholly objective nor subjective but instead constitutes a mediation between absolute subjectivity and absolute objectivity.

CHAPTER 9

1. Richard Palmer's *Hermeneutics* (1980) provides a useful summary of the hermeneutic tradition from Schleiermacher and Dilthey up through Heidegger and Gadamer. Hans-Georg Gadamer's *Philosophical Hermeneutics* (1977), Hans Robert Jauss's *Aesthetic Experience and Literary Hermeneutics* (1982), and Wolfgang Iser's *The Act of Reading* (1978) and *The Implied Reader* (1975) are a just a few of the major background works of the American reader-response movement.
2. Jane Tompkins's *Reader-Response Criticism* (1981) and Susan Suleiman and Inge Crossman's *The Reader in the Text* (1980) are the two major anthologies of American response criticism available today. Stephen Mail-

loux's *Interpretive Conventions: The Reader in the Study of American Fiction* (1982) provides a useful critical and metacritical text for American reader-response criticism.

CHAPTER 12

1. I wish to acknowledge here the guidance I have been given in this discussion by Robert Strozier's article "Saussure and the Intellectual Tradition of the Twentieth Century." Used by permission of the author.

CHAPTER 13

1. I have used in this chapter the form of documentation common among Peirce scholars, which is to cite from the *Collected Papers* by volume and section number according to the textual divisions established by Charles Hartshorne and Paul Weiss.

2. See Jacques Derrida's "The Supplement of Copula: Philosophy *Before* Linguistics" (1979) for an extended discussion of this grammatico-ontological problem. Derrida's analysis of Emile Benveniste's own critique of the historical relationship between the categories of grammar and the categories of metaphysics is particularly pertinent here.

3. It should be noted that Peirce's thought is teleological, but only in an asymptotic sense. That is, as the community of knowers seeks to learn as much as it can about reality, it ever improves its knowledge without necessarily arriving at any final conclusions. As Peirce writes: "It has been held that a real object is that which will be represented in the ultimate opinion about it. This implies that a series of opinions succeed one another, and that it is hoped that they may ultimately tend more and more towards some limiting opinion, even if they do not reach and rest in a last opinion" (1931–66: 5.609).

4. One might note in this regard the considerable popularity among social scientists of Thomas Kuhn's *The Structure of Scientific Revolutions* (1962), which, in spite of Kuhn's reiterated claims to the contrary, has been widely interpreted as arguing for the incommensurability of the structural "paradigms" of scientific research, and thus for the discontinuity of human knowledge. Given the structuralist predilection for epistemological rupture, this is hardly surprising.

CHAPTER 15

1. To distinguish between the ordinary "world" of social experience and the ontological "World" that human being-there constitutes in its quest for Being, I have written the former with a lowercase *w* and the latter in uppercase. This typographical distinction does not appear in Palmer's text. I employ it here to avoid confusion.

2. "To be a poet in a destitute time means: to attend, singing, to the trace

of the fugitive gods," Heidegger writes in "What are Poets For?" (1975:94). "This is why the poet in the time of the world's night utters the holy." What the poet attends to is the Being that technological human beings have forfeited in their will to truth and knowledge.

3. One might note in this context Michael E. Zimmerman's Heideggerian call for a certain passive opening toward Being in the nuclear age in the hope that such an openness might lead us to transcend our present technologically obsessed consciousness on behalf of a new, as yet unemergent understanding that would make war obsolete. I sympathize with this hope but would add that it is hardly a realistic political program in the face of the nuclear referent. See "Anthropocentric Humanism and the Arms Race," in *Nuclear War*, edited by Michael Allen Fox and Leo Groarke (New York: Peter Lang, 1985), pp.135–44.

CHAPTER 17

1. Edward Said has proposed his own model for the critic which resembles that of the "guerilla" criticism of Michel Foucault. This is the "disaffiliated" critic who operates on the margins of both the "affiliated" cultural power center and the "filiated" family. See Said's *The World, the Text, and the Critic* (1983).

2. One might note here Luce Irigaray's project to deconstruct the masculine-dominated, logical discourse of the West by developing a poetically feminine "lover's" discourse. Such a gesture may indeed overturn the dominant discourse of political life, but it does so at the expense of contributing to political debate, because it isolates itself from the norms of political speech by constituting its own noncommunicative "group" idiolect. See *Ce sexe qui n'en est pas un* (1977).

3. Richard Rorty makes a distinction between the "epistemological" desire of intellectuals to belong to "a group united by mutual interests in achieving a common end" and the "hermeneutic" (or pragmatistic) affirmation that all of us are "united by civility rather than by a common goal, much less by a common ground" (1980:318). In Rorty's terms, then, my argument for a potentialist realism is obviously epistemological, but in the face of the nuclear referent, it seems to me we are all engaged in an epistemological project and that hermeneutics cannot serve our interests nearly as well. Paradoxically, this is essentially a pragmatic argument against pragmatism.

Bibliography

Adorno, Theodor W. 1973. *Negative Dialectics.* New York: Seabury Press.
Althusser, Louis. 1984. *Essays on Ideology.* London: Verso.
Aristotle. 1928. *De Interpretatione.* In *The Works of Aristotle Translated into English.* Edited by W. D. Ross. Oxford: Clarendon Press.
―――. 1936. *The Metaphysics.* Books 10–14. Loeb Library edition. Translated by Hugh Tredennick. Cambridge, Mass.: Harvard University Press.
―――. 1946. *Poetics.* Loeb Library edition. Translated by W. Hamilton Fyfe. Cambridge, Mass.: Harvard University Press.
―――. 1947. *The Metaphysics.* Books 1–9. Loeb Library edition. Translated by Hugh Tredennick. Cambridge, Mass.: Harvard University Press.
―――. 1957. *The Physics I.* Loeb Library edition. Translated by Philip H. Wicksteed and Francis M. Cornford. Cambridge, Mass.: Harvard University Press.
―――. 1971. *Poetics.* In *Critical Theory Since Plato.* Edited by Hazard Adams. New York: Harcourt Brace Jovanovich.
―――. 1979. *The Metaphysics.* Translated by Hippocrates G. Apostle. Grinnell, Ia.: Peripatetic Press.
―――. 1983. *The Categories.* Loeb Library edition. Translated by Harold P. Cooke. Cambridge, Mass.: Harvard University Press.
Atlan, Henri. 1983. "Metaphysical Postulates and Methods of Research." *SubStance 40* 12, no. 3:43–47.
Baker, G. P., and Hacker, P. M. S. 1984. *Frege: Logical Excavations.* New York: Oxford University Press.
Barthes, Roland. 1979. "From Work to Text." In *Textual Strategies.* Edited by Josue V. Harari. Ithaca, N.Y.: Cornell University Press.
Bernstein, Jeremy. 1983. *Einstein.* Glasgow: Fontana.
Bohr, Niels. 1958. *Atomic Physics and Human Knowledge.* New York: Wiley.

Booth, Wayne C. 1974. *Modern Dogma and the Rhetoric of Assent*. Notre Dame, Ind.: University of Notre Dame Press.
Boundary 2. 1982–83. 11, nos. 1, 2 (Fall and Winter).
Bové, Paul A. 1982–83. "The Ineluctability of Difference: Scientific Pluralism and the Critical Intelligence." *Boundary 2* 11, nos. 1, 2 (Fall and Winter):155–76.
Copi, Irving. 1976. "Essence and Accident." In *Universals and Particulars: Readings in Ontology*. Edited by Michael J. Loux. Notre Dame, Ind.: University of Notre Dame Press.
Coppay, Frank. 1983. "In the Thick of It: An Introduction." *SubStance* 40 12, no. 3:7–10.
Cornford, Francis M., and Wicksteed, Philip H. 1957. Introduction to Aristotle's *The Physics I*. Cambridge, Mass.: Harvard University Press.
Crane, R. S. 1971. "Toward a More Adequate Criticism of Poetic Structure." In *Critical Theory Since Plato*. Edited by Hazard Adams. New York: Harcourt Brace Jovanovich.
De Man, Paul. 1979. *Allegories of Reading: Figural Language in Rousseau, Nietzsche, Rilke, and Proust*. New Haven, Conn.: Yale University Press.
Derrida, Jacques. 1972. "Structure, Sign, and Play in the Discourse of the Human Sciences." In *The Structuralist Controversy*. Edited by Richard Macksey and Eugenio Donato. Baltimore, Md.: Johns Hopkins University Press.
———. 1978. "Force and Signification." In *Writing and Difference*. Translated by Alan Bass. Chicago: University of Chicago Press.
———. 1979. "The Supplement of Copula: Philosophy *Before* Linguistics." In *Textual Strategies*. Edited by Josue V. Harari. Ithaca, N.Y.: Cornell University Press.
———. 1980. *Of Grammatology*. Translated by Gayatri Chakravorty Spivak. Baltimore, Md.: Johns Hopkins University Press.
———. 1981. *Positions*. Translated by Alan Bass. Chicago: University of Chicago Press.
———. 1982a. "Différance." In *Margins of Philosophy*. Translated by Alan Bass. Chicago: University of Chicago Press.
———. 1982b. "Signature Event Context." In *Margins of Philosophy*. Translated by Alan Bass. Chicago: University of Chicago Press.
———. 1984. "No Apocalypse, Not Now: full speed ahead, seven missiles, seven missives." *Diacritics* 14, no.2 (Summer):20–31.
De Saussure, Ferdinand. 1978. *Cours de linguistique générale*. Edited by Tullio de Mauro. Paris: Payot.
Diacritics. 1984. 14, no. 2 (Summer).

Draper, Theodore. 1983. *Present History: On Nuclear War, Détente, and Other Controversies.* New York: Random House.
Eco, Umberto. 1979a. *The Role of the Reader.* Bloomington: Indiana University Press.
———. 1979b. *A Theory of Semiotics.* Bloomington: Indiana University Press.
Engels, Frederick. 1968. "*The Eighteenth Brumaire of Louis Bonaparte.* By Karl Marx. F. Engel's Preface to the Third German Edition." In *Karl Marx and Frederick Engels: Selected Works.* New York: International Publishers.
Fish, Stanley. 1980. *Is There a Text in this Class?: The Authority of Interpretive Communities.* Cambridge, Mass.: Harvard University Press.
Foucault, Michel. 1981. *Language, Counter-Memory, Practice: Selected Essays and Interviews.* Translated by Donald F. Bouchard and Sherry Simon. Ithaca, N.Y.: Cornell University Press.
Frege, Gottlob. 1980. "On Sense and Meaning." In *Translations from the Philosophical Writings of Gottlob Frege.* Translated by Peter Geach and Max Black. Totowa, N.J.: Rowman and Littlefield.
Gadamer, Hans-Georg. 1977. *Philosophical Hermeneutics.* Edited and translated by David E. Linge. Berkeley: University of California Press.
Goudge, Thomas A. 1969. *The Thought of C. S. Peirce.* New York: Dover.
Hammond, Alexander. 1982. "Rescripting the Nuclear Threat in 1953: the Beast from 20,000 Fathoms." *Northwest Review* 22, no. 1:181–94.
Hawkes, Terence. 1977. *Structuralism and Semiotics.* Berkeley: University of California Press.
Heidegger, Martin. 1962. *Being and Time.* Translated by John Macquarrie and Edward Robinson. New York: Harper & Row.
———. 1968. *An Introduction to Metaphysics.* Translated by Ralph Manheim. New Haven, Conn.: Yale University Press.
———. 1969. *Identity and Difference.* Translated by Joan Stambaugh. New York: Harper & Row.
———. 1973. "Metaphysics as History of Being." In *The End of Philosophy.* Translated by Joan Stambaugh. New York: Harper & Row.
———. 1975. "What are Poets For?" In *Poetry, Language, Thought.* Translated by Albert Hofstadter New York: Harper & Row.
Heisenberg, Werner. 1961. "Planck's Discovery and the Philosophical Problems of Atomic Physics." In *On Modern Physics.* New York: Clarkson N. Potter, Inc.

Hochberg, Herbert. 1970. "Things and Descriptions." In *Essays on Bertrand Russell*. Edited by E. D. Klemke. Urbana: University of Illinois Press.

Horton, Susan. 1979. *Interpreting Interpreting*. Baltimore, Md.: Johns Hopkins University Press.

Irigaray, Luce. 1977. *Ce sexe qui n'en est pas un*. Paris: Editions de Minuit.

Iser, Wolfgang. 1975. *The Implied Reader: Patterns of Communication in Prose Fiction from Bunyan to Beckett*. Baltimore, Md.: Johns Hopkins University Press.

———. 1978. *The Act of Reading: A Theory of Aesthetic Response*. Baltimore, Md.: Johns Hopkins University Press.

———. 1981. "The Reading Process." In *Reader-Response Criticism*. Edited by Jane P. Tompkins. Baltimore, Md.: Johns Hopkins University Press.

Jakobson, Roman. 1971. "The Metaphoric and Metonymic Poles." In *Critical Theory Since Plato*. Edited by Hazard Adams. New York: Harcourt Brace Jovanovich.

Jameson, Fredric. 1981. *The Political Unconscious: Narrative as a Socially Symbolic Act*. Ithaca, N.Y.: Cornell University Press.

———. 1983. "Science Versus Ideology." *Humanities in Society* 6, nos. 2, 3 (Spring and Summer):283–302.

Jauss, Hans Robert. 1982. *Aesthetic Experience and Literary Hermeneutics*. Translated by Michael Shaw. Minneapolis: University of Minnesota Press.

Kripke, Saul. 1977. "Identity and Necessity." In *Naming, Necessity, and Natural Kinds*. Edited by Stephen P. Schwartz. Ithaca, N.Y.: Cornell University Press.

———. 1980. *Naming and Necessity*. Cambridge, Mass.: Harvard University Press.

Kuhn, Thomas. 1962. *The Structure of Scientific Revolutions*. Chicago: University of Chicago Press.

Leitch, Vincent B. 1983. *Deconstructive Criticism*. New York: Columbia University Press.

Lentricchia, Frank. 1980. *After the New Criticism*. Chicago: University of Chicago Press.

Levin, Samuel R. 1981. "Allegorical Language." In *Allegory, Myth, and Symbol*. Edited by Morton W. Bloomfield. Cambridge, Mass.: Harvard University Press.

Lenin, V. I. 1968. "Frederick Engels." In *Karl Marx and Frederick Engels: Selected Works*. New York: International Publishers.

Lukács, Georg. 1973. "The Ideology of Modernism." In *Issues in Contemporary Literary Criticism*. Edited by Gregory T. Polletta. Boston: Little, Brown.

Lyons, John. 1979. *Semantics*, vol. 1. Cambridge: Cambridge University Press.
Lyotard, Jean-François. 1984. "The *Differend*, the Referent, and the Proper Name." *Diacritics* 14, no. 3 (Fall):4–14.
Mailloux, Steven. 1982. *Interpretive Conventions: The Reader in the Study of American Fiction*. Ithaca, N.Y.: Cornell University Press.
Maniquis, Robert. 1983. "Pascal's Bet, Totalities, and Guerilla Criticism." *Humanities in Society* 6, nos. 2, 3 (Spring and Summer):133–38.
Marx, Karl. 1968. *The Eighteenth Brumaire of Louis Bonaparte*. In *Karl Marx and Frederick Engels: Selected Works*. New York: International Publishers.
Mielke, Robert. "Imaging Nuclear Weaponry: An Ethical Taxonomy of Nuclear Representation." *Northwest Review* 22, no. 1:164–80.
Morin, Edgar. 1983. "Beyond Determinism: The Dialogue of Order and Disorder." *SubStance 40* 12, no. 3:22–35.
Ong, Walter J. 1971. *Rhetoric, Romance, and Technology*. Ithaca, N.Y.: Cornell University Press.
Owens, Joseph. 1978. *The Doctrine of Being in the Aristotelian Metaphysics: A Study in the Greek Background of Mediaeval Thought*. Toronto: Hunter Rose.
Palmer, Richard E. 1980. *Hermeneutics: Interpretation Theory in Schleiermacher, Dilthey, Heidegger, and Gadamer*. Evanston, Ill.: Northwestern University Press.
Peirce, Charles Sanders. 1931–66. *Collected Papers*, 6 vols. Edited by Charles Hartshorne and Paul Weiss. Cambridge, Mass.: Harvard University Press.
Plato. 1921. *Sophist*. Loeb Library edition. Translated by H. N. Fowler. New York: G. P. Putnam and Sons.
Popper, Karl R. 1968. *Conjectures and Refutations: The Growth of Scientific Knowledge*. New York: Harper & Row.
———. 1982a. *Quantum Theory and the Schism in Physics*. Edited by W. W. Bartley, III. Vol. 3 of *Postscript to the Logic of Scientific Discovery*. Totowa, N.J.: Rowman and Littlefield.
———. 1982b. *The Open Universe*. Edited by W. W. Bartley, III. Totowa, N.J.: Rowman and Littlefield.
———. 1983. *Realism and the Aim of Science*. Edited by W. W. Bartley, III. Totowa, N.J.: Rowman and Littlefield.
Prigogine, Ilya. 1983. "Law, History . . . and Desertion." *SubStance* 40, 12, no. 3:36–42.
Putnam, Hilary. 1977. "Is Semantics Possible?" In *Naming, Neces-*

sity, and Natural Kinds. Edited by Stephen P. Schwartz. Ithaca, N.Y.: Cornell University Press.
Quine, W. V. 1971. "Two Dogmas of Empiricism." In *Readings in the Philosophy of Language.* Edited by Jay Rosenberg and Charles Travis. Englewood Cliffs, N.J.: Prentice-Hall.
Rorty, Richard. 1980. *Philosophy and the Mirror of Nature.* Princeton, N.J.: Princeton University Press.
Rosen, Stanley. 1974. *G. W. F. Hegel.* New Haven, Conn.: Yale University Press.
Russell, Bertrand. 1971. "Descriptions." In *Readings in the Philosophy of Language.* Edited by Jay Rosenberg and Charles Travis. Englewood Cliffs, N.J.: Prentice-Hall.
Ryan, Michael. 1982. *Marxism and Deconstruction: A Critical Articulation.* Baltimore, Md.: Johns Hopkins University Press.
Said, Edward W. 1983. *The World, the Text, and the Critic.* Cambridge, Mass.: Harvard University Press.
Schwartz, Stephen P. 1977. *Naming, Necessity, and Natural Kinds.* Ithaca, N.Y.: Cornell University Press.
Searle, John. 1979. "The Logical Status of Fictional Discourse." In *Contemporary Perspectives in the Philosophy of Language.* Edited by Peter A. French, Theodore E. Uehling, and Howard K. Wettstein. Minneapolis: University of Minnesota Press.
Shapiro, Michael. 1983. *The Sense of Grammar.* Bloomington: Indiana University Press.
Silliman, Ron. 1978. *This.* In *Ketjak.* San Francisco: Small Press Distribution.
SubStance 40 1983. 12, no. 3.
Suleiman, Susan, and Crossman, Inge. 1980. *The Reader in the Text: Essays on Audience and Interpretations.* Princeton, N.J.: Princeton University Press.
Thom, René. 1983. "Stop Chance! Silence the Noise!" *SubStance 40* 12, no. 3:11–21.
Thucydides. 1982. *The Peloponnesian War.* Edited by T. E. Wick. New York: Modern Library.
Tompkins, Jane. 1981. *Reader-Response Criticism.* Baltimore, Md.: Johns Hopkins University Press.
Vail, L. M. 1972. *Heidegger and Ontological Difference.* University Park: Pennsylvania State University Press.
Van Dijk, Teun. 1979. "Cognitive Processing of Literary Discourse." *Poetics Today* 1, nos. 1, 2:143–59.
Virgil. 1972. *The Aeneid of Virgil.* Translated by Allen Mandelbaum. New York: Bantam Books.
Weinsheimer, Joel. 1983. "The Realism of C. S. Peirce, or How Ho-

mer and Nature Can Be The Same." *American Journal of Semiotics* 2, nos. 1, 2:225–63.

Wells, Rulon S. 1970. "De Saussure's System of Linguistics." In *Structuralism*. Edited by Michael Lane. New York: Basic Books.

White, Hayden. 1980. *Metahistory: The Historical Imagination in Nineteenth-Century Europe*. Baltimore, Md.: Johns Hopkins University Press.

———. 1985. *Tropics of Discourse: Essays in Cultural Criticism*. Baltimore, Md.: Johns Hopkins University Press.

Wieland, W. 1975. "The Problem of Teleology." In *Articles on Aristotle*, vol. 1. Edited by Jonathan Barnes, Malcolm Schofield, and Richard Sorabji. London: Duckworth.

Yeats, William Butler. 1976. "Among School Children." In *Selected Poems and Two Plays of William Butler Yeats*. Edited by M. L. Rosenthal. New York: Macmillan.

Zimmerman, Michael E. 1985. "Anthropocentric Humanism and the Arms Race." In *Nuclear War*. Edited by Michael Allen Fox and Leo Groarke. New York: Peter Lang.

Zins, Daniel L. 1985. "Teaching English in a Nuclear Age." *College English* 47, no. 4:387–406.

Index

Absence: 52, 53, 55–60, 101, 212–14, 216, 250, 261
Actuality: 28, 34–35, 46–53, 59–61, 64ff., 73, 83, 90, 97–99, 101, 113–14, 118–19, 121–23, 139, 144, 151, 153, 165, 179–82, 193–98, 201, 216–18, 225–26, 230–31, 235, 255, 260, 274
Adorno, Theodore: 239, 270
Aestheticism: 14
Aesthetics, 43, 104
Aletheia: 230, 234, 236
Allegory, 148
Alphabet, eidetic: 57; *see also* Plato
Althusser, Louis: 247–51, 256, 264
Analytic philosophy: 125, 128, 134, 170
Anglo-American philosophy: 129, 145; *see also* analytic philosophy
Antithesis: 54ff.
Apocalypse, nuclear: 18–19, 23, 26, 274
Apostle, H. G.: 72
Appearance: 57
Arche: 72
Archeology: 210; *see also* Foucault, Michel
Archive: 14, 24–26, 29–31, 36–37, 45, 48, 50, 102–103, 177, 202, 204, 244–45, 248–49, 252, 259
Aristotle: 16, 36, 75, 79, 82, 97–99, 103–104, 113, 138, 178–79, 187, 193–94, 197, 207, 229–30, 235–36, 238; *De Interpretatione,* 28; *Poetics,* 41–43, 49–50; *Metaphysics,* 51, 54, 60, 62–73, 180–81; *Physics,* 51–62, 64; *Categories,* 185

Arms race, nuclear: 22–23, 163–64, 217, 224, 272; limitation of, 102; *see also* nuclear freeze movement; referent, nuclear
Arnold, Matthew: 10, 32
Artistic text: 119–21, 123
Athens, Greece: 43, 46
Atlan, Henri: 77–78, 82
Austin, J. L.: 125–26

Baker, G. P.: 130–31
Barthes, Roland: 11, 13, 121, 158
Bartley, W. W.: 84
Baudrillard, Jean: 264
Beardsley, Monroe: 122
Becoming: 41, 48–50, 52–54, 58, 60, 62, 100–101
Bedeutung: 130–36, 138, 149–50; *see also* reference
Being: 10, 34, 250; in Aristotle, 52, 56, 60, 62–71; in Pierce, 184–87, 189, 191–93; in Foucault, 208, 209; in Derrida, 212, 214–15, 218–19; in Heidegger, 225–43; *see also* essence; ontology; substance
Benveniste, Emile: 279n.
Bernstein, Jeremy: 87
Bezeichnung: 130
Big Bang: 70
Black, Max: 130
Bohr, Niels: 85–86
Bomb: 127, 224; sign of, 263–66, 269
Booth, Wayne: 273–74
Born, Max: 88, 91; and Born-Jordan interpretation, 87
Boundary 2: 15
Brisure: 20
Brute facts: 126–27, 144

289

Capitalism: 255
Categories: 59, 63, 183–89, 191–92, 208, 237–38, 242
Causality: 41, 231, 251; Cartesian, 247; Galilean, 247; Hegelian, 247, 256; in history, 247; Newtonian, 247–48, 250; Viconian, 248; structural, 249–50
Cause: final, 41, 53, 56, 59, 62, 68–69; formal, 41, 53, 55 ff., 69; efficient, 53, 56, 69; material, 53, 55 ff.; absent, 249–51, 260; *see also* causality; matter
Caws, Mary Ann: 6, 277 n.
Certainty: 28, 112
Chance: 76–78, 80–81, 209, 226–28; *see also* indeterminism
Change: 28, 51 ff.
Cicero: 136
Civil Defense Administration: 29, 102
Class: 66–67, 129–31, 145, 147–50, 153, 172, 180–82, 197–98, 207; social, 246, 252–54, 258–60; *see also* natural kind
Clinamen: 70
Code, in semiology: 170, 177, 202, 204
Cold War: 6, 8, 224
Coleridge, Samuel Taylor: 9
Committee on the Present Danger: 51
Complementarity: 85
Computer simulation: 101
Conceptualism: 117–18, 148–49
Conjecture: 83, 89, 93; and refutation, 94–96, 128, 151, 202, 259, 261–62; scientific, 97, 100–102
Connotation: 129–30, 132, 134, 137–38, 140, 142, 185
Consciousness, transcendental: 116
Contradiction: 53 ff.
Contrariety: 54, 63
Conventionalism, linguistic: 171–72
Copenhagen Interpretation: 85, 90, 99
Copi, Irving: 146–47

Coppay, Frank: 74, 76
Cornell University, colloquium on nuclear criticism at: 5–6, 8–9, 15, 17
Counterfactuals: 134–36, 139, 142, 170
Crane, R. S.: 113
Criticism: 5, 25, 36, 74–75, 103–104, 238–40, 272, 274–75; nuclear, defined: 5; political, 6, 14–15, 37, 111, 217–18, 241–42, 262; American, history of, 9–15; New, 9–11, 117, 122, 129, 134, 155; archetypal, 10; feminist, 10, 258, 280 n.; Marxist, 10, 14–16, 29, 124, 243, 244–62, 264, 268, 270; nuclear, 10, 15, 17, 20, 23, 30, 34, 37, 75, 104, 111, 151, 153–54, 217–19, 224, 261, 272–73, 275; Yale School of, 13; reader-response, 37, 112–23, 142, 278 n.; Chicago School of, 113; Konstanz School of, 115; Geneva School of, 116; guerilla, 265–66; 268–71, 274
Crossman, Inge: 278 n.
Cuban Missile Crisis: 6

Darstellung: 15, 249, 252, 255
Dasein: 226–27, 232–34
Day After, The: 7
Deconstruction: 11, 13, 15–16, 25, 33, 74–75, 82, 114, 162, 169, 177, 184, 205, 211, 213, 216–18, 242–43, 261, 271–74; *see also* Derrida, Jacques; poststructuralism
Deinon: 233, 238
Deleuze, Gilles: 266–67, 269; *Différence et répétition*, 207–208, 210
De Man, Paul: 13, 112, 154, 159, 160–62, 164–65, 169, 215; *Allegories of Reading*, 155–58; on misreading, 156, 164
Denotation: 130–31, 134, 137–38, 141–43, 185; defined, 129

Derrida, Jacques: 11, 13, 16, 49, 59–60, 83, 100–102, 104, 109, 151, 153, 169, 172–73, 176–78, 184, 190, 203–206, 219, 227, 241–43, 245, 248, 264, 277n., 279n.; "Structure, Sign, and Play," 12; "No Apocalypse, Not Now," 17–31, 51, 216, 218, 260; "Signature Event Context," 197, 214–15; "Force and Signification," 210–11; "Différance," 211–16
Designation: 130
Destinerrance: 27, 35, 100–101
De-struction: 219, 228, 230, 235, 237–38, 242–43
Détente: 8
Determinacy: 278n.
Determinism: 31, 35–36, 48, 74ff., 95, 98, 114, 245, 247–48, 250–51, 253
Deterrence: 23, 26, 109, 162–63, 218, 224
Diacritics: 5, 30, 110, 277n.
Dialectics: 15–16, 25, 27–28, 37, 45, 48, 54, 124, 208–209, 244, 258, 260–61, 270
Differance: 12, 16, 20, 31, 45, 59, 99, 176, 178–79, 205–206, 211–19, 227, 242, 272
Difference: 26–27, 30–31, 37, 44–45, 57, 59, 72, 81, 101, 121, 161–62, 184, 196, 198, 203, 205–214, 216–17, 219, 227–29, 237, 242–43; structural, 11–12; ontico-ontological, 63, 219, 228, 235, 238, 242–43, 251; as essence, 64; and potentiality, 98–99, 197; and semiology, 165, 169, 172–82; political, 262, 265–66, 268, 270–72, 274–75
Dilthey, Wilhelm: 115–16, 223–26
Discourse: 38, 44–45, 126; historical, 9–10, 41–50, 241, 244–62; scientific, 9–10, 29, 74ff., 103–104; poetic, 10, 41–43, 49–50, 238–39, 241, 273; political, 16; literary, 32, 74–75, 103–104, 111, 126, 154–58; post-Marxist, 248, 262–71; prophetic, 253–58
Disorder: 78–81
Doctor Strangelove: 7
Donato, Eugenio: 15
Donnellan, Keith: 134
Doxa: 23, 36, 157, 208, 218
Draper, Theodore: 152–53, 163
Dualism: 71, 96–97
Dunamis: 49–50, 63, 68, 72, 99–100, 194, 233
Dynamic Object: 199–201, 218

Eco, Umberto: 149, 200, 202
Écriture: 43, 177
Eidos: 230–31, 235–36
Einai: 229, 231, 234
Einstein, Albert: 81, 91, 95; and special theory of relativity, 87
Eleatic Stranger: 57
Electron: 86–87, 90–91, 96
Eliot, T. S.: 127
Empiricism (British): 145
Energeia: 49, 64, 193–94; 230–31
Engels, Frederick: 245–46
Enzenburger, H. M.: 264
Épistémè: 23, 36, 157, 218
Épochè: 25–26, 30
Erlebnis: 223, 225; *see also* lived experience
Errance: 98
Eschatology: 277n.
Essence: 49, 63–64, 139–41, 179–80, 214, 229–31; nominal, 145–47; real, 145–47
Essentia: 229–30
Evolution, biological: 69
Existence, Heideggerian: 229–31; *see also* Being
Existentia: 229–30
Existentialism: 10–11; in Heidegger, 226–27

Facts, institutional: 126–27, 143–44
Falsifiability: 36
Ferguson, Frances: 277n.
Feyerabend, Paul: 103

Feynman, Richard: 143
Fiction, nuclear: 22–23
Figure: *see* trope
Firstness: 182, 192–98; *see also* Peirce, C. S.
First principles: 37, 62
Fish, Stanley: 104, 112, 122–28, 137, 141–43, 156, 162, 199, 255
Fission: 27
Form: 58–73, 113, 120, 178–81, 194, 197; in semiology, 172–74, 176–77
Formalism: 37, 113, 117, 122, 128; Czechoslovakian, 9; Russian, 9; American, 14
Foucault, Michel: 37, 207–11, 245, 248, 262, 264, 266–69
Free play: 31
Frege, Gottlob: 130–36, 138, 149–51
Freud, Sigmund: 264
Frye, Northrop: 10, 13
Fusion, nuclear: 27

Gadamer, Hans-Georg: 115–16, 278n.
Geach, Peter: 130
Geertz, Clifford: 261
Gelb, Leslie: 23–24
Genealogy: 13, 208–11
Genette, Gerard: 158
Genus: 57, 64–68, 80, 97, 138–39
Geworfenheit: 226
Gödel, theorem of: 74
Gorbachev, Mikhail, administration of: 271
Goudge, Thomas: 184
Grammar: *see* De Man, Paul
Grammatology: 169
Green party: 271, 274
Ground: 27, 29, 32, 47, 188

Hacker, P. M. S.: 130–31
Haig, Alexander: 162–64
Hammond, Alexander: 277n.
Hawkes, Terence: 159
Hegel, G. W. F.: 16, 28, 185, 246–48

Heidegger, Martin: 12, 115, 219, 223, 239–43, 251, 278n., 280n.; *Identity and Difference*, 204; *Being and Time*, 225–28; *End of Philosophy*, 228; "Metaphysics as History of Being," 228–31; *Introduction to Metaphysics*, 228, 232–38
Heisenberg, Werner: 75, 85–86, 88, 91, 99–100, 278n.
Heraclitus: 233
Hermeneutics: 24, 36–37, 48, 112, 115–19, 121, 127–29, 137, 142, 223, 225, 274, 278n.; potentialist, 105, 112–13, 123, 142; dialogical, 115, 118–19
Hiroshima, Japan: 48–49, 83
Historicism: 101, 248, 255, 264
Historicity: 208–12, 216–19, 224–26, 239–42, 244–62
History: 36, 124–25, 203–206, 209, 223; New Critical attitude toward, 9; and post-structuralism, 13–14; in the nuclear era, 19; and poetry, 41–43, 49; as objective reality, 44, 241, 244, 271; metaphysical, 210–11, 248
Hochberg, Herbert: 129
Homer: 42, 136
Horton, Susan: 118
Humanities: 30
Hume, David: 92, 146
Hupokeimenon: *see* substrate
Husserl, Edmund: 10, 242
Hyle: *see* matter
Hylomorphism: 56

ICBM: 110
Idealism: 82, 125, 246
Identity: 31, 37, 45–46, 49, 140–43, 150, 175, 179–82, 198; in history, 207–11; and totality, 208, 270–71
Ideology: in Althusser, 256–57
Illocution: 161
Immediate object: 199–200

Indeterminacy: 278n.
Indeterminism: 48, 75 ff., 98, 114, 245, 251
Induction: 89, 95–96
Intentionality: 165, 198, 211
Interdisciplinarity: 32, 261
Interpretant: 188–91, 199; logical, 200–202; final, 202
Interpretive community: 123–28, 142, 145, 162, 255; see also Fish, Stanley
Intertextuality: see archive
Irigaray, Luce: 280n.
Irony: in new Criticism, 9; poetic, 10, 155
Iser, Wolfgang: 112, 118–23, 278n.
Itara: 177, 181, 197
Iteration: see repetition
Ithaca, New York: 6

Jakobson, Roman: 158–60
Jameson, Fredric: 14, 37, 244–49, 251–60, 262, 271
Jauss, Hans Robert: 278n.
Johns Hopkins University, colloquium at: 12, 15, 17

Kant, Immanuel: 183–84, 189–90
Kerckhove, Derrick: 277n.
Kermode, Frank: 10
Knowledge, absolute: 25, 27, 202
Kripke, Saul: 134, 136–43, 170
Kuhn, Thomas: 279n.

Lacan, Jacques: 256, 264
Lacedaemon: 42–43, 46
Language: see discourse
Language, constative: 126
Langue: 34, 165, 173–76
Laplace, Pierre-Simon: 75, 79
Legisign: 196–98, 201; see also type
Leitch, Vincent: 13, 277n.
Lenin, V. I.: 245–47
Lentricchia, Frank: 10, 12, 14
Levin, Samuel: 148
Lévi-Strauss, Claude: 11–13, 204
Lewis, David: 134

Lifton, Robert: 48
Linge, David: 116
Linguistics: see semiology; semiotics
Literary criticism: see criticism
Literature and the nuclear referent, 24–26
Lived experience: 216–19, 223–27, 239, 242–45, 261
Locke, John: 145–46
Logic: 32–33, 54, 184, 209, 227, 231–32, 236–37, 239; modal, 134, 136
Logocentrism: 184, 264
Logos: 56, 148, 232–38
Lucretius: 70
Lukács, Georg: 16, 239
Lyons, John: 129–31, 178–79
Lyotard, Jean-François: 34

McCandles, Michael: 277n.
MacCannell, Dean: 277n.
McGann, Jerome: 277n.
Mach, Ernst: 145
Macksey, Richard: 15
Mailloux, Stephen: 278n.
Mallarmé, Stéphane: 74, 171
Maniquis, Robert: 262–66, 269
Marginality: 265–72, 274–75; see also difference, political
Marx, Karl: 16, 216, 245–48, 253–54, 258
Materialism: historical, 219, 240–41, 243; dialectical, 245–46
Matter: 58–73, 99, 113, 118–20, 235, 246–47; in semiology, 171–76, 178–81, 194, 197–98, 201, 206, 213
Maxwell, James: 87
Meaning: see Bedeutung
Merleau-Ponty, Maurice: 12
Metahistory: 13–14, 43–46, 49, 245, 252
Metaphor: 26, 111, 157–60
Metaphysics: 27, 35–36, 45, 48, 52–73, 76, 78, 82, 99, 111, 113, 178–79, 197, 228–31, 235, 237–38, 241–42, identitarian,

Metaphysics (continued)
  10–11, 15, 33; see also Aristotle; Derrida, Jacques; Heidegger, Martin; Popper, Karl
Metonymy: 157–60
Mielke, Robert: 277n.
Mill, John Stuart: 129–30, 134, 137–38
Milton, John: 127
Mimesis: 20, 37, 236; see also representation
Missiles, Pershing: 271
Monod, Jacques: 77–78
Morin, Edgar: 77–82, 251
Morpheme: 174, 180

Nagasaki, Japan: 83
Names: proper, 130, 133, 135, 137–39, 141–45, 148, 150–51; fictional, 144, 148–51
Narrative, historical: 43–44, 248, 251–55, 258–61
National Security Council: 151
Naturalism, linguistic: 171
Natural kind: 137–41, 170, 207
Natural law: 32, 36, 73, 79–80, 95, 99–100, 195
Nature: 54–55
Necessity: 41–42, 78, 81, 183; in referential theory, 134, 139–40; in historical materialism, 245–47
Negation: 54–60, 183, 270; see also Not-being
New Historicism: 15, 245
Newton, Isaac: 73, 75, 86–87, 95
Nietzsche, Friedrich: 14, 81, 157, 208, 210, 225, 241, 248, 253, 269
Nixon, Richard: 141–43, 274
Noein: 231, 233–34, 238
Noise: 77–78, 80–81
Nominalism: 83, 192, 201
Northwest Review: 277n.
Not-being: 52, 56–60, 215; see also privation
Nuclear freeze movement: 162–64, 271, 274

Nuclear referent: see Referent, nuclear

Objectivism: see realism
Ong, Walter J.: 101, 112
On the Beach: 7
Ontology: 59, 61–73, 127, 169, 176, 178–79, 182, 191–92, 200, 208, 219, 225–28, 232–39, 270
Onto-theology: 63, 242
Order: 78–81
Organicism: 41, 68, 73, 278n.
Otherness: 57; see also Plato, *Sophist*
Ousia: 54, 63, 228, 230–31, 237; see also substance
Owens, Joseph: 68–69, 181

Palmer, Richard: 223, 225–26, 278n.
Paradigmatics: 158–61
Parmenides: 56–58, 233–34
Parole: 165, 173–74, 176
Particle, atomic: 71, 79, 82, 85–88, 96–97
Particulars: 41–43, 62, 66–67, 70, 72, 139, 141, 181, 194, 197
Pascal, wager of: 263
Peirce, C. S.: 36, 165, 182–205, 212, 217, 279n.
Peloponnesian War: 42–48
Pharmakon: 109, 218, 261
Phenomenology: 10–11, 116–18, 121, 183–85, 191, 226
Phoneme: 174–75, 179–80, 182
Phonemics: 173–75, 180
Phonetics: 170, 173–76, 179–80
Phonology: see phonetics
Photon: 82, 87, 91–92
Physics: 36, 79–80, 82–88, 90–100; classical, 73, 84, 86, 99
Physis: 230, 232–36, 238
Planck, Max: 87
Plato: 35, 68, 229–31, 235–36; and forms, 57, 181; *Sophist*, 57; *Cratylus*, 136, 171, 187; see also realism

Pluralism, interpretational: 46, 259, 261
Poetry: New Critical attitude toward, 9; and history, 41, 43–49; in Heidegger, 238–39, 241
Popper, Karl: 35–37, 75, 82–84, 88–101, 103–104, 126, 128, 145, 201–203, 259, 278n.; *Quantum Theory and the Schism in Physics*, 82, 84, 90, 98–99; *Postscript to the Logic of Scientific Discovery*, 84; *Realism and the Aim of Science*, 97; "Truth, Rationality, and the Growth of Knowledge," 90
Positivism: 82–83, 145
Possibility: 28, 41, 49–50, 80, 226–27
Possible worlds, theory of: 134–36, 139
Postmodernism: 15
Post-structuralism: 13–14, 16, 29, 37, 44, 53, 59, 103–104, 111–12, 154, 164–65, 170–71, 182, 199, 202, 205, 217, 244, 248–49, 259, 264, 270
Potentialist metaphysics: 31, 35, 73, 100; *see also* realism, potentialist
Potentiality: 27–29, 31, 34–35, 37, 46–53, 60–61, 63–73, 75–76, 80, 83–84, 89–90, 95–101, 103, 105, 110, 112–14, 118–23, 139, 144, 147, 151–53, 164–65, 179–82, 186, 193–98, 201, 203, 216–17, 225–27, 233, 238, 240, 255, 274
Potentiality-*and/also*-actuality: 67, 71–72, 99; *see also* power-*and*-difference
Poulet, Georges: 10, 12, 116
Power: ontological, 49–50, 63, 71–72; as propensity, 147–48, 150; as potential, 180, 197, 201; in Heidegger, 226–27, 232–33, 236, 238, 240, 242; political, 268–72, 274–75

Power-*and*-difference: 71–72, 197
Pragmaticism: 198, 202
Pragmatics: 21, 117
Pragmatism: 117, 125–26, 145, 199, 202, 280n.
Prediction: 28, 35, 81–83, 86–87, 90, 95, 101, 147; historical, 246, 253–54, 256, 260
Presence: 11, 14, 45–46, 52–53, 55–56, 58–60, 62, 79, 101, 193–94, 205, 210, 212–19, 230, 232, 237, 249–51, 275
Pre-Socratics, philosophy of: 229–31, 235–36
Prigogine, Ilya: 77–78, 82, 251
Primary substance: 63
Prime Mover: 59, 68–69, 71
Privation: 53–60, 66–67, 71; *see also* Not-being
Probability: 29, 31, 35, 41–43, 73–74, 76, 79, 81–82, 84, 86, 88, 91–101, 104, 112, 141, 147, 152, 227
Production, mode of: 246, 250, 254–55
Propensity: 29, 31, 35, 46–48, 93–103, 112–13, 145, 147, 201–202, 216, 224, 227; *see also* potentiality
Propensity interpretation: 73, 82, 92, 94–95, 98–101
Proust, Marcel: 158, 160, 162
Psychology: in semiology, 170–73, 180
Putnam, Hilary: 140

Qualisign: 196–98
Quality: in Peirce, 183–84, 186–93, 196
Quantum mechanics: 75, 82–86, 90–92, 95, 99
Quine, W. V. O.: 134

Randomness: *see* chance; indeterminism
Rationality: 37, 232–33, 236–39
Reader, informed: 123

Reagan, Ronald, administration of, 8, 24, 110, 271
Realism: in literary criticism, 16; potentialist, 31, 33, 35–37, 50, 53, 73, 98, 100–102, 105, 128, 146–47, 203, 226, 275, 278 n., 280 n.; Platonic, 31, 37, 57, 68, 80; scientific, 31, 35–36, 48–49, 73, 82–84, 90, 101, 103–104, 125, 128; naive, 128; in Kripke, 137; in Peirce, 192, 201–203; historical, 217, 219, 243–44, 259, 262; see also potentialist metaphysics
Reference: theory of, 129–54; in Frege, 130–33, 136, 149–50; descriptive theory of, 130, 134–36; see also Bedeutung; referent
Referent: 9–10, 13–17, 22, 26, 29–33, 37, 43–46, 49, 94, 103–104, 110–11, 125, 128, 133–36, 138–39, 141, 143–44, 149–53, 157, 165, 169–72, 177–78, 182, 190–91, 199, 202, 204, 210–15, 245, 248–49, 251–52, 254–56; nuclear, 17, 20–24, 26–37, 47, 49–52, 83–84, 100, 102–105, 150–51, 153, 177, 203–206, 217–18, 240, 260–62, 265, 271–75
Refutation: *see* conjecture
Relation: in Peirce, 184, 188–89, 191–92
Relativism: 30, 121
Repetition: 47, 175, 177, 180–81, 197–98, 208
Representation: 212, 231–32, 234–38, 251–52; of nuclear war, 23; of history, 43; in Peirce, 184, 188–92, 199
Ressentiment: 209
Revolution: 16, 218, 258, 261–62, 264–65, 269, 271; *see also* criticism, guerilla; difference, political
Reykjavik, Iceland: summit at, 102
Rhetoric, 5, 20, 24–26, 30, 43, 49, 104, 109–112, 127, 151, 153–64, 215, 260, 274; nuclear, 8, 109–10, 153–54, 162–64, 224
Rigid designation: 135, 137, 141–42, 170; *see also* Kripke, Saul
Rimbaud, Arthur: 171
Rorty, Richard: 232, 280 n.
Rosen, Stanley: 57
Russell, Bertrand: 135–36, 138, 149
Ryan, Michael: 15–16

Said, Edward: 14, 112, 280 n.
SALT: 8, 110
Sartre, Jean–Paul: 10, 12
Saussure, Ferdinand de: 12, 159, 165, 169–80, 198, 203–206, 210–11, 213, 217, 219, 242–43
Schelling, F. W. J. von: 210
Schleiermacher, F. D. E.: 115–16
Scholastic philosophy: 62
Schrödinger, Erwin: 88, 91; wave function of, 87, 90–91
Searle, John: 126
Secondness: 182, 192–95, 197–98; *see also* Peirce, C. S.
Semantics: 11, 32
Semiology: 5, 158, 160, 165, 169–70, 172–73, 177, 181–82, 196–98, 202–203, 205–206, 210–13, 219
Semiosis, unlimited: 199
Semiotics: 36–37, 165, 180–82, 190–92, 196–99, 202–205, 212, 217
Sense: 130–34, 136, 138, 149–51; *see also* Sinn
Serres, Michael: 78
Shakespeare, William: 136
Shapiro, Michael: 199–200
Shortage: *see* privation
Sign: 22, 110–12, 129–33, 150, 159, 165, 170–71, 176–77, 179–82, 190–92, 194–204, 206, 212–13, 216–19, 234; iconic, 190; indexical, 190; *see also* Peirce, C. S.
Signifiant: 170–71; *see also* signifier

Signifié: 170–71; *see also* signified
Signified: 26, 170–72, 174–75, 204, 213, 248
Signifier: 26, 170–72, 174–75, 177, 204, 213, 248; floating, 170
Silent Majority: 274
Silliman, Ron: 113
Sinn: 130–34, 136, 138, 142, 149; *see also* sense
Sinsign: 196–98
Skepticism: 82, 146, 201, 273
Socrates: 64, 66
Sofia, Zoë: 6, 277 n.
Sophocles: 233
Spain, Republic of: 269
Species: 64, 66, 69, 146–49, 207
Speech act theory: 125–26
Spivak, Gayatri: 14
Stambaugh, Joan: 228
Standard story: 125–27, 142, 144, 199, 255
Star Wars (Strategic Defense Initiative): 110
State, the: 265, 269–70, 272; *see also* power, political
Statistics, as measurement: 82, 88, 90–92, 94, 96
Steresis: 56; *see also* privation
Stevens, Wallace: 10
Strategic Defense Initiative: *see* Star Wars
Strozier, Robert: 279 n.
Structuralism: 11, 29, 44, 160, 165, 182, 203–206, 217; in linguistics, 169–80
Subject: 55; *see also* substance
Subjectivism: 37, 75, 81–84, 86, 89, 94, 103, 114, 121, 123, 128, 145, 273–74, 278 n.
Substance: 49, 54–55, 62–73, 79, 139, 147, 169, 173–80, 184–87, 189, 191–94, 206, 212–13, 228, 230, 237, 254
SubStance: 74–75
Substrate: 55–72
Suleiman, Susan: 278 n.
Sunolon: 64, 67
Supplement: 177; *see also* Derrida, Jacques

Symbol, in Peirce: 190
Syntagmatics: 158, 159–60

Technology, nuclear: 6, 240–41
Teleology: 16, 70, 199, 248, 279 n.
Telos: 70, 72
Terrorism: 265, 269–70
Testament: 7
Textuality: *see* archive; trope
Theology: 36, 62
Theory, critical: *see* criticism
Thirdness: 182, 192, 194–95, 197–99, 201–202; *see also* Peirce, C. S.
Thom, René: 76–78, 82, 245
Thucydides: 42–48, 278 n.
Todorov, Tzvetan: 158
Token: 182, 196–98, 212
Tompkins, Jane: 117, 278 n.
Tone: 196–97
Totalitarianism: 264, 266, 270
Totality: 46, 48, 72, 98, 202, 208, 210, 213, 247, 253, 263–70, 274
Trace: 20, 26, 30, 60, 176–79, 203, 211, 216, 242
Transcendentalism: Platonic, 57; theological, 68–69; in Heidegger, 239
Tredennick, Hugh: 69
Trojan War: 109–112, 150
Trope: 14, 32, 43–45, 104, 111–12, 155–58, 160, 162, 252
Tropology: 13–14, 17
Truth conditions: 32, 54, 130, 149
Type: 182, 196–98, 212; *see also* legisign

Uncertainty: 32, 35
Uncertainty principle: 73, 75, 85, 88, 91, 100
Undecidability: 27, 98, 100, 103, 214, 218
Union of Concerned Scientists: 29, 102, 261, 274
Union of Soviet Socialist Republics: 8
Universals: 41, 43, 66–67, 70, 72, 83, 139, 141, 181, 187
Utopia: 254, 257–58

Vail, L. M.: 239
Van Dijk, Teun: 117–18
Vietnam War: 273–74
Vorstellung: 132–33

War, nuclear: 6–7, 17–18, 21–22, 24–25, 49, 51, 83, 100, 151–53, 163–64, 224–25, 263–65, 269, 272; *see also* arms race, nuclear
Waves (atomic): 87–88, 91, 96–97
Weimar Republic: 269
Weinberger, Caspar: 151–53
Weinsheimer, Joel: 201
Wells, Rulon: 174

White, Hayden: 13–14, 43–46, 245
Wieland, Wolfgang: 70
Wimsatt, W. K.: 122
Winter, nuclear: 100–102
Wittgenstein, Ludwig: 138
World War I: 150
World War II: 150
Writing: 24; as differance, 176–78; and Derrida, 242; *see also écriture;* trace

Yeats, W. B.: 155–57, 160

Zimmerman, Michael: 280n.